Lorna Sage, Dean of the School of English and American Studies at the University of East Anglia in Norwich, is the author of a brief study of Angela Carter in the new 'Writers and Their Work' series for the British Council. She has also written *Women in the House of Fiction* (1992). She was a friend of Angela Carter, and has been a partisan of her writing since the mid-1970s.

Flesh and the Mirror

Essays on the Art of
Angela Carter

EDITED BY LORNA SAGE

Published by VIRAGO PRESS Limited, August 1994
42–43 Gloucester Crescent, Camden Town, London NW1 7PD

*A CIP catalogue record for this book is available from
the British Library*

Printed in Great Britain by Cox & Wyman Ltd., Reading, Berks

For Mark and Alexander

Acknowledgements

Passages from the work of Angela Carter are reproduced by kind permission of the Estate of Angela Carter c/o Rogers, Coleridge & White Ltd., 20 Powis Mews, London W11 1JN

Contents

A Brief Biography of Angela Carter

1940	born Angela Olive Stalker, May 7th, Eastbourne, Sussex, spends the war in Yorkshire with her maternal grandmother
	educated direct grant school in Balham
1959	junior reporter, *Croydon Advertiser*
1960	marries Paul Carter
1962–5	reads English at the University of Bristol, specializing in the medieval period
1966	first novel, *Shadow Dance*, published
1967	wins John Llewellyn Rhys prize for second novel, *The Magic Toyshop*
1968	wins Somerset Maugham Award for third novel, *Several Perceptions*
1969–72	visits, then lives in, Japan
1972	divorced from Paul Carter
1976–8	Arts Council of Great Britain Fellow in Sheffield
1977–	settles in South London, with Mark Pearce; member of Virago advisory board; Virago commission *The Sadeian Woman* (1979)
1980–81	Visiting Professor on the Writing Programme at Brown University, Providence, Rhode Island, USA, substituting for John Hawkes
1983	son Alexander Pearce born
1984–87	teaches part-time on the Writing MA at the University of East Anglia in Norwich
1984	writer in residence, University of Adelaide, South Australia: *Company of Wolves* (based on *The Bloody Chamber*, 1979) released on film; *Nights at the Circus* published by Chatto & Windus (joint winner of the James Tait Black Memorial Prize for 1985)
1985	teaches in Austin, Texas
1986	teaches in Iowa City, Iowa
1988	teaches in Albany, New York State
1991	publishes her last novel, *Wise Children*
1992	dies on February 16th

Introduction

LORNA SAGE

All at once the pungency and power of Angela Carter's style and the carnival mayhem of the late-comedy plots she ended up with seem self-evidently timely – representations of a certain *fin-de-siècle* sensibility we can recognise ourselves in. This is the right fun-house mirror after all, the one where we catch intimate, fugitive reflections of our own strangeness.

I say 'after all' because so much of her life as a writer, and so much of the life *in* her writing, was intransigent, bloody-minded, mocking, self-conscious and excessive. These were qualities that kept her for many years unassimilated, a figure identified with 'fantasy', Gothic, otherness. . . . Though she had always taken the line that fantasy was not the shadow-side of a binary opposition, but had a real life history. Being was marinated in magic, and (conversely) imaginary monsters had no separate sphere.

One of the heroes of her generation of writers, and a hero of hers, too (which didn't always follow), was Gabriel García Márquez. He liked to tell interviewers that he arrived at the style of *One Hundred Years of Solitude* by modelling himself on his grandmother's story-telling technique. Grandma would make the transition from realistic events to impossible imaginings without any change of expression, he said – with 'a brick face'.[1] Márquez's 'magical realism' certainly helped Carter's confidence in the continuity you could create between these supposedly disparate ways of describing the world. She herself played – or, better, played at – the grandmother role often during the last decade or so, in fact from the retold fairy tales of *The Bloody Chamber* (1979) onwards. Fantasy was an everyday, *domestic* business, she'd say. The ancient metaphor of yarn-spinning connected literature with the world of work. Cooking and quilt-making also had a lot in common with the craft of fiction, if you went back to pre-novel precedents. In 1990 she wrote, in the Introduction to the collection of *Fairy Tales* she edited for Virago:

> fairy tales, stories from the oral tradition, are all of them the most vital connection we have with the imaginations of the ordinary men and women whose labour created our world. . . . Ours is a highly individualised culture, with a great faith in the work of art as a unique one-off, and the artist as an original, a godlike and inspired creator of unique one-offs. But fairy tales are not like that, nor are their makers. Who first invented meatballs? In what country? Is there a definitive recipe for potato soup? Think in terms of the domestic arts. 'This is how *I* make potato soup.'[2]

Her discovery of this voice for herself didn't happen all at once, but bit by bit over the years. It was a witty, witchy idea. Also, ironically, a sign of her originality. She rightly discerned that a woman's inventiveness had still a whiff of original sin, and the grandmother-guise of the yarn-spinner was a splendid cover for a speculative, unsatisfied mind. She was the wolf in Grandma's nightcap.

The nostalgia for anonymity, for the archaic powers of the narrator whose authority rests precisely on *disclaiming* individual authority, is real, though, and goes deeper.

Angela Carter has become almost alarmingly 'central' for all sorts of readers and researchers. (We're told by the President of the British Academy, Sir Keith Thomas, that last year alone – 1992–3 – there were more than forty applicants wanting to do doctorates on Carter, making her by far the most fashionable twentieth-century topic.) This is not just because – as Gore Vidal mischievously pointed out once upon a time – death can be a very wise career move for the artist, but because she found a way of speaking for a longed-for loss of singularity. Not the death of *this* author, but The Death of The Author, no less. We want our representative works to be multivoiced, dialogic, hybrid. The author's dissolution into different and diverging sub-selves on the page has become for us the text's utopian promise. I'm paraphrasing Italo Calvino, another kindred spirit for Carter. In his posthumously published *Six Memos for the Next Millennium* (1988) he put it this way:

> the modern books that we love most are the outcome of a
> confluence and a clash of a multiplicity of interpretative
> methods, modes of thought, and styles of expression. Even
> if the overall design has been minutely planned, what
> matters is not the enclosure of the work within a
> harmonious figure, but the centrifugal force produced by it
> – a plurality of languages as a guarantee of a truth that is
> not merely partial.[3]

It's a vision born out of intense self-consciousness, self-doubt and the dangerous pleasures of demystification (demystify the individual self, and where are you?). Angela Carter arrived at her present pre-eminence the hard way, after a lot of picaresque adventures.

*

The first words of her first novel, *Shadow Dance* (1966): 'The bar was a mock-up, a forgery, a fake: an ad-man's crazy dream of a Spanish patio. . . .' Her début is all pastiche – set against the background of the sixties' camping-up of the cultural heritage, and (to multiply and intensify the effect) done in a style that is itself littered with quotations and allusions. Looking back, she commented: 'I do think we're at the end of a line, and to a certain extent I'm making a conscious critique of the culture I was born to.'[4] At the time it was more like a fascination, an addiction even, the sign of an imagination preoccupied with the decay and discrediting of the real. Her reading list included Swift, Blake, Mary Shelley, Poe, Lewis Carroll, Bram Stoker. . . . A strong overlay of Gothic, in any case, which – together with her line in camp cruelties – lends this novel in particular a Hammer Horror atmosphere – though all the novels up to and including *Love* (written in 1969, published in 1971) share a deliberately 'decadent' fancy for 'the smell of dirt, poverty and graveclothes'.[5] It's the very whiff of the past – if you perceive the past not as a living heritage, but as *undead*, stuff to animate and galvanise and replay.

It's a classless society, so far as the allusions go: Orpheus is quite likely to come back from the Underworld hand in hand with the bride of Frankenstein in this sixties Bohemia. All the accumulated imagery that silts up the modern imagination is levelled out in the democracy of 'death' (always with camp quotes). Carter's education had had a touch of the autodidact's idiosyncrasy about it, which probably helped. She did go to university (Bristol) to read English, but later than usual, and already married (see potted biography on p. viii); and she cheered up the leftover Leavisite canon which was what one mostly got in those days (there are some fleeting, scornful references to this in her third novel, *Several Perceptions* [1968]) with medieval texts that led her into the territory of romance and folk tale and anthropology. She loved the French Symbolists, and the Surrealists, and the films of Godard and Buñuel too. The early books clash and mingle icons and images and signs with mischievous indifference to their history and background, their provenance. And the same – much more disconcertingly – is true of characters. It's sometimes an insidious effect, sometimes blatant, especially (no surprise) with the girls (Ghislaine in *Shadow Dance*, a 'ravishing automaton' [p. 7]). But all the people are pretty consistently treated like role-players, assemblages of gestures and ready-scripted lines who are liable at any moment to flatten out into shadows themselves.

This wouldn't matter if they didn't also strike one as, at the same time, recognisably human – but they do, so their violence to themselves and each other is horrible, as well as (often) black-comic. For instance: it is a measure of the shakiness of characters' identities that they prey on each other in order to *feel real*: '"I should like . . . to play chess with men and women"', says Honeybuzzard in *Shadow Dance* (p. 112); or again: '"I would like to have a cupboard bulging with all different bodies and faces"'; or simply '"I would like to wear him"' (p. 76). Jewel in *Heroes and Villains* (1969), who's been elaborately tattooed by his mentor, Donally, says: '"He might even make me up into a ceremonial robe and wear me on special occasions"';[6] and in the same book Marianne reveals herself as the fake-shaman Donally's successor when she says nastily to Jewel: '"What I'd like best would be to keep you in preserving fluid in a huge jar on the mantelpiece of my peaceful room"' (p. 137). (It's that wide-eyed, wistful, childish formula 'What I would like . . .' that gives these lines their chilling quality.) Prey and predator, killer and victim, can coexist in the same person. Annabel in *Love* steals the sixties' last scene when she operates this way on herself – goes to the beauty parlour, bleaches her hair, does herself up, and commits suicide, 'a painted doll, bluish at the extremities. . . . Flies already clustered round her eyes' (p. 124).

Carter's people are constructs in any case, not born but made. Much later on interviewers would ask her why her characters so seldom had mothers, and she realised (she said) that in the novels houses stood in for mothers – 'When mother is dead, all the life has gone out of the house. The shop in *The Magic Toyshop* gets burnt down, the old dark house, and adult life begins. . . .'[7] The house stands for 'the culture I was born to' (*not* the nature) and for that whole sense of the past as a store-room of properties and costumes to try on – including, more narrowly, literature's past, the house of fiction's heritage. The houses in these early books are fascinating, threatening places, most obviously the magic toyshop, though the ruinous mansion in *Heroes and Villains*, which Jewel and Marianne burn down, starting with the chapel, is equally suggestive. For houses may symbolise mothers, but they belong none the less to patriarchal proprietors.

It's a measure of Carter's ingenuity, and of the intensity with which she scrutinised these decaying images, that she was able to reanimate in them such telling associations. Her houses are churchy (*Shadow Dance*), mirror-lined mausoleums (*Several Perceptions*), wombs and tombs. And to get back to mother: in her much later triple revision of the Grimm version of 'Cinderella', 'Ashputtle: or, the Mother's Ghost', 'mother love . . . winds about these daughters like a shroud'.[8] In its ultimate transformation the tale yields a mother who, in setting up the happy ending, is really saying to her daughter: ' "Step into my coffin" ':

> 'No,' said the girl. She shuddered.
> 'I stepped into *my* mother's coffin when I was your age.'

> The girl stepped into the coffin although she thought it
> would be the death of her. It turned into a coach and
> horses. The horses stamped, eager to be gone.
>   'Go and seek your fortune, darling.' (pp. 119–20)

Another, much mellower later exploration of the womb/
tomb idea (death transmitted as life) is the story titled 'The
Curious Room', first published in *Swiss Papers in English
Language and Literature* (SPELL for short) in 1990. Here the
matrix of transformations is a Renaissance *Wunderkammer*,
or cabinet of curiosities:

> There's a theory, one I find persuasive, that the quest for
> knowledge is, at bottom, the search for the answer to the
> question: 'Where was I before I was born?'
>   'In the beginning was . . . what?
>   Perhaps, in the beginning, there was a curious room,
> crammed with wonders . . .[9]

In 1987 she went back to *Love*, revised it, and added an
Afterword in a parody of nineteenth-century realist convention, telling us what happened to the characters after the
book. But not, of course, Annabel, who stays definitely
dead, a sacrifice to the spirit of the self-fashioning age in
which Carter had her beginning as a writer. The book, she
said, was 'Annabel's coffin' (p. 114).

'Go and seek your fortune, darling . . .'. And so she did,
but not exactly Cinderella-style. She had won the Somerset
Maugham award for *Several Perceptions* – 'In 1969, I was
given some money to run away with, and did so. The
money was the Somerset Maugham Award and five
hundred pounds went further in those days; it took me as

far as Japan. . . .'[10] She left her first husband behind her,
and lived – first with a Japanese lover; later, it seems, alone
– in Japan for two years. Thus she completed a project of
estrangement, taking herself as far away from home as
possible. What she made of 'the empire of signs' (Roland
Barthes's phrase) can be seen in some of the stories in
Fireworks (1974), and the pieces she wrote for *New Society*
(some of them collected in *Nothing Sacred* [1982]). She was
compounding, multiplying and confronting her sense of the
artificiality of her own 'nature'. The short story 'Flesh and
the Mirror', whose title I have borrowed for this book,
describes with austere exactitude an erotic encounter in
Tokyo in which she/I steps out of the old identity she has
in a culture that *recognises* her and gives her depth, and
faces herself as existence and action, not essence. What
vanishes is her conviction that she has an inner sanctum of
consciousness – a kind of psychic virginity, now revealed as
duplicity:

> all the time I was pulling the strings of my own puppet. . . .
> I attempted to rebuild the city according to the blueprint in
> my imagination as a backdrop to the plays in my puppet
> theatre, but it sternly refused to be so rebuilt. . . . On the
> night I came back to it, however hard I looked for the one I
> loved, she could not find him anywhere and the city
> delivered her into the hands of a perfect stranger. . . .[11]

In the hotel the mirror on the ceiling records their reflections' truth: 'There was nothing whatsoever beyond the
surface of the glass. Nothing kept me from the fact, the
act. . . . Women and mirrors are in complicity with one
another to evade the action I/she performs. . . . But *this*
mirror refused to conspire with me' (p. 65). The story's plot
is this: she runs away from this too-honest mirror, finds the

lover, and spends the next night with him, in a performance of guilt and intimacy, but cannot sustain her sense of fake drama: 'his features were blurring, like the underwriting on a palimpsest. . . . Then the city vanished; it ceased, almost immediately, to be a magic and appalling place. I woke up one morning and found it had become home' (p. 70).

Home is where the heart isn't. There's at least one imaginative twist in the story's anti-moral. 'I had been precipitated', we are told, 'into knowledge of the real conditions of living' (p. 65). This bleak-but-liberated sentence – which occurs just about in the place where she should, conventionally speaking, have been describing orgasm or (at least) undifferentiated bliss – actually seems, on closer scrutiny, to mean something unexpected. On the face of things she is renouncing 'magic'; in fact I think she is denying that magic is alien or strange, and so becoming a citizen of strangeness. It is the sexual tourist, or – to put it more politely – the orientalist, who finds the city and the 'arbitrary carnival' of its streets exotic. A true denizen of the mirror, one who can accept 'the fact, the act', will be at home *because* she is naturalised, can acknowledge her own inalienable self-consciousness. . . . It was here, I think, that Carter's project of estrangement became truly her vocation ('the fact, the act'), a matter of experience. 'It was as if I had never experienced my experience as experience' (p. 63), she says of the story's self, before she levitates into the ceiling mirror. It's a line she uses again, about the journalist Jack Walser at the beginning of *Nights at the Circus* (1984), before *he* goes through the gruelling rite of passage in which he loses and finds a self. Magic becomes one's daily fare.

So Japan completed the work of the sixties. Looking back, she talked about that country and that piece of time in very similar terms. 'In Japan I learnt what it was to be a woman and became radicalised,' she wrote in 1982,[12] and in 1983:

I can date to that time . . . and to that sense of heightened
awareness of the society around me in the summer of 1968,
my own questioning of the nature of my reality as a *woman*.
How that fiction of my 'femininity' was created. . . .[13]

It was an experience of vertigo, and of the hollowing-out or
deconstruction of 'the nature of [her] reality'. Another
Fireworks story, 'Reflections', dramatises the dizzying step
into the looking-glass with a lyrical intensity that in the end
becomes murderous violence. These virtuoso passages
come from the description of the mirror-world:

> The first thing that struck me was, the light was black. My
> eyes took a little time to grow accustomed to this absolute
> darkness for, although the delicate apparatus of cornea and
> aqueous humour and crystalline lens and vitreous body and
> optic nerve and retina had all been reversed when I gave
> birth to my mirror self through the mediation of the looking
> glass, yet my sensibility remained as it had been. . . .
> (p. 93)

> I saw wild garlic and ground elder and the buttercups and
> daisies in the fossilised undergrowth now rendered in
> vivacious yet unnameable colours, as immobile arabesques
> without depth. But the sweetness of the wild roses rang in
> my ears like a peal of windbells for the vibrations of the
> perfumes echoed on my eardrums like the pulse of my own
> blood. . . . (p. 97)

This inside-out pastoral with its solid, viscous air and
backwards logic is a kind of apotheosis of the theme of the
beginning, 'when I gave birth to my mirror self'. The story's
atmosphere of palpable illusion – the sensation is like being
trapped in metaphysical treacle, a human fly in amber – is
reminiscent of her darkest earlier novels, *Shadow Dance* and

Love. But its plot anticipates the restless reversals of *The Passion of New Eve* (1977). The Carter who came of age in Japan would be on the move from here on. Her sixties fictions had had – to simplify shamelessly – two different kinds of structure. There's the cabinet-of-curiosities or mausoleum shape, which is not always death-bound (*Several Perceptions* [1968] has a celebratory and benevolent ending) but is essentially static. And there's the speculative and/or picaresque plot, as in *The Magic Toyshop* and *Heroes and Villains*. It's this style of allegorical adventure which provides the pattern for the novels of the next decade, *New Eve* and *The Infernal Desire Machines of Doctor Hoffman*, which was published the year she came back to England, 1972.

The other kind of travelling she had been doing was mental travelling – particularly in the realms of theory and, more particularly still, structuralist anthropology and deconstruction. In a sense she had already worked out her 'line' in terms of narrative images and the analysis of character-as-construct. During the mid 1970s, however, when she had a real struggle to re-establish herself as a writer in Britain, she used ideas as a kind of armour, and as a way of marking out a space for herself where none existed ready-made. *The Sadeian Woman* (1979) was the outcome of her idiosyncratic mix of ironic utopianism and militant materialism. This 'Exercise in Cultural History' was commissioned by the recently founded Virago Press, whose advisory group she was a member of from the beginning. She had by now recognised herself as a feminist – wholeheartedly, yet at the same time with an enormous reluctance:

> 'If the fool persists in his folly, he becomes wise.' I suppose that was how I came to feminism, in the end, because still

and all there remained something out of joint and it turned
out that was it, rather an important thing, that all the time I
thought things were going so well I was a second class
citizen.[14]

The quotation inside this quotation comes from William
Blake's *Proverbs of Hell*. Blake, along with de Sade (both
great guerrillas of the Age of Enlightenment), was a favourite source, because of his radical irony and the parodic
authority of his devil's aphorisms. Carter believed, too,
with Blake, in the power of 'mind-forg'd manacles'; hence
(she would argue) the need to take such a long way round
to arrive at a view of women now.

In the de Sade book she sets out to track down and
discredit the lure and prestige of suffering. So her feminist
book is also aimed against a certain sisterhood. Other
writers during these years were constructing women's traditions: it's characteristic of Carter that she was setting out
to identify and demolish one, as a means of opening up a
seemingly timeless zone to historical consciousness. De
Sade's beautiful, suffering, incurably innocent Justine had
offspring after all:

> This good little girl's martyrisation by the circumstances of
> adult life as a woman makes her the ancestress of a
> generation of women in popular fiction who find
> themselves in the same predicament, such as the heart-
> struck, tearful heroines of Jean Rhys, Edna O'Brien and
> Joan Didion who remain grumblingly acquiescent in a fate
> over which they believe they have no control. . . . There is
> presumably no direct literary influence from the eighteenth
> century philosophical pornographer to these contemporary
> women novelists, but, in the character of Justine, Sade
> contrived to isolate the dilemma of an emergent type of
> woman. Justine, daughter of a banker, becomes the

prototype of two centuries of women who find the world
was not, as they had been promised, made for them. . . .
These self-consciously blameless ones suffer and suffer until
it becomes second nature; Justine marks the start of a kind
of self-regarding female masochism, a woman with no place
in the world, no status, the core of whose resistence has
been eaten away by self-pity.[15]

If you locate 'the start' of the rot, you can begin to plot an
end, is one of the implications here. Another (this is why
I've quoted at length) is the relentless determination conveyed by the book's polemical style. The writing sets itself
against sympathy and against niceness, because they col-
lude with suffering, and so help to mystify the good
woman's lack of worldliness, and keep her 'in voluntary
exile from the historic world, in its historic time that is
counted out minute by minute . . .' (p. 106).

It's central to Carter's argument that this lack of 'a place
in the world' is not women's genuine condition but a piece
of mystification, a myth, a nonsense – and a nonsense that
is compounded by the sanctification of motherhood. The
same sort of double-take obtains here, however, as in the
seeming renunciation of 'magic' in the story 'Flesh and the
Mirror'. It's not only that we must unmask 'bankrupt
enchantments' (p. 109), but that they must be equipped
with a real, blow-by-blow life-story, a *history*. There is no
world but the world, in short. And that means that any
strategy that valorises women as outsiders is suspect. She's
speaking a language with an interest in power – not only
the oppressor's power, but its own, her own. Her difficulties in making a place for herself on the literary scene must
have fuelled her scorn for self-pity (and her dread of it).
Certainly the essentialism of some feminist arguments provoked her into standing up for artifice, and insisting on the

artificiality of women's 'nature'. Most important, though, was the new vividness with which she became conscious of *time* as the territory on which you had to stake your claim.

This nervy and aggressive show of confidence derives from the support she found in some very un-British theoreticians. Her closest affinities earlier on had probably been with Roland Barthes, but in the 1970s it was, I suspect, Michel Foucault who counted most. She lists his early book *Madness and Civilization* (1961) in the de Sade book's bibliography, but she was also thinking very much along the same lines as he had in *La Volonté de savoir* (1976), translated as Volume I of *The History of Sexuality* in 1978. He too is going back to the eighteenth century to locate the beginnings of the modern 'deployment' of sexuality and, like her, he's concerned to question the notion that sex is outside history:

> what was involved . . . was the very production of sexuality. Sexuality must not be thought of as a kind of natural given which power tries to hold in check, or as an obscure domain which knowledge tries gradually to uncover. It is the name that can be given to an historical construct: not a furtive reality that is difficult to grasp, but a great surface network in which the stimulation of bodies, the intensification of pleasures, the incitement to discourse . . . are linked to one another, in accordance with a few major strategies of knowledge and power.[16]

Carter's 'Flesh comes to us out of history' (*The Sadeian Woman*, p. 11) makes the same move. These sweeping, abstract assertions have an ironic air about them, for what they mean to herald is an anti-universalist style of thinking: 'we have also invented those aspects of our lives that seem most immutable' (ibid). We mythicise certain zones of experience, and so keep them subtly out of focus (even when they obsess us). Our patterns of thinking, Foucault argued – and Carter would have agreed – generate false entities and perpetuate dead conditions.

Some of the oddest and most gnomic passages in *The History of Sexuality* are about 'bio-power', by which Foucault seems to mean social engineering, public health and population control – 'this was nothing less than the entry of life into history. . . . Western man was gradually learning what it meant to be a living species in a living world. . . . For the first time in history biological existence was reflected in political existence . . .' (pp. 141–2) We need a 'bio-history' (p. 143) to chart these processes adequately, though first (regress threatens often in this book) we need to wean ourselves away from the habit of locating authority in one patriarchal place: 'We must at the same time conceive of sex without the law, and power without the king' (p. 91). Power doesn't simply forbid, it also instigates and creates (compare the role of Carter's Doctor Hoffman), and in any case it is divided, disseminated and diffused:

> The omnipresence of power: not because it has the privilege of consolidating everything under its invincible unity, but because it is produced from one moment to the next, at every point, or rather in every relation from one point to another. Power is everywhere; not because it embraces everything, but because it comes from everywhere. (p. 93)

Foucault's revisionist picture of (sexual) politics mirrors Carter's thinking during these years. Whether or not she made direct use of *The History of Sexuality*, it does exemplify the kind of intellectual company she kept. And in practice, in the writing of fiction, she was playing out what she preached. Her marvellous collection of rewritten fairy tales,

The Bloody Chamber, was published in the same year as the de Sade book, 1979. In it supposedly immutable and time-less aspects of experience – and the symbols and forms that represent them – are melted down, reworked, wound up again and set in motion.

She became a conscious and deliberate revisionist, draw-ing the representations of otherness and outsiderhood into speculative 'histories', picaresque allegories and polemical plots. At the same time she took on a new authority as a writer. It's a paradoxical authority, because it involves the multiplication and dispersal of the narrative voice ('power is everywhere'). This is performative and political writing, writing that means to *work*. One last quotation from *The Sadeian Woman*:

> Fine art, that exists for itself alone, is art in a final state of impotence. If nobody, including the artist, acknowledges art as a means of *knowing* the world, then art is relegated to a kind of rumpus room of the mind. . . . (p. 13)

That image – the 'rumpus room of the mind' – gives one pause, as do her attacks on 'bankrupt enchantments' and 'fraudulent magic' (p. 109), because she's coming danger-ously close to scorning the properties of her own fiction. In impure practice, of course, what she does is not to banish the unrealities, the past's legacy of lumber, but to rewrite them into mutability, pull them into a world of change.

It's a high-risk strategy, no doubt. I haven't, I realise, mentioned what was at the time the most obviously scan-dalous aspect of her approach: her conviction that the pornographer de Sade can be made over into an ally in the task of demystification. This got her into great trouble in 1979 and for years afterwards, though radical feminist attacks on her for bad faith carry less conviction these days in the face of the range and carnival good humour of the later work. In the 1980s, in her forties, she came into her own – assembled bit by bit the yarn-spinner, Mother Goose persona, and settled down in South London, which meant travelling all over the world to read, and to teach creative writing. Thinking about writing as a practical craft fitted in with her revulsion against 'fine art' (see above) and the character of the artist (isolated, the apotheosis of the out-sider) that went with it. This sort of work helped to pay the mortgage, too, though she did start earning enough from the writing itself to more-or-less break even, during the 1980s.

Readings recalled for her the story-teller's ancient role, and had something of the magic she found in writing for radio: 'the atavistic lure, the atavistic power, of voices in the dark . . . the writer who gives the words to those voices retains some of the authority of the most antique tellers of tales'.[17] Except that you had to play all the parts yourself. In fact, she didn't 'act' her stories in this sense – it wasn't the multiple voices one was aware of, but the teasing power of the narrator who would, within the same story, give you different versions, turn it around or inside out, transform it. Her reading style was stylised, charming in the strong and disconcerting sense of that word. More than most of her contemporaries, I suspect, she found performing her work not so much an afterthought as a dimension of its real life, something that entered into its nature. In the last two novels, *Nights at the Circus* (1984) and *Wise Children* (1991), the protagonists are performers – professional *artistes*, no less. The real point about this, though, is the skill with which she got the illusion of voices and bodies on to the page. She was a woman of letters, after all, and that's no small part of the humour of the granny role she invented for herself. She judged, anthologised, edited, introduced, all with zest.

The paradox remains: the wolf in Grandma's clothing. Grandma has been eaten up, in fact, by one of the boldest and most voracious imaginations of our time. There's the same sort of tension in the air when you start to analyse her authorial authority. True, she distributes the role of narrator with cunning largesse: stories within stories, switches of voice, and so on. Yet the whole project (one should never forget) is devoted to deconstructing the notion of transcendence, or of any soulful or metaphysical conception of creation. She wanted to *secularise* the art of writing, in the last analysis, and for her this was bound up with the demystification of motherhood which she undertook with such cruel gusto in the 1970s. The logic behind this was hinted at in the story 'The Curious Room'. We're obsessed with origins and originality, but though the womb in our heads/the *Wunderkammer* is indeed full of amazing things, the myths and the magic are of our own contrivance. . . . Demystify motherhood, and you abolish the last hiding-place for eternity.

Having exorcised the Holy Mother, she proceeded to have a child herself, in 1983. She and Mark Pearce had been living a settled-vagrant life together since the mid 1970s, based in South London and travelling when they could, and they went on doing so with their son Alexander until in the last year of her life, 1991–2, illness grounded her. Her death has sent us all back to her fiction with a different kind of attention. This book, however, aims to reflect something of the directness and freshness of people's responses to the work when it was still work in progress.

Some of the contributors to this collection are Angela Carter's fellow writers, some are academics and researchers, some freelance critics, and several of them combine a couple of these roles. On the whole the tone is celebratory, though that doesn't preclude or mask the ambivalence in people's responses. Indeed, you gather quite often, even if you're not reading between the lines, that part of what characterises Carter is her power to provoke. But then again, that is precisely what some readers are perverse enough to *relish*, which is why celebration clearly wins out. It was always a pleasure to argue with her, and some of the same effect lingers in the words on the page.

She is just not the kind of writer whose fiction abides interpretation with docility – for one thing she was an intellectual, of the vagrant self-appointed kind less common in Britain than in France or Italy; as a result, there's a generous amount of 'metafictional' critical reflection built in. And for another thing, her speculative fiction is designed to allow its images, characters and places to be squatted or intermittently possessed by ideas in time-honoured allegorical fashion. In order to underline her impatience with the notion that art was outside daily differences, she took to spelling out her position with challenging baldness: 'to explore ideas . . . for me . . . is the same thing as telling stories since, for me, a narrative is an argument stated in fictional terms'.[18]

Did she mean it? Yes, I think so, in the sense that she distrusted critical traditions – 1950s New Critical and 1970s poststructuralist alike, for once – which would cut textuality off from worldliness. She pitched fiction's dubious authority against authority. I've always thought that one of the reasons she so admired William Blake was the way he contrived to take the formal shape of the balanced, aphoristic sentence and use it to advance the most heterodox suggestions. For instance: 'You never know what is enough unless you know what is more than enough.' Or (a less subtle and more notorious example): 'Sooner murder an infant in its cradle than nurse unacted desires' (*Proverbs of Hell*, numbers 46 and 67). She multiplied and distributed and so strengthened the authorial voice, and that is why, I think, her writing resists the orthodox strategies of deconstruction. You can make it sound like *écriture féminine* only if you don't quote much. She picked and chose her literary influences: French theory, but not necessarily French feminist theory; Donne, but only in his cynical, dandy guise; Surrealists *except* when it came to women; in general, a range of reading so heterogeneous that it revamps the whole notion of handing on (tradition); and always a generous admixture of the non- or sub-literary in any case.

The pieces in this volume are arranged to cover the fiction chronologically, more or less, from the sixties on; and the first – by Marc O'Day – addresses directly that decade's flamboyant reinventions of the past, which Carter both exemplified and chronicled. She was, he argues, a kind of realist then, if you allow that reality had taken on a strange patina of impermanence. Sue Roe, overlapping on the last of those novels, *Love*, agrees, but sees the reality in question as even more savagely distorted. She focuses on the racked symbolism of the surreal as a way of analysing the heroine Annabel – the 'desiring hysteric' the Surrealists left out. Her Carter is at the end of something, on the verge of the unimaginable. Susan Rubin Suleiman, who concentrates on *Doctor Hoffman* (1972), is also describing a 'dark' literary collage that exposes the seemingly timeless role of the feminine, but in this novel she's able to trace shadows from the future, cast by postmodernism and the women's movement. History is getting in on the act.

The next group of essays deals mainly with the ideas and the speculative fictions, so it has its centre of gravity in the 1970s, with *The Passion of New Eve* and the book on de Sade. Margaret Atwood's title sets the tone: 'Running with the

Tigers'. Atwood and Carter eventually became friends, and I've always thought that the heroine's subversive sidekick in the brothel in *The Handmaid's Tale* was a tribute to Carter, in the form of a vignette from her kind of world. Be that as it may, both writers revisited and revised their earlier work during the 1980s. In her essay here, Atwood rereads *The Bloody Chamber* in the light of *The Sadeian Woman*, and the result is horrid and hilarious, and a tribute from one tale-spinner to another: 'She knows her motifs, and Wolf-Alice is in part a Frog Prince story – kiss the yucky thing, the really yucky thing, and it will get better; though the Duke, even when licked, is no prince.' Nicole Ward Jouve, by contrast, charts her own changing relations to and readings of Carter through gaps and estrangements over the years. Rapprochements too, of course. This essay, like Sue Roe's, is a sort of writerly 'close encounter'. That both of them are fiction writers as well as literary academics has something to do with it: they don't react to Carter's work only as critics; there's a special edge to their responses, to do with shared territory (and the doubt: but how far is it shared?)

Carter linked a lot of different worlds. Roz Kaveney describes one that's really several, the world of science fiction, and draws out what Carter got from the genre, and (perhaps more surprisingly) what she gave to it. This is an essay that gives remarks about the openness of Carter's texts a new and refreshingly particular meaning. Elaine Jordan, taking an overview of Carter's fifteen-year speculative journey from *Heroes and Villains* through to *Nights at the Circus*, argues that these novels provide a kind of traveller's companion-guide 'in a changing world where claims to universality struggle with different particular claims'. Her main topic is the allegory of gender, and also Carter's way of handling narrative and iconic devices themselves, so that they act in new, ambivalent ways. Carter also enjoyed –

and found food for thought in – transforming her own written words into 'voices in the dark' (for radio) and film images (*The Company of Wolves*, *The Magic Toyshop*). Guido Almansi, writing on the radio plays, conjures her up as a meaty, 'maximalist' writer, engaged not in 'a simple miscegenation of reality and dreams . . . but an overloading of the frequencies of real life'. Laura Mulvey revisits the history of cinema magic, and traces the affinities between cinema and (oral) story-telling. Where did the old monsters go? Into the 'new technologies of illusion' is one answer.

One of Carter's most successful pieces of illusionism was the process by which she made over her own authorial persona from the 1980s on. In 'Bottle Blonde, Double Drag' Marina Warner traces the provenance of the yarn-spinner, and the larger transition by which 'Gothic decadence turns into comic defiance', and (a double or even triple somersault, this) burlesque in turn becomes 'a last-ditch stratagem, even an admission of defeat' in the political climate of these times. Isobel Armstrong (again concerned with crossdressing, and dressing up) sees the Carter of *Nights at the Circus* as the heir to the Virginia Woolf of *Orlando*. *Nights*, with its stylised, external manner, 'as if all experience . . . is self-consciously conceived of as *display*', is the festive rival of the grey 'fiction of elegy' we've tended to associate with Woolf's legacy.

These closing essays, in fact, follow Carter home to roost, and explore the question of her place in British cultural tradition. Kate Webb's piece on the last novel, *Wise Children* (1991), looks at that novel's many-sided, comic claim to represent Shakespeare's bastard offspring, the 'other' line that's not content to stay on the sidelines. And finally, Hermione Lee takes issue with one of the more comprehensive posthumous tributes to Carter's nuisance-value, by John Bayley (also a target for Elaine Jordan), and again makes the Woolf connection. She is right, I am sure, to imply that what the British literary world makes of Angela Carter will be a sign – one of many, but a significant one – of our capacity to imagine the future into existence.

That takes readers as well as writers, and I'm enormously grateful to this book's contributors. Quite a few of them were Angela Carter's friends or acquaintances, so for them it was perhaps, in a sense, a labour of love, but even so. . . . Nearly all of these essays were originally written or specially revised for the occasion, for which many thanks. It's appropriate, too, that Virago is the publisher of this first collection on Carter, since she was, of course, one of Virago's fairy godmothers.

'Mutability is Having a Field Day': The Sixties Aura of Angela Carter's Bristol Trilogy

MARC O'DAY

Introduction: Realism and The Bristol Trilogy

> The first novel I wrote, *Shadow Dance*, was about a perfectly
> real area of the city in which I lived. It didn't give exactly
> mimetic copies of the people I knew, but it was absolutely
> as real as the milieu I was familiar with: it was set in
> provincial bohemia.
>
> (Angela Carter, interviewed by John Haffenden, 1984)

We have become too used to characterising Angela Carter's
fiction by the shorthand label 'magical realism'. The term
began to be applied to her writing, apparently with the
author's blessing, in the early 1980s, and it took a firm hold
with the publication of *Nights at the Circus* in 1984.[1] Later, in
some of the tributes and reassessments which followed her
death, it was retrospectively applied to the whole of her
oeuvre from the sixties onwards.[2] This is inaccurate: several
of the early novels actually invite readings in terms of quite
traditional literary realism. True, it is a sixties realism
saturated with domesticated gothic and psychological fantasy elements, but 'magic', in the sense of supernatural or
fantastic violations of the laws of everyday life, hardly
comes into it.

The works I have in mind here are the little-known *Shadow
Dance* (1966) and *Several Perceptions* (1968), and the much

better known *Love* (1971). These three novels, it seems to me, clearly belong together within Carter's *oeuvre*, because of the many formal and thematic elements they share. I label them collectively 'The Bristol Trilogy', for though Bristol is never named as the city in which they are set, external evidence makes the autobiographical connection clear.[3] The Trilogy novels offer realist representations of the 1960s 'provincial bohemia' which Carter herself inhabited. They deploy a similar motley array of characters, plot structures which can be read as variants of one another, comparable forms of narration, and a wide variety of themes and motifs concerning the sixties counterculture in which Carter moved. In all, they exude a fascinating period aura and are full of charming and nasty contemporary 'notations' – to use Roland Barthes's term for those descriptive details which construct the 'effect' of reality.[4] This essay aims to show that reading these early novels literally affords us valuable insights into the particular cultural and social moment from which Carter's writing derives much of its style, energy and historical vision.

How do these books produce their reality effects? Taking setting first, the events of the Bristol Trilogy 'happen' – very much in the sixties sense of 'happening', where art and life mingle so that life itself is often a form of art – in a variety of everyday, local private and public spaces. These include bedsits, flats and houses (derelict as well as occupied), cafés and coffee bars, pubs and shops, auction rooms, museums, libraries, hospitals, the Zoo and the Labour Exchange, and outdoor locations like the streets, the park and the Down. The locations are not identical. In *Shadow Dance* the auction room, the junk shop and the derelict houses are fore-grounded; in *Several Perceptions* it's the Down, the (anti)hero's bedsit and a large, shabby mansion; and in *Love* the park, the ballroom (must be a Mecca) and, most of all, the protagonists' two-room flat. There is, nevertheless, a strong sense that Carter is representing the same place over a period of time.

One American commentator describes the milieu of *Shadow Dance* as 'a British slum where streets smell of urine, vomit, and stale beer'.[5] Carter quoted with amusement reviewers' responses to her chosen locale, which certainly isn't all urine and vomit, though it's undeniably, gloriously seedy. She'd insist that the novel concerned 'a perfectly real area of the city in which I lived', while London-based reviewers tended to view it as 'a completely other world', nothing like the one with which they were familiar.[6] Of course, this was partly due to her use of gothic codes. Her implied criticism of the reviewers, too, is no doubt partly tongue-in-cheek, but it also conveys a truth about the mainstream metropolitan insularity of the reviewing Establishment.

The Trilogy's locations, then, are a fictional mediation of and an imaginative response to the particular place where the author lived, in marked contrast to the fictional worlds of the speculative fictions. Similarly, too, the motley, marginal, deviant and mainly countercultural characters in each of the novels are partly composites drawn from the people among whom she lived. Fashionable youth in various phases provide the core: if they aren't students at the university or the art school or pupils at the comprehensive school, they're liable either to be doing short-term jobs to earn a bit of cash or to be living on the dole. Some have 'square' jobs, like factory worker or teacher, but many are engaged in more self-consciously arty and bohemian pursuits, such as the second-hand trade, or art, or jewellery and handicrafts. (No one, as far as I can remember, is a writer.) Then there are other, often older, people whose lives have marginalised them from middlebrow society: an ageing prostitute, a faded actress, a former music-hall artiste, a tramp, as well as the locals who work in the shops and cafés. Authority is represented by parents who put in an occasional appearance, or lurk in the minds of their offspring; and by psychiatrists, who are increasingly prominent as the decade proceeds. But youth is at the centre of things and Carter, like anyone under thirty in the sixties (and, indeed, like many people over thirty), was intensely conscious of the sexiness of youth: witness her feeling that she was 'a has-been' when she published her first novel at the ripe old age of twenty-six.[7]

The plots of these novels are also similar: they circulate around youthful death. *Shadow Dance* and *Love* are particularly close to one another, since in each a love triangle involving two young men and a young woman is at the centre of events which conclude with the woman's death. In the earlier novel, the exhibitionistic, polymorphously perverse Honeybuzzard – bird of prey, sweet thing, bastard – tyrannises those closest to him, the weak, neurotic Morris Gray and the masochistic Arthurian moonchild Ghislaine, whom he has (probably) scarred and whom he finally murders in a blasphemous ritual. Honey and Ghislaine are 'twins for blondness and prettiness, with a wild innocence in their playing bred of sheer perversity . . . two golden beloved children destroying each other', while the unhappily grey Morris is often dangerously close to the locals whom Honey despises: '"They are all shadows. How can you be sorry for shadows?"'[8] The title switch between the British and American editions, from *Shadow Dance* to *Honeybuzzard*, reflects a shift of attention from the supporting cast to the monster himself.

Love represents, with frank intensity, the sadomasochistic and emotionally cannibalistic triangle involving two half-brothers: narcissistic schoolteacher Lee and his unstable brother Buzz (self-named, truncated descendant of Honey-buzzard), and Lee's equally unstable wife Annabel. It ends with Annabel's suicide. She's tried at least twice before, though each brother feels that the other is responsible.

Several Perceptions works the other way round, in a double sense: here death haunts a young man, Joseph Harker, instead of a woman; and his suicide attempt, in part a response to his girlfried Charlotte's departure, occurs in the novel's first chapter, not its last. Joseph's preferred mode, like Annabel's when she is finally successful, is gas (Morris, too, briefly contemplates a similar fate in the opening chapter of the first novel), but he fails. The remainder of the novel charts, among other things, his uneven recovery, and it closes with a positively carnivalesque and miraculous party. It's by far the most optimistic conclusion of the three.

The narratives that make up the Bristol Trilogy are set in a very precise cultural and historical moment – or rather, several moments within the wider history of the counterculture and the sixties. *Shadow Dance* – drafted in 1963 and/or 1964, but not published until 1966 – belongs to the 'post-beatnik, pre-hippie phase'.[9] *Several Perceptions* is signed 'March–December 1967' on the last page: this is the moment 'when things were peaking'.[10] *Love*, written in 1969 and revised in the winter of 1970, captures and grotesquely magnifies the waning of the sixties.[11] Carter herself once claimed that she initially thought of herself as a 'social realist'.[12] She may have been joking, but there is no doubt that these novels work over the terrain of the emergent counterculture in a recognisably realist form. More than this, however, they explore the relationship between the 'alternative' people and the postwar consumer society which also 'took off' fully in the 1960s. Before looking at the novels in more detail, I want to describe in brief the features of consumerism most relevant to Carter's techniques and concerns. The key words here are 'mutability' and 'fashion'.

Mutability: The Fashion System

> The inscrutable but imperative logic of change has forced fashion in the sixties through the barriers of space and time. Clothes today sometimes seem arbitrary and bizarre; nevertheless, the startling dandyism of the newly emancipated young reveals a kind of logic of whizzing entropy. Mutability is having a field day.
> (Carter, 'Notes for a Theory of Sixties Style', 1967)

Carter's article 'Notes for a Theory of Sixties Style' was prompted above all by the summer-of-love hippie fashions. Its title hints at a vignette for some grand structuralist project which would explain the workings and significance of fashion (in fact, Barthes's *The Fashion System* came out in the same year). What is the source of the 'logic of whizzing entropy' which the dressing-up (or down) of the hippies and the other youth subcultures typifies? Like any good structural analyst, Carter suggests that 'environment' rather than individuality is expressed by changes in fashion, as it is also in advertising, pop music, pulp fiction and second-feature films (but not in high culture, it seems!). If individual consumer preferences alone do not generate change, then neither, according to Carter, do those of the people involved in the fashion industry, the businessmen, writers, design-ers, models, retailers, buyers and window-dressers: 'They think they mould the public taste but really they're blind puppets of a capricious goddess, goddess of mirrors, weather-cocks and barometers, whom the Elizabethans called Mutability. She is inscrutable but logical.'[13]

I'll return to the codes of 1967 dress in the final section. For the moment, let us note that Carter was always a lover and chronicler of fads and fashions, in both her fiction and her journalism. She may not have been quite as resolutely intellectual as a Susan Sontag or as famously trendy as a Tom Wolfe, but in the context of conventional British literary circles her work was both loved and hated for keeping abreast of new trends and fashions, whether in books, film, intellectual ideas, or food and drink. Her work, in fact, consistently foregrounds the mutability of things, people, ideas and values. 'Mutability', whether in the form of the quaint, literary, apostatised version of the goddess or in its more mundane denotation of 'changeableness' or 'the quality of being changeable', captures her consistent focus on the malleability, flexibility, mobility and turnover in ideas, images and languages, selves and things, styles and lifestyles, reality itself; and on obsolescence, whether physical, technological, or stylistic.

The sixties are arguably the crucial period in which this logic of change became fully institutionalised as an objective feature of economic and social life. The label 'consumer society' captures the emergence of a society whose prosperity is founded on a regular turnover of images and styles orchestrated by the conflicting interactions of capitalist producers and private consumers, with marketing, advertising and the price mechanism mediating between them. There was nothing new in the sixties about many of the phenomena of consumerism, or the conflicts of class and status which underlay changing taste and consumption patterns. What *was* new was precisely the degree of institutionalisation, the regularity of change and turnover. In recognition of the systematic nature of regulated change, I should like to appropriate Barthes's notion of the fashion 'system' to describe the general mechanism of consumerism since the 1960s. Carter's 'Mutability', I think, is close to what I want to call the fashion system of consumer culture. Bernard Levin, writing at the end of the decade, registered how wide-ranging the fashion system was:

> Fashions changed, changed again, changed faster and still faster: fashions in politics, in political style, in causes, in music, in popular culture, in myths, in education, in beauty, in heroes and idols, in attitudes, in responses, in work, in love and friendship, in food, in newspapers, in entertainment, in fashion. What had once lasted a generation now lasted a year, what had lasted a year lasted a month, a week, a day. There was a restlessness in the time that communicated itself everywhere and to everyone.[14]

Even a right-wing commentator such as Levin was fascinated by the rapid turnover of images, ideas and things.

It may at first appear as though the counterculture was directly opposed to all that the fashion system stands for. It's certainly the case that the hippies and the Underground were consciously opposed to consumerism and to the capitalist state. However, the counterculture's own values and lifestyle were often only apparently in contradiction to the hegemonic values of consumer society. I'll return to this point on several occasions; suffice to say that the individualism, expressiveness, private fantasy, romanticism, self-indulgence and need for change espoused by the counterculture are all valorised as values and practices of consumerism itself. The Bristol Trilogy offers a brilliant response to the restlessness and malleability permeating all features of sixties society. The aura of these novels, set in a provincial clique, splendidly captures the mutability of the period. Indeed, mutability is almost the central theme of *Shadow Dance*.

Rubbish Theory: *Shadow Dance*

> The entire spree [of the sixties] was sustained by a buoyant
> economy; everybody was so very, very rich you see, due to
> sponging off the state or, I don't know, cornering the
> market in tie-dyed underpants or cover versions of aged
> Mississippi-blues singers or patchouli-scented candles. Or.
> But at that time Britain was a low rent, cheap food country
> with relatively low wages and high taxes – most people I
> knew lived on very, very little. We were early into recycling
> – second-hand furniture, old houses, old clothes were dirt
> cheap in the sixties, or else free. You could strip a derelict
> house, nobody else wanted the stuff.
>
> (Carter, 'Truly, It Felt Like Year One' [1988])

This, from her reminiscences in *Very Heaven: Looking Back at
the 1960s*, is a typical Carter passage. It begins by offering
one position and then turns it around into its apparent
opposite, yoking them together, via a snapshot bricolage of
trends, without resolving – or even caring to resolve – them.
We were rich/we were poor is the particular period opposition here, but the pattern of contradiction without resolution is repeated throughout her work. Elsewhere, for
instance, she says: 'It was the Sixties . . . I was very very
unhappy but I was perfectly happy at the same time.'
Perhaps, however, it's a hopelessly male or masculine
approach to talk about oppositions, contradictions and resolutions? It depends who you are, where you're perceiving
from, what values inform the act of perception, and how
these change. It was Anthony Burgess, of all people, who
liked *Shadow Dance* for its display of Carter's 'capacity for
looking at the mess of contemporary life without flinching'.
This sentiment – admiring her penchant for being at home
in 'mess' – is echoed in Margaret Atwood's tribute to Carter,

published just after her death: 'Nothing, for her, was outside the pale: she wanted to know about everything and everyone, and every place and every word. She relished life and language hugely, and revelled in the diverse.' And I can't resist quoting one more example here, from a 1977 letter, where she's describing changes to her south London house and garden: 'Sucks boo to Snoo's barley and bamboos; we're going to have a *real* Clapham front garden, the anarchist colours & pieces of motorcycle & broken bottles & used condoms lightly scattered over all. . . .'[15] Ah, the aestheticised, subcultural, domestic geopolitics of it all, as Carter might have put it.

Like Carter, at home in mess, junk and (frankly) rubbish, are Morris and Honeybuzzard in *Shadow Dance*. In particular, they are fictional representations of the recyclers she fondly identifies above, interested in the mutability of categories and values surrounding the reuse of things. What is discarded junk or rubbish in one context can be shifted to a new one, done up or combined creatively with other 'second-hand' things, and achieve a new function or purpose: making money, for instance. Morris and Honey specialise in stealing Victoriana from derelict old houses, due for demolition, which they can then sell to American tourists in Morris's junk (sorry, antique) shop:

> They were looking, primarily, for American-bait. . . . They looked for small, whimsical Victorian and Edwardian articles that could be polished or painted and sold as conversation pieces. Although there was always the chance of finding built-in furniture i.e. cupboards, corner cupboards, window-seats with backs, etc. that were the age of the house itself and, cunningly extracted from the house, cleaned and polished, could legitimately be termed Georgian or Regency, such finds were rare. Their mainstay

was what Honey called 'Observer Design-for-Living Gear' –
aesthetically pleasing tiles from fireplaces; fireplaces
themselves and occasional mid-Victorian pottery whimsies
like ornately decorated lavatories or wash-basins and even
chamberpots. They had once, one red-letter day, found a
bidet lovingly handpainted with a pastoral scene of nymphs
and shepherds, which they sold to a crew-cut,
incredulously giggling, advertising man on holiday from
Detroit. They also took early gas fittings that looked
charming fitted up for electric light, or so they told people
who turned them over in the shop – 'just a coat of paint,
and there you are.'

Oil-lamps, occasional pieces of fine china or pottery or
copper pans, or the pile of old prints crumbling in an attic
came but rarely and were precious. These were the high
spots of their collecting. (pp. 87–8)

There's a moment here, at 'built-in furniture', when the
thought that they might sell the whole house, were it
possible, comes to mind; instead of London Bridge, ship a
genuine Victorian terrace back to your private museum in
the States (I'm sure it's been done). Honey is the one who's
been reading the new Sunday colour supplements to find
out what's supposed to be trendy with gullible Americans,
and we see here, on a small and amateurish scale, the
packaging of Britain's past which was to mushroom into the
full-scale tourist 'heritage industry' of the 1980s.

We see also, in these activities, the provincial cousin of
Portobello Road (Dodo, Trad), Camden, and other street
markets, where the creative recycling of bric-a-brac and
clothing sprang up in the mid to late 1960s. And we can
see, too, the sense in which the same creative impulses
often underlay the British gift for the theft and recycling of
old things and images in the second-hand trade, and the
creation of new things and images (themselves often a

bricolage of the new and the old) in the commercial avant-garde of fashion and pop music (Mary Quant and Biba, the Beatles, the Stones and the Who), which was to coalesce into the prime sixties myth of 'Swinging London'. What both official and countercultural, commercial and anti-commercial (if there was really any such thing) practitioners shared – even if the latter wouldn't have agreed – was an ability to 'dress up' materials for consumption and a commitment to mutability and turnover, whether this involved using old or new materials. In this sense they all belonged to the overall fashion system, in which exchanges between the new and the second-hand, the new and the old, and the high and low, are crucial to the constant generation of fresh ideas and stylistic changes.[16]

Morris and Honey both enjoy 'the pleasure of creeping through the abandoned dark, of prying and poking' (p. 88) on their hunts. Their attitudes to junk, however, are quite different, and they are typical of a wide range of differences between them, which together add up to quite distinct notions of self.

Morris is a junk 'addict' (p. 72) – the metaphorical drug connection is spelled out explicitly – whose interest is nevertheless a genuinely human one. At an auction held in a former Edwardian department store, an early Carter tableau of 'vividly coloured plaster gnomes' (p. 26) leads him to reflect on the mutability ('Mutability, goddess of the auction room' [p. 26]) of human fortunes. His interest is sentimental and nostalgic, but above all genuinely motivated. It's all very Peter Blake-y, to invoke a contemporary pop art comparison. He's drawn to the sense of 'domestic catastrophe' (p. 26) – things have reached rock bottom when you have to sell your gnomes; or else you're dead – and the 'atmosphere of hope decayed' (p. 27), because this is how he sees himself, his marriage and his life. At the end of the opening chapter he feels 'totally impotent, helpless, useless as the junk in his shop' (p. 21), and he views the shop itself as a sign of failure rather than success. Morris looks like an El Greco Christ, a picture of suffering; he is a solitary, failed painter who can never be the artist he wants to be, keeps his paintings locked in his studio, and hates his wife for hanging them in their flat. Feeling trapped in a basically monogamous marriage, he suffers paroxysms of guilt over his part in Ghislaine's scarring, and fears that she'll return to get him. Introspective, indecisive and reactive, he is the type of what Elizabeth Wilson calls the 'authentic' self, albeit a rather miserable version.[17] As such, he fits the conventional image of beatnik (and later hippie) 'authenticity'.

Honeybuzzard, by contrast, has a style interest in junk. Promiscuous and polymorphous perverse, he meets his latest girlfriend, cool, detached south London Emily (sounds like the 'Carter' character to me!), at a theatrical costumiers while on a jaunt to find and steal new things to amuse himself (and perhaps to sell). His attitude to junk, as to people, is one of 'detached, amused interest' (p. 63). He sees them as props in his latest games or escapades. Casual, cool, whimsical, irresponsible, ever the joker, he externalises and lives out his fantasy life in an extrovert and exhibitionistic manner. Bricoleur, toymaker, and poser in his own porn pictures, he's a demotic dandy of ambiguous gender and sexuality who loves dressing up in new costumes: 'I like – you know – to slip in and out of me. . . . I would like to have a cupboard bulging with all different bodies and faces and choose a fresh one every morning' (p. 76). A self-conscious actor and performer, he adopts a notion of self based on images, surfaces, appearances, and the assumption that it's not psychological authenticity but stylistic artifice which is important. In contrast to authenticity, he is the type of what Wilson calls the 'modernist' self.[18] As such, he's an embodiment of the 'kinky', camp and dandy elements of sixties 'theatrical dresser' style, and he crosses over between beatnik/hippie and mainstream pop fashions (rather as the Beatles were later to do in their *Sergeant Pepper* phase). In this, I'd say, he reveals the degree to which hippie notions of naturalness and authenticity were themselves artificial, mythical constructs no less than the mainstream commercial products against which hippies defined themselves. No one can be simply natural or authentic any more: these are just options among a variety of roles and acts; they have to be cultivated just like the others.

Of course, Morris's and Honey's more obvious similarities shouldn't be overlooked. Both are bohemian, romantic, expressive individualists; both are narcissists, both are misogynists. They're perhaps the serious and frivolous sides of the same coin. And Morris's feeling that he himself is 'a second-hand man' (p. 21) – a feeling which the implied author almost certainly doesn't endorse – isn't far from Establishment and official cultural definitions of the people who comprised the emergent Underground subculture. Writing in *New Society* at the end of the decade, Michael Thompson, himself at the time a figure of ambiguous social status, notes in 'An Anatomy of Rubbish' that people who deal in rubbish (his example is second-hand car dealers) tend to be regarded as rubbish themselves: 'The people who buy, sell, do up and use these vehicles also fall within the "rubbish" category. Students and unmarried young men are really neither one thing nor the other.'[19] I'm not sure what the necessary connection is here, unless it's that most used-car dealers tend to be students or unmarried young men (unlikely?). The slippage from one to the other, however, is certainly symptomatic.

Thompson's article, and the book-length expansion of it, *Rubbish Theory: The Creation and Destruction of Value* (1979), are valuable intertexts in understanding the relationship between Morris's and Honey's recycling of things, their social and economic status, and wider questions concerning the valued and the valueless in the fashion system of sixties society (and, indeed, in any organised society). Thompson argues that on the basis of prevailing values, things tend to be assigned to one of three categories: 'durable', in which their value is increasing; 'transient', in which it is falling; and 'rubbish', in which it is zero or even negative. Durable and transient are overt, in the sense that they are visible in everyday life and take place in everyday time. Rubbish, by contrast, is covert and invisible, and inhabits a timeless limbo. It's the stuff which has fallen out of public visibility and waits to be revived from the dead, as it were.

Having established his categories, Thompson then analyses some of the control mechanisms at work in permitting or forbidding transfers of objects from one category to another. One of his most detailed examples is the career of Victorian Stevengraphs, the plaster ducks of their time, which began life as transient kitsch, disappeared into the rubbish category for the best part of seventy years, and were rediscovered in the early sixties, becoming nice little durables by the seventies. They're just the sort of thing that Honey and Morris would be looking to take advantage of. There's also a brilliant reading of the gentrification of Islington, in which housing was shifted from the transient, nearly rubbish category into the durable one by the efforts of some of the image and culture industries' 'young meteors'. And it isn't only things to which Thompson's analysis applies. It's also people, as I've mentioned, and ideas, and values themselves. The categories through which we view things are at least as important as the things themselves.

What is most interesting is why Thompson should have been exploring these issues when he did. Why was this such an apposite moment to be asking: 'Something transient can *become* durable: junk can become antique. How?' (p. 37). The short answer is that he observed a rapid speeding up and diversification of transfers between categories. Morris and Honey exemplify one area of this trend, by literally lifting things out of the rubbish category – unwanted objects in slum houses – and attempting to place them in the durable category (though they haven't quite mastered the latter!). In his original article Thompson picks up on the idea of 'camp' taste (his inverted commas), in which 'things are lifted out of the rubbish category "before their time",' (p. 42), causing conceptual confusion to those who haven't caught up with the latest trend. In the later book he notes that a whole system has emerged in which the turnover of fashions is orchestrated – this is close to what I am calling here the fashion system. The sixties counterculture, in among other subcultures and taste groups, played its part in the development and complexification of this system, which includes all Thompson's categories, both visible and invisible. In the nineties we're so accustomed to endless revivals, to instituted nostalgia and pastiche, that we forget how surprising it was when it happened on a grand scale for the first time.

What has all this to do with Angela Carter's writing? It's not only that Morris and Honey offer a period fictional representation of rubbish theory in dynamic action. It's also that the career of the Bristol Trilogy – as of any published fiction, or any art – functions within the cycles of the system, as does this piece, with its rhetorical plea that these novels should be shifted from the invisible category to which they have largely been assigned into the visible, value-increasing, durable one. And more than this, I'd

argue, since the relation between the valued and the valueless is so central to the forms, themes and reception of all
Carter's work – a point to which I'll return in the final
section.

Bomb Culture: *Several Perceptions*

> There's no denying that towards the end of the decade
> everyday life, even where I was living, in Bristol, took on
> the air of a continuous improvisation . . . the particularly
> leafy and graceful bit of Bristol where I lived attracted festal
> behaviour. *Carpe diem.* Pleasure. It didn't have to cost much,
> either.
>
> (Carter, 'Truly, It Felt Like Year One')

There's a passage in Jeff Nuttall's *Bomb Culture* where he's
describing the nineteenth-century aesthetics of fragmenta-
tion in the last book of Lautréamont's *Maldoror* and Rimbaud's *Illuminations*: 'Narrative becomes disconnected
incident, argument becomes verbal arabesque, description
becomes image, image dissolves into the berserk juxtapositions of schizophrenia.'[20] This is a *bit* excessive for *Several
Perceptions*, which is neither proto-surrealism nor symbolist
poem nor, indeed, stream-of-consciousness modernism, but
it's still intriguingly close to the novel's 'structure of feeling',
to use Raymond Williams's term. My only doubt is whether
there ever was any argument, as such, before or behind the
verbal arabesques of Carter's style in this particular novel.
Later, in the speculative fictions, there certainly is: the style
is sharply intellectual; characters represent ideas; tableaux
are rich with symbolism, accompanied by authorial commentary and interpretation; picaresque narrative branches
bristle with allegorical possibilities.

But *Several Perceptions* is different and special. While it demonstrates a precise and even touching hold on conventional codes for representing reality, it also goes right down (or is it up?) into the disorientation and discontinuity of the mid-1960s countercultural mind and lifestyle. Joseph the dreamer and his friends and acquaintances are a whimsically individualised provincial counterculture in its high period of waywardness, excess and flowering. They're the nearest British equivalents to Leslie Fiedler's 'new mutants', the organised, mainly student youth generation rising up to challenge the parent culture. And for Fiedler they were no less than a new species: mutability again.[21] Closer to home, Nuttall's contemporary insider account of the countercultural Underground's emergence is, in all its unevenness and confusion, an appropriate intertext for the period aura in which *Several Perceptions* is drenched. It's contemporary in a double sense, too: first, with the experiences and events it describes; second, with Carter's novel. Like Carter, Nuttall completed his manuscript towards the end of 1967, and it was published in 1968.

Superficially, *Several Perceptions* uses a similar narrative technique to that of *Shadow Dance*: a third-person retrospective narration, with focalisation through the consciousness of a single male character. Morris, like Joseph, is prey to all kinds of dreams and fantasies: his vision of suicide by gas, a blood-filled dream in which he slashes Ghislaine and his wife Edna, fantasies of escape or invisibility, the idea that he's the last man left alive on earth, a fantasy or memory of what happened to his mother when he was about seven years old. On a couple of occasions he fears that he's becoming psychotic or going insane ('"Do I need therapy?"' [p. 116]). But he isn't and he doesn't.

Joseph, however, crosses the boundaries between health and sickness, neurosis and psychosis, thinking about killing yourself and actually trying it. Things have moved on since *Shadow Dance*. A new, expressionist emphasis on the inner life of the mind as a dramatic (though by no means an empty) space is signalled by the title *Several Perceptions* and the epigraph, taken from David Hume: 'The mind is a kind of theatre, where several perceptions successively make their appearance, pass, re-pass, glide away and mingle in an infinite variety of postures and situations.' Joseph's Christian name allies him with his biblical namesake, a prophetic dreamer and interpreter of dreams; and the content of his dreams, fantasies and visions mixes the intensely private and the glaringly public:

> A picture of Charlotte was tacked over the gas fire. She was
> squinting into past suns. Her blonde hair blew over her face
> which did not in the least resemble the face he
> remembered, since that face reincarnated in fantasy,
> recreated nightly in dreams for months and months after
> she left, had become transformed in his mind to a Gothic
> mask, huge eyeballs hooded with lids of stone, cheekbones
> sharp as steel, lips of treacherous vampire redness and a
> wet red mouth which was a mantrap of ivory fangs. Witch
> woman. Incubus. Haunter of battlefields after the carnage
> in the image of a crow. After the bombs fell, in the ruins of
> the village, the rescue party surprised a woman gnawing
> gobs of flesh. His Madonna of the abattoir.[22]

It's no accident, then, that Joseph's surname is 'Harker' (and there's even an echo of 'Jonathan' in 'Joseph', to underline it). Here he dreams that he's the victim of the girlfriend who left him, one of the women at Dracula's castle, or Lucy (in the sky with diamonds?), or, more likely, a figure from the horror comics he loves so much. But this rich Gothic image is also condensed with another, from the

Vietnam War. Joseph, like those who took part in the increasingly violent riots in both the States and Britain at the time, is obsessed with *images* of the war. In his room he has books (and *new* books, at that), newspaper cuttings and scrapbooks. Vietnam, as well as being the war that the great postwar multinational capitalist power lost because of – among other things – popular resistance, was also a major media war.

The pictures tacked to Joseph's walls also confirm this mixing of the inner and the private and the outer and the public, and of sex, violence and death. There's Lee Harvey Oswald, the burning Buddhist monk, a sexy girl in a soft-drinks advertisement, Marilyn Monroe, Charlotte. It's an everyday pop collage, of the sort self-consciously re-created on the front cover of the 1970 Paladin *Bomb Culture* (the monk and Marilyn are actually there) and, more formulaically and even more self-consciously, on the sleeve of Jonathon Green's oral history of the Underground, *Days in the Life* (1988). Or – to take a period analogy from the intelligensia's darling film director – a montage from Godard's *Two or Three Things I Know About Her*, or *Weekend*. As Carter writes: 'I saw Godard's *Breathless* when it came out in 1959, and my whole experience of the next decade can be logged in relation to Godard's movies as if he were some kind of touchstone.'[23]

Joseph's sickness itself is also, of course, period-specific. There's no evidence of R. D. Laing lying around in his room – though Gilchrist's *Life of Blake* and *Alice in Wonderland* indicate the romantic and surrealist cast of his reading habits – but it's no accident, surely, that this is the exact moment when schizophrenia became a trendy form of resistance to and rejection of oppressive families and parents. *The Divided Self*, remember, was published in 1960, but it didn't catch on until later – even though, as Nuttall points out, deviant psychopathology was in vogue from the hipster onwards, reaching its height in the 'symptomatic delinquency' (p. 101) of the American Beats. Mental sickness and schizophrenia, he argues, are the legitimate responses of disaffiliated youth whose political hopes of banning the Bomb have been thrown back in their faces by the Establishment, and who fear the mass suicide of the species, the end of the world in a nuclear apocalypse. The violence and obsession with death and cruelty, in the counterculture and other youth subcultures, is a distorted and far less harmful mirror-image of the institutionalised violence of official culture. Joseph, incidentally, has a sparring, black-comic relationship with his psychiatrist, Ransome ('"May I call you Arthur?"' [p. 27]). His response to a diagnosis of immaturity and maladjustment is to send a piece of excrement to Lyndon Johnson. He's cured when he decides to be, at the novel's conclusion (which *is*, in some ways, rather romantic).

If the mind is a kind of theatre in this novel, so also is life itself. For all Joseph's despair, the novel's narrative structure and the everyday lives of the people it represents have an open-ended feeling of improvisation and even, at times, carnival, of the kind Carter notes as typical of the milieu she inhabited then. Lorna Sage captures this formal quality best: 'The novel is constructed rather like a strip cartoon, or a "flicker-book", in which the motion of the pages turning sets the separate frames in illusory motion.'[24] The action occupies a few months leading up to Christmas (the novel, as I've mentioned, was completed in December), but one is rarely conscious of this. 'Time passed' is a typical phrase marking transition from one narrative incident to the next. It's as though actions and interactions are not linked by cause and effect in linear or public time but happen within some other time, perhaps that of fairy tale, myth, dream, or a 'happening'. Joseph himself feels that he is outside time after his clock, which he calls 'Charlotte', stops at the precise moment of his suicide attempt, and there's an uncanny feeling that the same applies to the fictional world itself.[25] History in any traditional, progressive sense has stopped, and things just happen.

It's perfectly in accordance with the increasingly playful mood here that events should close with a carnival Christmas party held at the bisexual Kay's ramshackle mansion. Kay is a good version of the Honeybuzzard type, comparatively marginalised to the fringes of the action; he always seems to be passing by. Through the lens of conventional categories and values, most of the figures in this novel, both youthful and ageing, don't have much to look forward to. In the miracles at the party, things are put right (though it must be acknowledged that whether this is reality or fantasy is left ambiguous). Joseph makes friends with time again, and may even have found a new girlfriend. Anne Blossom, who has been betrayed, lost her child, and is mysteriously crippled, walks again. The ageing prostitute Mrs Boulder, mother of Joseph's friend Viv, is reunited with her old lover. And Old Sunny, the music-hall violinist who has lost his violin, suddenly has one again.[26] This isn't directly political, in the sense that the festive, carnival atmosphere of the early-sixties CND marches or the 1967 riots was a direct affront to authority, but it's utopian in a down-to-earth, human way, and it possesses something of the ' "collective dream" ' and 'contagious culture' (p. 8) which Nuttall sees as the political possibility of the counterculture.

The 1968 *Times Literary Supplement* reviewer notes that *Several Perceptions* might merely leave the reader with 'a fashionable whiff of despair' were it not for the author's comic bathetic touches, and claims that 'so circumstantial is much of the detail of Joseph's beatnik world that its allusions will be lost on readers a few years hence'.[27] The key words here are 'fashionable' and 'circumstantial' ('beatnik' is surely out of date, but would this have been of concern to your *TLS* reviewer or reader?). The implications are clear. To be merely 'fashionable' or too 'circumstantial' is to be superficial and ephemeral, as well as local, rooted in a particular time and place, and therefore without literary value which, in the great tradition favoured by the *TLS*, inheres in a text's permanent and transcendent qualities. The reviewer's observations are correct. This is indeed a fashionable and circumstantial work. But the implied judgements are not. There's no necessary contradiction between being fashionable and circumstantial and enduring literary value, not least because there is no longer any single standard of value. Here, as it happens, I'm arguing that it's these very qualities, of both expression and content, which give *Several Perceptions* and the other Bristol Trilogy novels value: they have an aura – a distinctive structure of feeling – rare in British fiction of the period.

Goodbye Baby and Amen: *Love*

> I was married most of the sixties – the sense of living on a demolition site was perfectly real, in one way, because we stopped being married in 1969. By which time the sexual revolution the papers were always going on about was more or less completed. . . . It turns out that human relations are very complex and often very painful regardless at what moment during their course sexual intercourse takes place. . . . It is the sex that people are really thinking of when they talk about the inexpressible decadence of the sixties. (And it wasn't just heterosex, either; oh, dear, no.)
>
> (Carter, 'Truly, It Felt Like Year One')

In her Afterword to the revised edition of *Love*, Carter describes the novel as 'the text that is Annabel's coffin', and acknowledges – or should one rather say revels in? – the tastelessness of resurrecting the other characters to write some more of their lives.[28] I remember being baffled at first by this act of revivification, and indeed by the revisions to the original text. The finality and irredeemability of the original *Love* seem to me fundamental to both its extraordinarily precious style and its heady aura of 'savage detachment' (p. 18/11) and 'inexpressible decadence'. 'Nothing but death is irreparable' (p. 124/112) are the novel's closing words. Death is the ultimate evidence of human mutability; you can't come back from it. Revision, in this light, looks like a bizarre, if not indecent, attempt to repair the irreparable. And the updating of lives in the Afterword, though wry and witty and socially insightful, only further dilutes the novel's hermetic intensity. It belongs to another genre – another species of writing – and to another time. It's generally agreed that *Love* is a farewell to the sixties and to myths of the sixties, written and set at the end of the decade. In the title of David Bailey's 1969 book of photographic portraits, which itself parodically mourns the passing of 'Swinging London', it's *Goodbye Baby and Amen*. I've always thought of the coffin on its cover as being, at least partly, Annabel's. Her death, too, symbolises the death of the sixties. This is dramatic, but as Robert Hewison puts it of *Goodbye Baby*: 'The end of every decade invites a miniature millenarianism.'[29]

It's pushing things too far to claim that the sexual triangle comprising Annabel, Lee and Buzz is a microcosm of the counterculture in any naive, reflectionist manner. No text, whether fictional or otherwise, can be that, and certainly not one characterised by such a fascinating mixture of realism and expressionism, analysis and fantasy. Nevertheless, the characters are fictional creations who in part typify various aspects of the social and sexual mobility opened up by the postwar expansion of educational opportunities, the welfare state, the widespread availability of the Pill, the 'permissive' attitudes officially marked by the reform of the laws on divorce and homosexuality, and counter-cultural hedonism. This, as I've suggested, is also true of other figures in the Bristol Trilogy novels. The difference in *Love* is in the kind and amount of detail we're given, and in the intense focus on the dynamics of the triangle.

Thus the Collins brothers represent two trajectories for the working-class boy born in the forties who moves out of the parent culture. Actually they're half-brothers, sharing a mother who went spectacularly mad, leaving them to be brought up by a stern leftist aunt, but with different fathers: Lee's a railwayman, Buzz's an American serviceman who, he becomes convinced, was an Indian. Brought up in south London, they move to the bohemian area of Bristol in 1963 or 1964 (it isn't possible to reconstruct the fable precisely on this point), when Lee gets a place at the university, and gain a reputation as bandits and alienated exotics, attractive because they are perceived as dangerous and sexually ambiguous.

Lee, twenty-three in 1969, is the conventionally beautiful one, with blond hair and blue eyes, who has moved ambivalently into the middle class via a grammar school and university education and a post as a comprehensive school teacher (he hasn't forgotten his aunt's socialism).[30] He's a self-conscious narcissist with an array of charming smiles and 'a chronic slum-child infection' (p. 19/12) which makes his eyes water, so that often no one, including himself, knows whether his tears are authentic or not. Romantic, sentimental, and devoted in the mid 1960s to a hippie ideal of individual freedom, he also possesses a strong puritanical conscience which desires clear concepts of sin and guilt. The Kantian moral imperative 'Do right because it is right', which he learned at school, remains his motto. He's the only one of the three with any recognisable sense of social responsibility.

Buzz, by my reckoning about twenty-one in 1969, is tall and thin, with an Apache or Mohawk hairstyle – an Indian to Lee's cowboy, a paradoxical working-class hippie drop-out in opposition to Lee's gradual incorporation into the 'paramount reality' – as Berger and Luckmann call it – of everyday life.[31] While Lee goes to grammar school, he goes to the local comprehensive. When Lee moves, he moves with him, working sporadically in factories, docks or cafés but mainly living off his brother or stealing. Melodramatic and malign, self-absorbed and perverse, he takes to the North African hippie trail in the winter of 1965–6, sending Lee hash and returning, in Lawrence-of-Arabia-style garb, with VD, to find that Annabel has moved in. Buzz, we're told early on, 'had been grievously exposed to his mother's madness' (p. 19/13), and his mother thought he was the Antichrist.

Annabel is the type of middle-class virgin who leaves home to enter the world of bohemia as an art student. Like Buzz, she's also about twenty-one in 1969, having been eighteen when she met Lee at a New Year's Eve party, as 1965 became 1966. Like Buzz also, she's tall and thin, with protuberant veins on her hands and feet, 'a sparse, grotesquely elegant, attenuated girl' (p. 35/27) with the long, Pre-Raphaelite hair favoured by many hippie women (she could never be that other hippie type, the Earth Mother; she's far too fragile). Still like Buzz, she steals, and this in spite of being the child of well-heeled middle-class parents. Later she emulates his work pattern, too, taking a variety of short-term jobs in the period leading up to her third, successful suicide attempt.

And, still like Buzz, she lives in a world of subjective fantasy, a Berger and Luckmann 'private enclave' which she has inhabited from an early age, having been secretive and withdrawn as a child.[32] Her madness, therefore, isn't the result of a decision to explore 'inner space' with the help of consciousness-expanding drugs, it's just the way she is. No reason is given for her psychological state, though it's perhaps implied that her bourgeois parents are responsible (the Marxist term 'bourgeois' was more in fashion then that it is now). More, even, than Joseph, she is Laing's suffering schizophrenic, with no clear sense of the boundaries between self and other, inner and outer, intra- and interpersonal, private and public, fantasy and reality:

> She had the capacity for changing the appearance of the real world which is the price paid by those who take too subjective a view of it. All she apprehended through her senses she took only as objects for interpretation in the expressionist style and she saw, in everyday things, a world of mythic, fearful shapes of whose existence she was convinced although she never spoke of it to anyone; nor had she ever suspected that everyday, sensuous human practice might shape the real world. When she did discover that such a thing was possible, it proved the beginning of the end for her for how could she possess any notion of the ordinary? (pp. 9–10/3–4)

Once again, the great difference from the earlier novels in the Bristol Trilogy, where fantasy, daydream, dream and nightmare are also sometimes fused or confused with everyday reality, is in the kind and amount of detail which this passage exhibits. This isn't focalised through Annabel's perception. Rather, it's scrupulously distanced, a penetrating analysis of her world and its relation to the real. The style is frighteningly pellucid.

The novel's short middle section is almost wholly given over to a dialogic analysis of the *ménage à trois* in the form of an interview between Annabel's psychiatrist – a sexy young woman – and Lee. This device, more concentrated than that of the Joseph–Ransome relationship in *Several Perceptions*, provides a space for an official version of the triangular relationship to be voiced. Annabel and Buzz are mutually stimulating in each other the psychotic disorder of *folie à deux*; Buzz must be removed from the household, while Lee must quit his extramarital affairs, one of which has precipitated Annabel's second suicide attempt, and devote himself to taking care of Annabel. It doesn't work.

As with the circumstantial and psychological detail, so the sexual detail of *Love* is more intensively focused. It's the sex, as Carter notes, which is central to the myth of sixties decadence. The primary sexual orientation here is undoubtedly heterosexual. Annabel's loss of her virginity is described in detail, in two different accounts, and the dénouement is marked by her sexual encounters with each of the brothers: the bitter disappointment of her adultery with Buzz, followed by the 'mutual rape' (p. 108/97) of violent sex with Lee. There's also plenty of evidence of the Collins brothers' promiscuity scattered throughout, and considerable attention is given to Lee's relationships with the unnamed philosophy tutor's wife, the student Carolyn, and his pupil Joanne, as well as his sexual fantasies relating to the psychiatrist. Most of the verbal dialogue in the novel takes place in these encounters, rather than within the triangle.

Heterosexuality rules, but Lee's and Buzz's incestuous homosexual desire for one another is also repeatedly stressed, and for Buzz, at least, Annabel is interesting only in relation to his brother. No explicit homosexual encounter is represented, but the desire is implied everywhere. Annabel, for instance, is dressed in Buzz's clothes when Lee deflowers her. At the party the brothers dance together, 'a put-on or come-on for which they were notorious, an exotic display' (p. 51/43). When Lee kicks Buzz out of the flat, he remarks: '"I'm not divorcing you, for God's sake"' (p. 75/66). In the Afterword, it's no surprise that the one thing Buzz admits he would like to do before he dies is to fuck his brother.

Where does Annabel figure in this? It's widely acknowledged by now that the sixties sexual revolution mainly concerned male pleasures, and that women played an all-too-traditional subservient role in the counterculture. Annabel's experience certainly bears this out. Though she's on the Pill and, in theory, a free agent (as the jargon goes), her sexual freedom amounts to little more than sleeping and living with Lee for a few months before her parents insist that they marry. The horrible Buzz is (I think I'm right in saying) her second partner. The imaginary invisibility she confers on herself using Buzz's magic ring seems an apt metaphor for young women's position in the counterculture.

It's well known that Carter disagrees with this reading of the sexual revolution, and it's true that Melanie in *The Magic Toyshop* (1967) and Marianne in *Heroes and Villains* (1969) demonstrate a growing sexual autonomy. But the women in the Bristol Trilogy – at least those who occupy any narrative space – have a bad time of it. It's also worth noting that there's a high degree of sexual and other violence towards women in two of these novels (certainly more than there is towards men), and that a total silence, again typical of the counterculture and of the period in general, surrounds any kind of lesbian sexual orientation.

It's unwise, however, to reduce sexual identities merely to sexual practices (just as it's unwise to reduce identities to sexual identities . . .). *Love* is, after all, just an updating of the (almost) eternal triangle plot. What's perhaps most fascinating about this particular triangle is the way in which perceptions of self and other are both created and mediated by various kinds of visual images. Here Annabel comes into her own, since it's through the manipulation of images that she gains control over Lee.

She takes over his room by painting a tree – he thinks it's a good tree of life; she knows it's an evil, poisonous one – and then painting the walls green after their marriage. She confuses his sense of identity by incorporating him into her private mythology in a series of drawings which range from herbivorous lion to castrated unicorn. Her imagination, unconsciously exercised, is romantic, gothic and surrealist; her favourite painter is Max Ernst. Next, she takes over Lee's body by having her name, surrounded by a heart, tattooed on his chest in green Gothic script. And then she steals his personal image by appropriating his repertoire of smiles and his self-consciousness, as she manipulates her madness for her own ends. Her final gesture in this direction is to change her own image completely, in preparation for her final performance, her suicide.

If Annabel's visual economy is based on her thoroughly middle-class knowledge of art history, Buzz's is located in photography, and especially pornography. He gives Annabel some hard-core photographs, and she attempts to emulate the model's expressionless expression. He takes pornographic photos of Lee and Annabel, and leaves them lying around the flat. Pornographer, voyeur and fetishist, he's actually terrified of women and indulges the classic male fear of the *vagina dentata*. One of the novel's most heavily ironic moments is when Annabel's parents admire him because of his camera. They think he may become a member of the 'new aristocracy' (p. 45/37), the media term which emerged in the summer and autumn of 1965 to describe the new, fashionable young things, including photographers such as David Bailey, whose photographs in *A Box of Pin Ups* were instrumental in creating the idea in the first place. This irony is undermined by the Afterword, since they turn out to have been not far wrong.

Lee, by contrast, has a quite different relationship to visual images. He knows a lot about cinema – some of the period allusions are removed in the revision – and is particularly depressed when he finds himself behaving like an actor in a 'B' movie. He's able to apprehend something of the relationship between self and image, whereas Annabel and Buzz do not understand 'the play of surfaces' (p. 31/24) or 'the cult of appearances' (p. 32/25), so thoroughly are they immersed in them. This is also why he's the only one of the three who has any sense of personal history, expressed by his three photographs – himself at school, with his aunt and Buzz, and with Annabel – which he eventually burns. Even he, however, can't see any continuity between them.

It's in this relationship between self and image that Carter's symbolic representation of the death of the counterculture overlaps with Bailey's ironic farewell to the pop sixties in *Goodbye Baby and Amen*. Bailey's world is unequivocally pop: it promotes the fast turnover of images and styles, and boldly assumes that there's no truth beyond surfaces and appearances. This, indeed, is the message of pop art and the essence of pop. Carter's world, for all its apparent opposition to the consumerist materialism for pop, is similarly obsessed by the power of images. Undoubtedly there is a truth other than that of surfaces – hence her representation of different kinds of selves – but the surfaces prove all too seductive in *Love*. Annabel's and Buzz's sickness, however defined, may have its origins in the family and early childhood, but the heady aura of their quintessentially sixties lifestyle provides an ample theatre for its development.

On the inside sleeve of *Love*, Carter describes it as 'a tragedy of contemporary manners . . . a total analysis of a complex emotional situation, leaving nothing out, and being as honest as possible'. A bit grand, possibly, and there are moments where it's just as easily read as the blackest of comedy, rather than tragedy. However, in its aestheticist style, its sheer, relentless precision, and its distilled aura of inevitable doom, it does have claims to be her great novel. I personally prefer *The Passion of New Eve*, but in many respects it just isn't – to draw on an impressionistic aesthetic notion – as achieved as *Love*.

Bricolage and Fashion: The Bristol Trilogy, Carter's *Oeuvre*, and the Contemporary Canon

A young girl, invited to a party, left to herself (no mother to guide her), might well select the following ensemble: a Mexican cotton wedding dress (though she's not a bride, probably no virgin, either – thus at one swoop turning a garment which in its original environment is an infinitely potent symbol into a piece of decoration); her grandmother's button boots (once designed to show off the small feet and moneyed leisure of an Edwardian middle class who didn't need to work and rarely had to walk); her mother's fox fur (bought to demonstrate her father's status); and her old school beret dug out of the loft because she saw Faye Dunaway in *Bonnie and Clyde* (and a typical role-definition garment changes gear).

(Carter, 'Notes for a Theory of Sixties Style')

Not quite such a young girl: Carter was probably twenty-seven when she wore this outfit. Maybe it isn't autobiographical, but all the generational and topical details fit. This is her prime example of fashion mutability in 'Notes for a Theory of Sixties Style', hence the voguish finishing touch of the beret: *Bonnie and Clyde* was at the centre of the 1920s and 1930s revivalism which also peaked, along with flower power, in 1967. We're back with Honeybuzzard again, the fictional exemplar of the dandy self as work of art. This, however, is a journalistic deconstruction of fashion bricolage, in which 'eclectic fragments' are lifted from their original contexts and recombined 'to form a new whole'.[33] A semiotician's and cultural critic's dream, this outfit mixes – though it certainly doesn't match – the old and the new, the high and the low, the indigenous and the foreign, the first-hand and the second-hand, antique and junk (but which is which?). In retrospect, it's a perfect postmodern outfit. And it provides a perfect analogy for Carter's fictional styles and strategies.

For bricolage and fashion – not just fashion in dress but fashion in all areas of the fashion system of consumer culture, from music, art, architecture, films and literature through to places, people and ideas – are central to all Carter's work. They are what connects the Bristol Trilogy to the speculative fictions, since all are concerned to provide an imaginative and a critical response to 'the mess of contemporary life'. The difference, of course, is that in the speculative fictions, beginning fully with *Heroes and Villains*, she drops any residual realist or naturalist conventions and recombines, instead, pre-novelistic narrative forms, popular generic elements, and non-fictional discourses. With her penchant for intellectual bricolage, and her desire to write fiction with strong doses of criticism, the shift to fantastic and allegorical picaresques was a brilliant one, though it ruined her reputation with lovers of the so-called novel proper. Quite right, too, in a sense: *The Infernal Desire Machines of Doctor Hoffman* and *The Passion of New Eve* aren't novels, if by that one means the narrow, though undeniably glorious, tradition of formal realism. But they fit much better into the longer history of narrative forms sketched out in the sixties by Robert Scholes and Robert Kellogg in *The Nature of Narrative* (1966) and given a sharper theoretical focus with the rediscovery of Bakhtin in the seventies and eighties.

As I hope is now clear, what the Trilogy novels give us (as also do some of the tales in *Fireworks*) which we don't get so recognisably elsewhere in her *oeuvre* is a sense of at least a part of the milieu from which Carter's ongoing revaluation of the boundaries between the valued and the valueless – whether in terms of forms and kinds, ideas, people or things – proceeds. It's long been customary to notice that postmodern aesthetics involves the renegotiation – though not, surely, the effacement – of the boundary between the high and the low, the serious and non-serious or frivolous, art and kitsch, the durable and the rubbish in the arts, the media, and culture more generally. The Trilogy mixes realism and gothic, in a way that fits quite neatly into the revival of a domesticated gothic in the sixties; but more than this, it shows clearly how the sixties were a laboratory – or perhaps, rather, a battlefield – in the relativisation of all kinds of values: aesthetic, moral, spiritual, economic, political.[34]

In the literary sphere this resulted in an assault on the traditional canon, and indeed on the very idea of a canon. The canon has certainly weathered it, but there's no doubt that now we have no single agreed set of standards or values to define what counts as great literature. It's now quite respectable to study popular fiction and culture, and in any case you have to know about them to understand much of what is categorised as serious fiction, which is awash with cross-fertilisations, mutations and new hybrid species. Literary criticism itself, in line with many other trends in the fashion system, diversified into a variety of approaches with their own oppositions and cross-fertilisations, while the genre of 'Theory' emerged as a new sphere of intellectual bricolage in its own right. They're all symptoms of and responses to the constantly changing mess of contemporary culture. It's no longer a question of what is, in any final sense, valuable, but of what is of value to whom in what circumstances.

Angela Carter enjoyed all this, she revelled in it. Michael Thompson, that unsung deconstructor of value systems, is right in saying that you have to understand the relationship between the durable, the transient and the rubbish to see how an economy, or any of its parts, is functioning at any given moment. In myriad ways, all Carter's fiction helps us to do just that. But the Bristol Trilogy, by virtue of its setting in a particular time and place, offers us a special flavour of the aura of mutability in a period when our value systems went excitingly crazy.

Max Ernst: 'Men Shall Know Nothing of This', oil on canvas, 1923

The Disorder of *Love*:
Angela Carter's Surrealist Collage

SUE ROE

I   Outlaw/Photomontage

In her essay on Surrealism, written in 1978, Angela Carter
defends the Surrealists, mourns the passing of this inimita-
ble phase in the history of art, and reminds us of the febrile,
fragile nature of love: its shakiness, when it is subjected to
any kind of intellectual theory; its inspirational quality; and
its problem, once it emerges as an aspect of the creative
process, with women. It is refreshing to see a profoundly
intellectual artist embracing the raw edges of artistic practice, as Carter does here and in her fiction. It reminds us (if
we should need reminding) not to subject her work to rigid
intellectual controls. Surrealist art, she holds, was 'a way of
life, of living on the edges of the senses'. The Surrealist
poem lived, loved, and changed sides: 'A poem is a wound;
a poem is a weapon.'[1] Beauty, for the Surrealists, was
'convulsive. That is, you *feel* it . . . yet the beautiful does
not exist *as such*. What do exist are . . . objects, or people,
or ideas, that arbitrarily extend our notion of the connections it is possible to make.' Surrealist art was disordered,
irreverent, and consisted in releasing and revealing drives
that cannot be contained within the social order. But the
Surrealists were not good with women. 'That is why,' Carter
laments, 'although I thought they were wonderful, I had
to give them up in the end.' At the end of 'The Alchemy

of the Word', though, she looks back longingly at the Surrealists' struggle, and asks whether it might not continue. 'Why not. Give me one good reason. Even if the struggle has changed its terms.'[2]

Actually, Carter has answered her own question: both here (the Surrealists were not good with women) and in the novel in which she makes a sustained and troubled fictitious collage composed of imagery of the Surreal and the real. *Love*, written in 1969, is Carter's fifth novel. Following on from her studies of schizophrenia, silence and desire,[3] it predates by most of a decade her return, in *The Bloody Chamber*, to mythology as a way of dealing with the problems of destabilising the social order of sexual relations. In 1969, she had not yet moved over to the animal kingdom of drives and desires which would enable her to comment on human behaviour in her own uniquely symbolic notations, looking askance and with pleasure at her own gift of story-telling. Here, she had not yet moved into what was to become her determinedly symbolic mode of retelling as reinterpretation. Where the *folklorique* was later to determine and stabilise the shapes of her plots, here, in *Love*, the prevailing form is that of disorder, and we are placed firmly – if not entirely mimetically – within the social world of 'Nescafé and the Welfare State':[4] materialist, postwar Britain. The pendulum of Carter's axis swings, in *Love*, between a kind of freedom and repression, between 'liberation' and despair; caught up in its mechanisms is a heroine held captive by the expectations of an earlier generation, of which we catch barely more than a glimpse.

Love is neither, directly, a product of Carter's thinking about the postwar English provinces, nor a fabrication of the kind she would later come to be known by: the dazzling acrobatics out of which she would effect her radiant metamorphoses – in *Wise Children*, for example, or *Nights at the*

Circus. (The books go on working their transformations after leaving the author's hands. I received a card from the bookshop notifying me that *Nights at the Circus* was ready for collection; anything was always possible.) *Love* is different. It has more in common with the earlier, riskily realist *Shadow Dance*, but formally it stands alone within her *oeuvre*. It goes into dark and dangerous territory without a hint of pastiche: into the *terra incognita* of anonymity, despair and the paralysis of the will. It is mainly about the effects of repression. It recognises the power of the unconscious to break down under the pressure of influences which are barely visible. It deals with psychic waste, the silent beating of neglect and outlawed desire. Unlike all the other productions of Carter's magic-trick box, it cannot offer the female an endless range of playful disguises. Annabel is the victim of everything that has produced her and thereby outlawed her from herself; it may be that *Love* should really stand among Carter's most important works, in that it leads the reader deeply into the question of how to render the problem of outlawed femininity in artistic form. It offers itself no escape routes. In her later works Carter deals robustly with the return of the repressed, turning the sweatshop of the female unconscious to theatrical advantage. Here she deals with rehearsed and re-rehearsed repression: not only of desire, but of *self*. This daughter, Annabel, has not been *formed* in *Love*. As a result, the very world she inhabits does not quite contain her. It has no contours, any more than she has. *Love* is Angela Carter's Surrealist poem for the forlorn daughter, a poem which cannot take Annabel as its subject, except as *peinture-poésie*, photomontage, *cadavre exquis*, collage.

The novel has a tripartite structure ('triple-distilled', Carter later called it in her Afterword) of which the second part holds some of the keys to the nature of Annabel's plight; other signs of it are affixed throughout the work. She, Annabel, appears formless against a backdrop of fantastic forms. A still point in a moving collage of the real, she is no richly subversive centre, she is incapable of misrule; she is, simply, marooned in an unnameable position outside the self: 'as if [she] never experienced experience *as* experience' – the Carter of the later short story 'Flesh and the Mirror',[5] except that Annabel, unlike that heroine, is not even 'pulling the strings of [her] own puppet'. Annabel is not even subject: by the end of the novel, she still 'did not speak often and she laughed even less' (p. 108). She is incapable even of demonic laughter, oblivious of the ruses of subterfuge; she exists outside even the traditions of female Gothic which, like other literary solutions in this novel, have, it is hinted, broken down along with much else. The Gothic take on heroines might have afforded 'the mad girl'[6] the backhanded compliment of the vivid and unforgettable (and unforgetting) role of those revenants who haunt the interstices of the narratives of their own unspoken drives in ways that enable them, eventually, to take up a position of subversive articulacy. Not so Annabel. The spectacle of eclipse, which she is seen glimpsing at the opening of the novel, makes her behave like a Gothic heroine – 'she flung up her hands in a furious gesture of surrender and pitched herself sideways off the path' (p. 3) – but in gesture only. Gesture obliterates her; actually, she is 'the helpless pivot of the entire universe as if sun, moon, stars and all the hosts of the sky span round upon herself, their volitionless axle' (ibid.).

Nothing in *Love* is quite overthrown. Nothing is placed, nothing is fully formed; but at the same time, it is the intactness of this endless, pointless revolution that has driven Annabel into psychic captivity. Where fantasy in literature typically enables the posing of fundamental questions about the order of things, Annabel's interior world is a world where *nothing* is discarded. Annabel's is a world of nothing-adds-up, and no-questions-asked. The *real* criminality of her making is (almost) invisible, and has resulted in a kind of autism: the anorexia of the real. Carter's world, in *Love*, is flamboyant, uncontrollable, but it is not quite the outlaw's world. The outlaw enters into it, but Annabel herself is fixed in the object-woman's hall of mirrors, lacking her rite of passage from.girlhood, possessing, identifying, trying to draw something from it, and getting very tired. If she wants to be an outlaw she will have to get (possess, make love to) one: the double-bind of feminine lock-out is barely articulable, except in hopeless, helpless gesture. If she wants self, she will have to find a way of getting out of being locked outside herself. But how will she ever find a way of getting out of her (lock-out) self, when what is being outlawed is her interiority?

To explore all this, Carter must devise a narrative which obeys some of the laws of mimesis (the repressive is always spectacularly, materially real), but in collage. Annabel is a mess. This has to be said, in contexts as well as in things. *Love* presents the world as Annabel sees it: a messy collage of the imaginary and the real. '"I thought you were an incubus," she said to Lee . . . they had to make tea and so on, in the false cheerfulness of five in the morning' (p. 35). As this conversation takes place, there are albatrosses frozen in the middle of the ceiling. The consequence seems to be that Annabel and Lee get married. Surreal.

Annabel's favourite painter is Max Ernst. Carter gives us the gift of this clue to her method while we are still in the middle of a collage of drawings, derelict parks, indifference, and love of a kind, attempting to puzzle out where in the story the novel has begun, which came first, what came next and what exactly had happened to whom. When

Annabel and her boy-husband make love, they do so in the dust of the coloured chalks which Annabel has used to make her picture of a tree, so that each becomes 'involuntarily patterned by those workings of random chance so much prized by the Surrealists' (p. 34). For Max Ernst, the activity of painting became an arena in which a dialogue between conscious and unconscious could be staged;[7] for all the Surrealists, as for Freud, the arena of the unconscious was involuntarily patterned with all that had had to be repressed in the interests of maintaining a civilised order.

Where Freud's investigations took him into the difficult practice of working with a very few symptoms, the Surrealists littered their work with the 'symptoms' of artifice. They worked consciously within a new medium which aimed to bring together painting and poetry – *peinture-poésie* – in order to make compositions made up entirely of *context*: psychological, theological, scientific, historical; always blatantly material. The paintings of the mentally ill, which he investigated in his local mental hospital, together with his enthusiastic readings of Freud, enabled Ernst to investigate his interests in mental illness and primitive cultures – the two pre-civilised orders. His contribution to the Dadaist movement – the art world's most direct and overt attack on the prevailing cultural order – took the form of collage, his interest being focused not on abstraction but, rather, on the impact of juxtaposition.

Ernst's 'collage novels' consisted of a series of cut-up and reassembled nineteenth-century book illustrations; the collage novel offers a direct attack on nineteenth-century literary realism, by being composed of loosely related episodes patched together out of sequence and with no discernible ending.[8] In his juxtapositions of word and image, words interact with images and function *as* images: the collages are made up of engravings and photographs. Ernst

progressed to the 'collage novel' from his earlier experimentation with photomontage. The context produced is that of
love memory, erotic dream or half-sleep; the subject is
latent, has not yet been produced. The formal style is –
necessarily – that of disorder: where the subject is outlawed,
the objects are placed in spaces which often contradict
either their modelling or their perspectival arrangement.
Often they are thrust towards the picture frame in dramatic
foreshortening. The effect – of something seen in close-up,
too close for us to get a real visual take on it – is used by
Carter in many of Love's descriptions: of landscape, of
couplings, of Annabel, 'pitched sideways' so that she effec-
tively disappears from view. What we see is simply the
impact of distortion; or a glimpse of her, whole but flattened
out, as it were, as she crosses our vision.

For the Surrealists, love was the buzz word. Its most
audible spokesman was usually André Breton: in his
Recherches sur la sexualité he records a discussion on the
subject with fellow Surrealist Antonin Artaud, who insisted
that in their discussions of sexuality they must 'begin by
linking the question of sexuality to that of love. The whole
point of this investigation is, in love, to establish what
part belongs to sexuality.'[9] Years later, Breton was to
supplement that remark in an 'Inquiry into Erotic Representations': 'Would we believe in the words of love if they did
not carry the hope of that union of the real and the
imaginary of which the lovers' encounter forms the allegory?'[10] They managed to stage all such discussions without
any investigation at all into the nature of femininity; the
idea that their wives might have a part to play in their
investigations surprised and even rather shocked them.[11]
There were, however, two important female Surrealists,
one of whom is surely silently present in Angela Carter's
work. Gertrude Stein spent her lifetime's oeuvre on the

problem of simultanism integral to Surrealist presentations of the real; Leonora Carrington was Max Ernst's lover and companion for at least three years. He valued her stories, Marina Warner has perceptively suggested, perhaps even more than her paintings, for her experiments and discoveries with words would have supplemented rather than challenged his own experimentation. In Carrington's story 'Cast Down by Sadness', we can surely see some of the seeds of Carter's investigation, in *Love*, into the idea of the female body as accompaniment to self:

> I have wept so much here . . . I find that my beauty is very touching. For entire nights I have trailed my luxuriant hair in the water, and washed my body, telling it, 'You rival the moon, your flesh is more brilliant than its light.' I said all this to offer it pleasure, for my body's so jealous of the moon. One evening I'll invite you to meet it.[12]

Annabel is hiding from the moon; too abject for worship, but estranged from her own form in the same way. It is intrinsic to the design of *Love* that Carter will never apologise, never explain, but the explanation might, perhaps, have run something like Carrington's in 'My Mother is a Cow':

> To be one human creature is to be a legion of mannequins. These mannequins can become animated according to the choice of the individual creature. He or she may have as many mannequins as they please. When the creature steps into the mannequin he immediately believes it to be real and alive and as long as he believes this he is trapped inside the dead image, which moves in ever increasing circles away from Great Nature. Every individual gives names to his mannequins and nearly all these names begin with 'I am' and are followed by a long stream of lies . . . Suffering

is the death or disintegration of one or more of these mannequins. However, the more dead mannequins a creature leaves behind, the nearer he or she comes to leaving the human condition for ever. The only trouble is that when a being is obliged to abandon the invented presence of a disoccupied mannequin, he or she is quite often busy again building bigger and better mannequins to live in.[13]

In *Love*, the lie is the *cadavre exquis*[14] of the wedding ceremony (of which more later). For Carrington within Surrealism, the body must be put on, taken off, worn, fashioned, named, addressed. What comes across most strongly here (in contrast to the male debates, which focused on such issues as procreation, buggery, impotence) is the parodied but still dead-serious treatment of the distinction between female subject and female form – and, most strikingly of all, the *unfamiliarity* of the female body, which has somehow never been viewed as a given reality.

To Carter, Carrington seemed 'prim',[15] and she takes the defamiliarisation of the female body one stage further, into complete dissolution, until Annabel re-emerges, in the third part of *Love*, as embodied masquerade. She's a more subtle psychologist, of course, than Leonora Carrington. She has been dubbed the 'female Nijinsky' of modern fiction, 'Our Lady Edgar Allan Poe'. She is the Aubrey Beardsley, the Huysmans, the Maeterlinck, the Hoffman, the female Polanski of our day.[16] It's an impressive line-up: a good inheritance of experimentation, decadence, taste for the theatrical and the Dionysian. It's a male line, of course, so in the very act of trying to identify what it is she does, she disappears again. From every angle, the feminine seems to disappear, but this is what Carter is trying to show us. From the start, in her fiction, women are desperate, violent, attacking, silent, or parodied in their reasonableness (as is Emily, in *Shadow Dance*). By the time we get to *The Magic Toyshop*, Melanie 'discovers she was made of flesh and blood'[17] the summer she is fifteen, but not without discovering that she must keep her place as Leda to Uncle Philip's Swan in the mythology of awakening in which women blossom into shuddering subordination. Throughout her work, Carter's heroines sign themselves up for display, so that we read the way they have become accustomed to being treated: in that sense she is consistently realist. Appearing as it does in the cultural context of postwar upward mobility, *Love* is Carter's deepest investigation, in her early work, into the confounding artistry that must go into the business of paralysing the daughter: that forlornly mute by-product of upward mobility. In it – *without* using masquerade, and devastatingly without wit – she investigates Annabel's lack of femininity and the impact of that lack, the near-madness that cannot speak its name; the inarticulate body.

'Mixing the grim, the exotic, the farcical,' commented Anita Van Vactor in *The Listener*, 'Miss Carter traces the growth of a three-way symbiosis, a hermetic mythology decorated by Annabel's suicide attempts.'[18] This works as a kind of Photofit description of Annabel's dilemma, but it doesn't break through to Carter's position on it, which is indeed exotic; grim, on her own admission; and farcical up to a point, beyond which it is dead, dead serious. What is missing from the critical reception of *Love* is any acknowledgement of Carter's quiet, stealthy emphasis on the fluidity of the hysteric's desperate artistry, which moves across the canvas of inexpressible desire, projecting individual, disconnected figures. An object-daughter is an empty vessel. It is possible to castrate interiority. (This may be what Freud discerned, in his 'castrated' women.) Annabel sees in simultanism because she is spectacularly unintegrated into the world, to which she belongs only as an observer. She knows she sees, and so, in her forlorn way, she makes a living out of her determination to show what little she knows – which means putting her lack (of vitality) on display, an act which may often be confused with sluttishness.

In the eighteenth-century park in which all that remains of the former mansion is a portico which now functions (like Annabel) 'only as a pure piece of design', Annabel runs through herself in synaesthesia, seeking the Gothic North – the language of the missing literature of the nineteenth century which would privilege sensibility over sense and thereby release *something* in excess. Recognising, at some subliminal level, that her portico is both dismantled *and* locked (a possibility realisable only in the language of simultanism, which is why the Surrealists insisted on juxtaposition), Annabel has resorted to seeing as the only way she has of believing. At the beginning of the novel, and the crux of the story, we flash-forward to the night of her first suicide attempt, following the superposition of one oedipal triangle upon another. We have already had (earlier in the story, later in the narrative) the graphic disorderliness of the wedding, which focuses in gory close-up on her parents' designs on her as the subordinate *objet trouvé* of their upward mobility. On this night (the night on which the sun and moon can be seen in juxtaposition, in the ruins of the park) the triangle forms again. With the penetration into her house of her husband's new subsidiary love-object, she tilts towards the total closure of suicide, and sees double. With this feat of 'natural' astrological alchemy, with its hint of eclipse, Annabel knows, with the dependable intuition of the hysteric, that she herself has been tilted once too

often into the impossible position of being the empty
reflector of others' refracted desires.

The park, at this moment, is irradiated by a light source
which renders it a stage: a 'premeditated theatre where the
romantic imagination could act out any performance it chose
amongst settings of classic harmony or crabbed quaintness'
(p. 2). Annabel is thereby positioned as the source of this
Expressionist vision which establishes her, the obvious
projectionist, as the volitionless actress in her own, inarticulable theatre of the unconscious. This style of things seen
at one remove, foreshortened or displaced, is typical of
Annabel's style of seeing. It apes a method she has grown
up with, the style of reasoning that looks *through* a daughter, as a window on to parental prospects. Annabel might,
here as elsewhere in *Love*, be exposing a version of what de
Chirico revealed to Max Ernst: the Surreal as a 'culture of
systematic displacement'.[19] Ernst, like Carter, relished in his
collages the possibility of envisaging the effect of one
cultural impossibility juxtaposed against another, peppered
with the unintegral imagery of figures of desire; like Ernst,
Carter, here in *Love*, ultimately effects a *rejection* of the
Surrealist 'resolution' of dreams and reality which takes us
right up to the edge of the *néant* of Dada. *Love* effects a
superb layering of visible and barely visible monsters which
are conjured up, Surrealist-style, to mock man's reliance on
his 'rational' powers; Carter juxtaposes sixties art school
liberation with fifties upward mobility and asks: What are
the monsters? Madness? Love? Mad love? Mother? Or is
the monster entirely silent, unseen, unrepresented: the
néant of Dada, language collapsed into unmeaning; or, in
this case, Daddy (who exists, in *Love*, only as the silent
appendage to Mummy). Or is it just the apparatus of the
real, the social machinery, which subjects Annabel to a
ceremony that layers oedipal triangle on oedipal triangle,

obliterating the 'I am', except as a pack of lies, creating increasingly *fewer* real figures out of which the openly Surreal image emerges: that of the eerily unattached, free-floating eye?

'The basic feat of simultanism', Roger Shattuck has commented of the nexus of work which collates Post-Impressionism and the Surreal, throws us back on 'a desperate effort of assimilation.'[20] The Surrealists knew that creativity is interiorised, and wanted that productive interiority reflected as hard surfaces, inclining planes, in contexts which allow one thing to comment on, rather than lead to, another. Carter, in *Love*, plots in superposed images: the park; the wedding; the party. Annabel, crossing the park of reason to get to the other side, gets to the other side (which is *inside*), but it is disordered, overdetermined, bloody. The castle of herself has never been introduced to her, and is therefore impenetrable. Flitting across the surface of this impediment to vision is – paradoxically – the outlaw – in-law.

Brother-in-law Buzz, also a stranger to himself, liberates Annabel through an act of love: he shares his treasures with her. He, like the figure of the bird in the Surrealists' work, is an unhinged, unattached thing: 'It sharpened its knives; it splashed in its acids; it snipped, stitched and dyed its commedia dell'arte rags; it rolled its joints; . . . it squatted for hours on the floor . . .' (p. 64). Buzz is the flagrantly asocial on display; he is also the seeing eye. His camera, the signature of the new aristocracy for Annabel's mother, is the opposite of a sign for Annabel: it is a source. Empty, unattached to the symbolic realities of this novel's mimetic signatures, a stranger in her own text, selfless in the twentieth-century sense, Annabel signifies nothing. She is unconstructed, welded firmly in place, all eyes, with nothing to say. Something makes Buzz gravitate towards her: perhaps the complexity with which the world is mediated through to her. Carter likens her to 'a blind man at a firework display who can only appreciate the fires in the air by interpreting their various degrees of magnificence through the relative enthusiasm of the noisy crowd. The nature of the dazzlement was dimly apprehended, not known' (p. 24). When later she is driven to apprehend more directly, her desire to possess will render her tawdry, but in her earlier state, stranded with the fragility of her robbed imagination, she is approachable, for someone like Buzz, because her act of transgression is clearly yet to come. Carter was later struck by her own 'icy treatment'[21] of Annabel, identifying the original idea for her novel in Benjamin Constant's *Adolphe*, the early-nineteenth-century novel of erotica in which passion dies down once it has achieved its transgressive aim.[22] For the forlorn daughter, what has been outlawed is, precisely, the possibility of transgression, which requires the corruption and collusion of the self. Annabel, living in pieces, cannot do more than *identify* with the desire to transgress, positioning herself somewhere in the inarticulable between: between subject and object, seer and seen, she must draw (the world to) herself. She does it by looking *and* modelling. Her first fellow-intermediary is Buzz.

Buzz is the authentic outlaw: the source of drugs, erotica, lawlessness. We meet him when he gives Annabel some images he thinks will please her. His taste is for pornography, the outlaw's natural device for keeping sex at a distance, and he makes her a present of his treasures because he likes her enough to want to touch her with his gifts.

A glum, painted young woman, the principal actress (torso and legs sheathed in black leather, sex exposed) eyed the

> camera indifferently as though it were no business of hers
> she was blocked at every orifice; she went about her
> obscene business . . . with the abstract precision of the
> geometrician . . . (p. 4)

Annabel, seeing herself ('all she wanted in life was a bland, white, motionless face like that of the photographic whore so she could live a quiet life behind it') derives solace from these images of arrest. Outlawed from self, she can identify herself as the model of the outlaw, with as many layers of dissociation as that implies. Carter plunges us, then, into the middle of her story with the heroine's projections, themselves beyond representation, here juxtaposed with a spectacle of identification which is itself a displacement. Annabel, it seems, would (desire to) be (like) Buzz. Except that she has no will.

The photograph makes a subjective moment – an essentially Expressionist act – into a document, conferring on the image the status of a record: this (has now) happened, it is (here) fixed in time.[23] Buzz thereby gains authority, and stability, for Annabel. He is a fixed point; they share a knowledge of something unsayable, unsaid: a graphic emptiness. As she moves, though, from being a spectator to demonstrating her own skills as a graphic artist, she begins to emerge for the reader in a collage of scraps of the *here and now*, which is her only reality (just) outside the realm of the imaginary. The tree she draws has a gaudy parrot on its topmost branch; it is executed in coloured chalks from which a coloured dust rains down on to the bed on which her husband, brother of Buzz, first deflowers her – or, more graphically, 'invades the castle of herself' (p. 32).

Earlier in the narrative, as Lee and Annabel lie together on the narrow mattress like 'lovers in the jungle' (p. 29), beneath a wall decorated with a 'forest of trees, flowers, birds and beasts . . .', Annabel's parents make their intrusion on the scene. They take their daughter away until Lee promises to marry her. 'One January morning' it snows. The room is full of white light reflected from the outside, and Annabel takes 'a technical pleasure' in observing the play of snowlight on Lee's shoulders as he lies sleeping:

> She found him continuously interesting to look at but it hardly occurred to her the young man was more than a collection of coloured surfaces. . . . She did not even think of herself as a body, but more as a pair of disembodied eyes – when she thought about herself at all, that is. She was eighteen, secretive and withdrawn since childhood.
> (pp. 30–31)

She tries on Buzz's clothes, masquerading Buzz. She gets out her pastel crayons and draws a tree on the wall. This section of the novel is layered up in a series of images which seem to have no clear causal or temporal connection. The deflowering of Annabel is very bloody: 'she quickly interpreted [Lee] into her mythology but if, at first, he was a herbivorous lion, later he became a unicorn . . .' (p. 34). Waking in the night, she sometimes sees white birds – for the Surrealists, the ubiquitous symbol of repressed desire. So it goes, one image being stuck up against another, with no process, no development, no flow. Closed down as if in anticipation of just such a moment, the body registers no surprise at the parental interference, for the language of the text does not even bother to signal the arena of taboo.

Like Freud's hysterics, Annabel has been rendered nearly inarticulate; like Ernst, she collects scraps of her untold story and puts them together to create not images, but contexts. She is in an impossible position: girl and woman; subdued and exposed; painter and model; artist and subject;

she sees, but signifies nothing. A mite less disabled, she might have occupied the already troublesome, unclear-cut position of woman-artist. But this is 1969, she is a child of the postwar, respectable, inarticulately ambitious, co-ordinated 1950s, and she is addicted both to the transformation of the real *and* to remaining in hiding. She cannot draw from life, she draws from her robbed imaginary. At large in the landscaped park, she seeks the Gothic North; loved, she becomes deranged. Betrayed, she seeks the solace of the natural world, and in the sky she sees a repetition of what is intolerable because it is constantly being repeated: the simultaneity of things which should follow, things which should move, in due time, one into the other. I think, too, that she is shown eclipsed, in this first part of the novel, by the shadow of the painting Max Ernst called 'Men Shall Know Nothing of This' (1923), in which the movements of sun and moon are shown together in a geometrical shape which is both phallic and cervical. The collage juxtaposes metronome; gender symbols; parachute; acrobat; conception, and birth. The back of that canvas bore a poem:

> The crescent moon (yellow and parachute-like)
> prevents the little whistle from falling to
> the ground
> Because someone is paying attention to it, the
> whistle thinks that it is rising to the sun.
> The sun is divided in two, the better to
> revolve.
> The model is stretched out in a dream-like pose.
> The right leg is bent back (a pleasing and
> precise movement).
> The hand shields the Earth. By this motion,
> the Earth takes on the importance of a sexual
> organ.
> The moon goes very quickly through its

phases and eclipses.
The picture is odd in its symmetry. The
two sexes balance each other there.[24]

II   *Cadavre Exquis/Folie à Deux*

Artaud's periodical *La Révolution Surréaliste* (1924) considered such topics as 'Is Suicide a Solution?'; 'What Kind
of Hope Do You Put in Love?'[25] Ernst was a signatory. The
group of twenty-six signatories enjoyed playing Surrealist
games, the purpose of which was to share genius in
common without loss of individuality. One of the most
popular games was *'le cadavre exquis'*: a sentence or drawing
composed by several people in turn, none of whom was
allowed to see the previous contributions. *La Révolution
Surréaliste* published the results of these games of consequences; Paul Eluard stressed the ritual nature of the
occasions: in this 'collectively determined poetry' the Surrealists 'gambled with images'.[26]

The game of chance extended outwards more generally:
Ernst defined collage itself as the 'alchemy of the visual
image' which worked on a principle he defined as 'the
exploitation of the chance meeting of two remote realities
on a plane unsuitable to them'.[27] The *cadavre exquis* of *Love*
is the wedding ceremony, that monologic montage of image
and speech which admits the outlaw as seer, repeats the
insult of parental intrusion, and collates the *'folie à deux'* –
in duplicate – which Annabel must then undo if she is to
extract a modicum of individuality.

In the final section of the novel Annabel, by turning aside
from the diagram of the couple and lured by the talisman of
outlawed desire, herself taboo, must find a way of representing herself as outlaw to her in-laws. At a subliminal

level, she redesigns the geometry of relationships by form-
ing an allegiance with Buzz's dead mother, thereby creating
for herself what she most needs: a new past. This time, she
will *take after* a woman who wore her heart on her sleeve.
Nakedness and cabalistic signs will take the place of the
stifling intrusions of instant results and the obsession with
exteriority which Annabel's mother displays. This process
begins with the wedding, where each player takes a stand
and has something to say, seemingly in isolation from and
oblivious to the verbal or topological positions of the other
players.

There's no bride stripped bare at Annabel's wedding: she
has a white sheath, within which she will secrete herself if
she remembers. She doesn't marry as a woman or as a
daughter, she marries as a thing. '"Oh my darling. . . . It's
not what I would have wished for you,"' is Annabel's
mother's line (p. 36). The consequence is, ultimately,
attempted suicide. Nothing happens at the wedding, except
nostalgia and regret, and the takeover of central place by
Buzz, Apache-style, in remembrance of his father. While
Lee goes through his rite of passage, remembering his aunt
and her hopes for him and for the Revolution, the parents
fix on Buzz as potentially the most upwardly mobile because
of his camera. 'No wonder', Carter intervenes wryly, in case
we should have missed the point, 'the daughter saw only
appearances' (p. 37). Lee catches the mood:

> 'Betrayed to the bourgeoisie!' he thought and, once outside,
> lurched against the wall as if to face the firing squad. The
> brilliant morning shot him through the eyes with darts of
> glass and he was crushed by the conviction that he had
> done something irreparable. He saw the man and the
> woman grimacing at his brother and his new wife, their
> daughter, and all transmitted signs and messages not one of

> which any of the others could interpret. Words flew out of
> their mouths like birds, up and away. . . . (p. 36)

Materially, the postwar culture of which Annabel's mother
is so clearly a part went for instant substitutes. The Collins
brothers can remember when this was not so. The photomontage of memory, activated by the snapshot collage of
the wedding scene, brings back memories of their aunt,
who named Lee after Trotsky, and of a Romantic hope of
Revolution and the faith in things that might take a long
time. Their memories have depth: Lee's mother had 'gone
mad in style', with 'a spectacular psychosis in the grand,
traditional style of the old-fashioned Bedlamite', bursting
into the school playground in the middle of the festival to
celebrate Empire Day 'naked and painted all over with
cabbalistic signs' (p. 10). Lee's father was an honest railwayman, but Buzz's was an American serviceman who had left
behind him the 'crude, silver finger-ring decorated with
skull and cross-bones' that makes Buzz believe that he must
in fact have been an Apache or a Mohawk: certainly, with
tribal origins.

The brothers have history, then; Annabel has none. She
is, here, ' "Nothing-But" Daughter',[28] the Jungian creature
'so identified with the mother that her own instincts are
paralysed through projection', thrashing impotently under
the fire-blanket of not having chosen this condition. She *is*
taboo, embodying the forbidden, and 'a mocking memory
to the mother', as Carter puts it in *The Sadeian Woman*: 'As I
am, so you once were.'[29] It works both ways, moreover: the
mother is, thenceforth,

> a horrid warning to her daughter. 'As I am, so you will be.'
> Mother seeks to ensure the continuance of her own
> repression, and her hypocritical solicitude for the younger

woman's moral, that is, sexual welfare masks a desire to
reduce her daughter to the same state of contingent
passivity she herself inhabits, a state honoured by custom
and hedged by taboo.[30]

(In other words: 'Oh my darling. . . . It's not what I would
have wished for you.') Lee and Annabel sign themselves up
to this, but when – not much later – Lee's bit-on-the-side
comes to the party, Annabel signs out, putting her name to
another *cadavre exquis*:

disparate sets of images shuffled together anyhow. A
draped form on a stretcher; . . . a knife; an operating
theatre; blood; and bandages. In time, the principal actors
(the wife, the brothers, the mistress) assembled a coherent
narrative from these images but each interpreted them
differently and drew their own conclusions which were all
quite dissimilar for each told himself the story as if he were
the hero except for Lee who, by common choice, found
himself the villain. (p. 43)

Section two of the novel is brief, functional. The collage
comes unstuck; the problem of the couple is re-rehearsed,
under-studied, sujected to transference. This latter Carter
deftly subjects to the repetition and object fixation which is
psychiatry's key subject. Her sleight of hand is that the
transference is Lee's, not Annabel's; it distils the triple-
structure of the series of triangles into one, surreal encounter. His orgy with the shrink may be real or imagined, he
may be enacting it on his own behalf or on behalf of any
combination of any of the other couplings; it is the most
graphic, the most 'real' incident in the book. This, too, is
(probably) imagined. Surreal.

Here we get the explanations, the labels, the names.

Annabel is mad. She exists only in shadow, she has no femininity: 'She's like a shadow that sits and remembers and probably the things it remembers never happened' (p. 58). She is Jung's emptied woman.[31] She has eaten her wedding ring and believes she can survive by continuing to be invisible, if she displays the skull ring – the link with Buzz's past which also links her to Buzz. This ring is the story's central love token; that story, at the heart of *Love*, shrinks to a section of ten pages and to two dimensions, taking, now, the form of a dialogue. Here Carter introduces a new player, the psychiatrist who gives disorder a name: '*folie à deux*'. But which two?

The greatest taboo may be to wish your mother dead. Annabel finds ways of wish fulfilment, as she must if she is to move out of the shadows and undo herself, break the seal. The past is hard to swallow, but Annabel swallows it when she swallows her wedding ring. Transference is a hit-and-miss affair, involving, often, misplaced lust, displaced emotions, misalliance. No matter: it does at least take place, enabling Annabel, obliquely, to effect a reversal which has its due reverberations: 'now the circumstances were altered. Annabel freshly defined Lee as having no life beyond that of a necessary attribute of herself alone' (p. 64). If she will repossess him, now, she will have it show. 'Far more radiant than she had been as a bride' (p. 70), Annabel will now effect her own, ultimate form of mastery of herself by labelling her husband as hers, in her own tribal ceremony, which borrows from all she has observed of the outlaw in whose footsteps she must follow. She will mark her husband in flesh, now, in the way she must also mark herself if she is to break the seal of the castle. In marking him thus – in a conflation of totem and taboo – she will sign him with the full impact of her interiority (which spells, in one language, sorrow, in another, lack – there are endless words for this) and Lee, in the perverse reversal of the ceremony which makes two into one flesh, becomes the feminine receptacle. 'Sometimes she thought of him as a mean, black fox and sometimes as a metamorphic thing that could slip in and out of any form he chose . . .' (pp. 74–5).

Here is the plumage, then, to Annabel's gaudy parrot. Though we must take with us into the remainder of the novel Max Ernst's warning about the (lack of) narrative of the collage: if the plume makes the plumage, it's not the glue [colle] that makes the collage. The wound won't disappear. We aren't going to be able to *stitch it up*.

III   'Artist in Flesh': Mother RIP

Under the influence of psychoanalysis, history repeats itself, but this time the scars are on show. In his *Surrealist Manifesto* of 1924, André Breton claimed a similar project for Surrealism, which should take as one of its aims the attempt to re-evaluate the past, and to explore obscure and neglected areas of human experience. In so doing, 'we cross what the occultists call dangerous territory'.[32] The imagery of Leonora Carrington's breakdown, following Max Ernst's arrest, repeated that of her earlier experimentation, in her writing and painting,[33] but in the process of regression, the abiding characteristic of her language is that it throws up images which are divided and split. Carrington, in the midst of her breakdown, puzzles over the composition of the egg, and of the split, seeing self:

> The egg is the macrocosm and the microcosm, the dividing line between big and small which makes it impossible to see the whole. To possess a telescope without its other essential half, the microscope, seems to me a symbol of the darkest

incomprehension. The task of the right eye is to peer into the telescope, while the left eye peers into the microscope. . . . I felt that, through the agency of the Sun, I was an androgyne, the Moon, the Holy Ghost, a gypsy, an acrobat, Leonora Carrington, and a woman.[34]

The signature – Leonora Carrington – is but one fragment of the shattered self, the plume of the plumage rather than the *colle* of the collage,[35] yet deconstructing its assumed power to bind the other selves does not strip it of its import. On the contrary.

To see the part, and yet the whole, is, paradoxically, to lay claim to the incidental, the contingent nature of our vision. This is what Surrealists such as Dali were getting at when they painted floating eyes along with leaden-looking birds, or when they harnessed timepieces, or when they painted words. I am puzzled that Angela Carter should think Leonora Carrington's work 'prim', but perhaps there is, ultimately, a railing *against* chaos in Carter's work which makes her the more profound artist: 'Be bold, be bold, but not too bold,'[36] as the psychoanalysts say. That holding back, that 'not too bold', she did not achieve in *Love*, as the self-defensive witticism of her Afterword to the novel shows. But as collage it is huge, fine, complex, a narrative 'decalcomania':[37] a stain, of sorts, pressed between the leaves – or leavings – to make a pattern; but then worked up, carefully wrought.

For the revitalisation of the past, achieved with such a wry, glancing delicacy in *Love*, involves the territory of taboo: that which may be indicated; named, even; but which you sign yourself up to only in great pain. Taboo is an experience, rather than a thing. It finds a shape, a figure, becomes visualised as a psychic stain which begins as randomness and forms itself, gradually over time and through repetition, into a pattern, emerging out of the *clair-obscur*; composed, in collage, out of a mixture of the searching imagination and the *objet trouvé* or the telescopic and the microscopic. The Surrealists loved junk, were regular *flâneurs* at the local flea market, always searching for the appropriate find, the object possessing an attraction as if never before seen.[38]

For Annabel, in psychic regression, the taboo is herself: she embodies all that is outlawed. The major taboo in the upwardly mobile family, with mother on show and father silenced, is her own development, so that she must now get back for herself something she never had. What gets called on is the junk box of her own imaginary. She turns up, quite by chance, a formative experience:

> When she was two or three years old, her mother took her shopping. Little Annabel slipped out of the grocer's while her mother discussed the price of butter and played in the gutter for a while until she decided to wander into the middle of the road. A car braked, skidded and crashed into a shop front. Annabel watched the slivers of glass flash in the sunshine until a crowd of distraught giants broke upon her head, her mother, the grocer in his white coat, a blonde woman with dark glasses, a man with four arms and legs and two heads, one golden, the other black, and many other passers-by, all as agitated as could be imagined. 'You might have been killed!' said her mother. 'But I wasn't killed, I was playing,' said Annabel . . .
>
> However, this was not the memory of a real event but of a particularly lifelike dream she had under sedation in the hospital although she now believed it to be perfectly true. (pp. 75–6)

This is not a memory, it's a retrospective Identikit precedent for later events: as such, it will serve her present purposes.

Of course she can't really remember play, she has been trained not to play, let alone to remember. But the greatest taboo, for the '"Nothing-But" Daughter', is touch, which for Annabel has been transferred into the practice of drawing. Re-enacting the past as she is, in the process of withdrawing from it, she must, then, stage another prohibition. If she cannot (again) leave Mother's side, well then, she must cease to draw. And live a little. Which means getting her own back. What is the matter with Annabel is Annabel's *matter* – psychic canvas, the *néant* of her own substance, or simply this: flesh. Getting to flesh involves undoing the whole damned edifice, so that all that is left is *material*:

> The world unshelled itself or she unshelled the world and she found, beneath the crust of spiked armour, a kernel of plasticine limply begging to be rendered into forms. As she grew more confident this was so, she drew a final picture of Lee as a unicorn whose horn had been amputated. Her imagery was by no means inscrutable. Then her sketchbooks were put away for good. . . .
> She guessed the institution of a new order of things in which she was an active force rather than an object at the mercy of every wind that blew; no longer bewitched, she became herself a witch. (p. 77)

Becoming a witch means re-enacting, and this time showing the other up: turning the tables, laying claim. At the centre of this new endeavour is a horrid double-bind. Annabel must still choose either to go on being wounded or to wound, since in removing her displacement activity she must sacrifice her talent, the gift that has kept her alive while also ensuring her sustained removal from deep subjectivity, or simply contact of the kind of which Buzz is searingly, Lee gently, capable. Refusing, any longer, the status of object, she limply begs to be rendered into forms. She becomes material. What is denied is artistry, since that is a lifetime's process, a learned skill, and she has just renounced her only skill. Why, then, she'll *fit* them all (in the Shakespearian sense): she'll show them.

Actions speak louder than words. In the final section of *Love*, Annabel goes about her reclaiming in another tripartite structure: she possesses her husband, she reconstructs herself, and she acts out her sexual desire. In other words, she becomes an artist in flesh: the sexy woman who will surely kill her mother. Or herself. She'll live in sin, she'll totemise herself and others, she'll synthesise the world. What is significant about all this is that, taken as complete collage, it 'simply' re-enacts the first part of *Love*. Annabel was *already doing all this*. She must do it again, though, and this time with a clear perception that written into *this peinture-poésie* is the likelihood of her own destruction. Surreal . . .? Yes, but with an extra cutting edge. The witticism seems to be missing. Releasing the imagery of the unconscious for this woman-artist, this character, has something odd about it, something absolutely un-jaunty. It *sounds* different, somehow, from the work of the Surrealists (with the exception, of course, of the work of Carrington in regression, which synthesises, in a quasi-scientific, pictorial piece, all the elements of *Love*): it's *so like the original*.

We're in, now, to double-syntax. If Annabel has so far existed (except for Lee, but he doesn't know how to put his insights into practice) only as representation, she must now form herself into a representative of herself. Masquerading (the protective skin, the fashioning of self as object of desire[39]) is *nearly* it, but not quite. What Annabel goes on to

do, in the final section of the novel, has just a shade more
in common with what Buzz does, in the first. She dresses
up, makes up, acts up. That isn't the same as the dressing-
up she does in the wedding dress, nor even the same as
bleeding under a muzzle of bandages. It's closer to the
source. It's more like play. It *looks* more like regression, but
it's not, it's acting. Not ham acting, real acting. The kind
where you get out of yourself into the part that then
becomes a part of you. The kind that involves an inexpres-
sibly subtle negotiation of self and other, the construction
of a kind of objective-correlative self: impersonality as
poetry – and, of course, as paint.

Annabel as *peinture-poésie* begins by signing herself as
Lee's wife, as she has done, of course, from the start – it
was just that she couldn't sign all of herself, for the reasons
which keep emerging. But the ' "Nothing-But" Daughter'
Annabel which makes Annabel less than whole cannot
remould herself into the newly formed Annabel overnight.
She must begin somewhere, and at first actions will go on
seeming to be divided from words. She takes her husband
to the tattooist, that 'Artist in Flesh' who takes Surrealism
on to the canvas of the body:

> Men turned into artificial peacocks displayed chests where
> ramped ferocious lions, tigers or voluptuous houris in all
> the coloured inks which issued from the needle. One man
> had the head of Christ crowned with thorns. . . . Some had
> flowers, memorial crosses and the words: MOTHER R.I.P.
> (p. 69)

She signs him her possession, making him uncomfortable
and endowing him with 'the status of any other object in
her collection' (p. 70), though it should be remembered that

all her *objets trouvés* are valuable, precious, and at some level stand in for Annabel.

Carter permits some reversals: tattoo – the mingling, as Annabel herself is, of totem and taboo – enables Annabel to sign herself. Her signature, as Leonora Carrington's was for her, is only one fragment of the self to be composed, or decomposed, or, perhaps, handed over. The reconstruction following psychoanalysis enables the handing over of some of the pieces that don't properly belong: now it is Lee, bearing Annabel's name, who suffers an 'unmotivated absence of pleasure that dulled the colours of the approaching spring and took the dimensions from the things around him so everything was reduced to flat, ineffectual shapes. He raised his arm and no shadow fell for Annabel had taken out his heart, his household god, squashed it thin as paper and pinned it back on the exterior, bright, pretty but inanimate' (pp. 73–4).

This is her way of signing Lee her possession *and* the only way she can think of to effect the mingling of flesh that will make him truly hers. She is not humiliating him but signing him, with a rosy-red heart crossed with her signature, in green – an ambiguous gesture which, from her point of view, constitutes proof of sexual possession. From where Lee sits, she achieves her aim, since it is he, now, who experiences pain, discomfort, confusion and the sense that his body is no longer his own. For the reader conscious of Carter's wider purpose, what may be recalled here is Freud's study, within primitive cultures, of the traditional conflation of totem and taboo in the totem which *illustrates* taboo, rendering it paradoxically both officially outlawed *and* inscribed within cultural iconography.

Lee, too, is now branded outlaw, in a ceremony which reinscribes the wedding ceremony, this time reversing sexual roles, reordering the triangle and making Lee subject to Annabel's psychic order (which is *dis*order). *Folie à deux* is self-perpetuating, though each time it occurs it will take a different form. Where Freud collapsed totem and taboo, Annabel takes this process a step further. She collapses other into self, self into totem, through the essentially subversive artistry of the tattoo, which is a threat to sign out of cultural uniformity, a graffiti of feelings of unbelonging. Lee, now (possessed by) Annabel, becomes subject to the psychic numbing experienced by the outlaw suffering feelings which cannot be named, except by signing them taboo. It *nearly* works, this cultural practice of rendering self into totem which traditionally reaches its apogée in the figure of woman struck dumb and rigid in the form of mannequin, the doll figure dressed up to represent the condition outlawed by familial prohibition, modelling femininity as masquerade. The trouble is, these are feelings which cannot be shared: we know, really, that this isn't his *actual* heart (or hers).

She needs his heart, she always has. His understanding keeps her alive. But he cheats on her, so she demonstrates this heartlessness by giving him a new one, more in keeping with the tenor of events. His new, visible heart is 'rosy red' (p. 70), but no longer secret. What is on display is there to be raided, no longer hidden, no longer private – Buzz (with his pornographic images) knows this. Well then, if Lee is no longer secret, no longer private, Caroline's for the asking, Annabel will put his heart on show. She knows about the essentially artificial game of taking a lover to dissipate the sheer philosophical confusion of the one-flesh of the marriage ceremony, and she will put this on show too. We know she knows it because she demonstrates it: our reading of Annabel, like much in this third section, has to go into reverse. In this final section, what you see is what you get – it's the first part of the book that was cryptic.

Again the conventions of narratology go into reverse, and we can hardly believe our eyes: this daughter is getting so naughty. This daughter says what she means and means what she says. *Confusing*. No convention has prepared us for this. ('Taboos, we must suppose, are prohibitions of primeval antiquity . . .'[40])

Freud, on the question of taboo, is amusingly tentative and suddenly outrageously emphatic, a bit like Surrealism. He notes the closeness between taboo and 'touching phobia'; it might be maintained, he suggests in *Totem and Taboo*, 'that a case of hysteria is a caricature of a work of art' (p. 73). Annabel, when she takes a job in the local ballroom, *shall* go to the ball, even if it means working for her living; here she is both artist and work of art, writer, painter and *peinture-poésie* and something else: a sixties working girl, astray in the swinging provinces, *modelling* herself, as women have done since primeval antiquity – and doing something else to boot. In section three she goes on to a kind of auto-pilot, hell-bent on rewriting the reality principle, and perhaps also revising Breton's novel *L'Amour fou*.[41] The *Surrealist Manifesto* offers a telling spoof-dictionary definition of 'surrealism': 'surrealism, noun, masc., pure psychic automatism by which it is intended to express, either verbally, or in writing, the true function of thought'.[42] 'Surrealism, noun, masc.' Janet, along with Jung, was their key philosopher: Janet, who believed that 'to limit the life of man to this clear and distinct thought process Descartes speaks about, is to suppress, in my opinion, three-quarters of this human life and to leave aside what is most attractive, the shadows and the *clair-obscur*'.[43] Angela Carter had to move from *Shadow Dance*, her first novel and study of schizophrenia, out into the light of a mythology of the unconscious, via the chaos and disorder of *Love*; the Surrealists knew what was involved (the unleashing of desire) but not, really, that this would involve the speaking voices, and the articulate bodies, of desirous women.[44] A relatively unknown Surrealist, Austin Osman Spare, wrote a book entitled *The Book of Pleasure (Self Love): The Psychology of Ecstasy*,[45] which argued that art is the instinctive application of knowledge latent in the unconscious; Luce Irigaray, in *This Sex Which Is Not One*, reminds us that the 'self-affection of women' does not really exist in our cultural grammar.[46] Annabel knows this too, but because *Love* is art, not philosophy, Carter can give us something the philosophers cannot offer: a kind of enlightenment-through-decadence which lets out something which we have to know about. Love can *unhinge* 'self-love': it's this unhinging that *Love* does best.

The ballroom is an objective correlative for psychoanalysis: that which is impossible in the realm of the real, 'A synthetic reduplication without an original model', which is why it has to maintain a room of its own. Annabel gets it in one – 'Here, since everything around her was artificial, she and her first, carefully contrived, if tentative reconstruction of herself as a public object passed for a genuine personality' (p. 78). She smiled 'her borrowed smile', she served drinks and washed out glasses, and got on.

'She worked in this place for five nights out of the week, from seven . . . to eleven . . . on Monday, Tuesday and Wednesday and from seven . . . to one the next morning on Friday and Saturday.' Just like life, really. When Lee arrived at the club, she 'hid for a while behind a plastic tree' (p. 79), for all the world like a character in a rehearsal of *A Midsummer Night's Dream*. He looked out of place in the environment of the ballroom, 'for he still looked more than ever like a handsome outlaw' (pp. 79–80), and it is in this moment that Carter effects some tiny, radical change in the generic nature of her narrative, since in this moment the cut-out technique of collage gives way to an instant of double-exposure in which we are suddenly invited to do what Annabel is supposed to do, from here on in. Remember.

The memory of the 'hermetic triangle'[47] of Annabel, Lee and Buzz, itself fashioned to remodel the oedipal triangle which smothers Annabel in her role of '"Nothing-But" Daughter', reminds us of what has driven her mad: the ceaselessly, seemingly self-perpetuating pattern of triangles set into play again by Lee's infidelity. In the relentless disorder of space and time which is reality, in the *absence* of meta-fictitious play (the play-within-the-play of Shakespeare's comedy; the mythology-within-mythology of Carter's later fictions), too much 'contactless sociability' (p. 85), too much of a 'gaping hole in the fabric of everyday behaviour' (p. 86), ends in the padded cell. Annabel's release from the mental institution, and then from the ballroom into the pub, pitches her again into the 'endless conversation of silences and allusions' (p. 84) in which the Collinses (all three) maintain their enigmatic, suggestive hell of constant, unremitting back-to-the-future. When Lee publicly embraces his bit-on-the-side, leaving Annabel with Buzz, the horror of the '"Nothing-But" Daughter' surfaces again, but this time Annabel isn't going to just sit with it. Outlawed, she'll make love to the outlaw (which by this time is Buzz *and* Lee): it's the one act that's absolutely taboo, and which therefore takes care of the past in more ways than one. It's incest (of a kind); it's *folie à deux*, which will enable her to disobey the shrink. It's putting herself on display for the photographer, but this time without a man at her side; it's touching herself.

The problem, of course, is that Buzz, like Annabel, is

unformed, except as a practitioner. His camera is his tool; he is – as she is – a specialist in the art of look-but-don't-touch. He's seen her, many times, in the shadow dance of his imagination, but here she is real. That's different:

> he faltered between her real self on the bed and her many shadows on the wall, determined to have her but thwarted by his inability to feel as intensely in situations that were actual as he did in the supercharged events of his imagination. (p. 93)

'The more he caressed her, the stiffer and colder she seemed to grow' (p. 93). This is, for both of them, the supreme re-enactment of everything that's gone before to *prevent* the authenticity – and the implications – of sexual contact; as such, it is itself as provocative as it is preventative. And yet she is full of desire: 'She wanted this desperately. So they began a duel of mismatched expectancies in which Annabel was bound to be the worst hurt . . .' (p. 93). Buzz's mother had given him 'many fears about the physicality of women; all the nightmares that had ever visited him rushed back into his head at once and he flinched from Annabel's mouth, which numbed him' (p. 94). It's the *real* that seems to get in the way. The here and now. Flesh. 'It is always a dangerous experiment to act out a fantasy,' Carter soberly intervenes, 'but Annabel suffered the worst for she had been trying to convince herself she was alive' (p. 95). Quite so.

This is as far as it's possible to go with the *néant* of the desiring hysteric, the excruciating double-bind Carter would have, in her subsequent novels, to move off from. It's impossible to rewrite the reality principle; the only thing it's possible to do is to *rewrite* history, fiction, myth. Which, of course, is precisely what she has to go on to do. Before she abandoned realism, however (because *Love* still incorporates realism, of a [feminist] kind), she did allow herself one last feminist-realist act: the final act of Annabel's lovemaking, in which 'a changeling Annabel attacked Lee with gross, morbid passion' (p. 97), the 'mutual rape' which elicits from her behaviour which has 'no place in the order of things': 'She cried out in a lonely voice and bit and tore at him so savagely he wondered if he would survive the night for he had never known a more tempestuous performance from anyone . . .' (p. 97). We're glad she finally made it, aren't we? Even if it killed her?

Annabel dies because this ultimate embodiment of primitive woman has no precedent in the male imagination; she dies, in artistic terms, partly because Carter's project for *Love* was to rewrite Benjamin Constant's *Adolphe* from the point of view of the female (thus, the transgressive act must be the end of all loving). If the Romantic hero's problem is that once woman is loved into subjectivity she is knowable, and therefore unlovable, the heroine's – any heroine's – problem is that she can never be passionate in any sustained process. The act of love, for the emerging female, might involve a devastating series of destructions of all the graven images with which she has masqueraded the female self. But that would be too terrifying. It's that lonely voice that haunts *Love* for me. *That* voice is one I never heard in any fairy story. I don't know how to make sure its timbre may be separated from the timbre of insanity. Nor did Leonora Carrington. Nor did Angela Carter. But there it is, after such struggles, such pain. Which is why the greatest manifestation of her gifts, to my mind, even if not exactly her most polished, or her most cheerful work, is *Love*.

I like to think that this meeting of outlaws in the act of love might have worked in another time, another place. It could not, in the here and now of Carter's fiction, because

– contrary to all appearances – Annabel was more knowledgeable than Buzz; she had tipped herself over the line which separates present from past, and reached into the abyss, and fished up a few *objets trouvés*. In a sense, she knew what she was doing, whereas Buzz – wedded to the past, and to Mother – was still in the *cadavre exquis* of not knowing who or what would make the next move, or even who or what had made the previous one, really.

Because their solution doesn't work, he paradoxically gives her the gift of her own flesh, which is left poised in its desirous state because she's gone, with Buzz, *beyond* fantasy, beyond the imaginary world of substitutes and endless perpetuation. Paradoxically, this is the only moment in the narrative when Annabel finds herself *as Annabel* in the real world: that's why she can transcend the 'order of things' to which her behaviour no longer belongs; that's why, aptly symbolic, she commits suicide beneath a 'fornicator's moon'. No sun. No androgyny. No bride, stripped bare or dressed up. No ambiguity. Suicide is like photography: you want it – the world – to stop *there* (now). And with this bit of lateral thinking, the vertical narrative appears, the central graphics of *Love* which Carter has set before us earlier, at the story's flash-forward beginning: the description of the Gothic park *as* Gothic, the description of sun-and-moon *as* (androgynous-)Surreal; Annabel's vision *as* (specifically) Expressionist. We can see it all now, in retrospect, opening up again before us in sequence, like the work of a projectionist – the wedding, followed by the eating of the ring; the psychiatrist saying '*Folie à deux*', then leaning back against the wall. The ballroom. And the central question which binds together this collage of snippets, the text's different planes, swims back up: we have heard it asked before, but now it makes 'sense'. At the interface of the Surreal relationship between conscious and unconscious,

Expressionism and silence, the jungle and the city, writing and speech, paint and flesh, Carter asks a question so plangent that it almost seems to come from the place we may fear most, as readers – a place just on the borders of this project, which intimates that Annabel has done something to the author, rather than the other way round:

> if one should do right because it is right, why should she have been forced to simulate a life-likeness that did not satisfy her? (p. 112)

In answer, Carter, again like the psychoanalyst, concentrates not on the solution (there isn't one – at least, not one *within reason*) but on the effect:

> now she lay in her ultimate, shocking transformation; now she was a painted doll, bluish at the extremities, nobody's responsibility. (p. 112)

But it's not as if we can't see that there were precedents. We have, at least, moved on that much.

Afterword

What would really have happened next? There would have been no solution for Annabel: sixteen years on, Carter herself was still confident of this: 'Even the women's movement would have been no help to her and alternative psychiatry would only have made things, if possible, worse' (p. 113). Instead, Carter, in her 1987 Afterword to the novel, wittily itemises the possible fates of the minor characters. The bit parts. Annabel, in retrospect, whichever way you look at her, is – one way of putting it – sexuality locked in the

imaginary. *Love* takes the predicament of woman-as-object
as far as it can go; the narration's vertical axis reads: 'Refuse'.
In one sense, the novel is the ultimate in bad taste: a feminist
Adolphe for the sixties, drug-induced surreal; the pursuit and
merciless exposure of that monster, the '"Nothing-But"
Daughter'; woman as totem, women's language as taboo.
The doll figure, liberated from its nineteenth-century connotations of 'goodness', objectified by even a hint of Gothic,
denied sense *and* sensibility, saddled instead with impossi-
bly 'right' action,[48] in a state of sexual paralysis.

In the face of the novelist's own (appropriate) refusal to
define Annabel, the taboo of *Love*, unpacked, unpeeled,
exposed,[49] might read something like this: a distillation of
all the narrative planes – madness, silence, inactivity, the
lack of a dependable accomplice, the search for recognition.
As the axes of the novel tilt, we are pressed up close – too
close – to yet another, and yet another geometry that
excludes Annabel as subject. The collage (once the novel
falls into shreds again, as the novelist plays her next
perspectival trick) might be entitled something like this:
'Beyond Representation'. No, that's too empty, too theoretical. Something borrowed, perhaps: *Men Shall Know Nothing
of This*? *My Mother is a Cow*? The monster reinvented,
perhaps, by the symbolism of the Surreal: lots of birds,
eyes, unicorns, timepieces, rings, all monstrous. The *cadavre
exquis* of everybody speaks, nobody knows. But put them
all together and there's no 'beyond', no consequences, as
Carter's wry, mock-dutiful Afterword should chasten us into
remembering. All she can do is show us the predicament.
She's already given it a name – the difficulty is that the
word, like Annabel, has had to put up with so much: use,
abuse, overuse. So much shadow-show, so much sorrow.
The conditions change; the condition doesn't, really, reciprocal or not, requited or not. It's called love.

The Fate of the Surrealist Imagination in the Society of the Spectacle

SUSAN RUBIN SULEIMAN

> Imagination alone offers me some intimation of what *can be* . . .
>
> (André Breton)

> In Japan I learnt what it is to be a woman and became radicalised.
>
> (Angela Carter)

What does Japan have to do with it? That requires a little story. In 1991, I decided to write an essay on an early novel by Angela Carter, *The Infernal Desire Machines of Doctor Hoffman* (1972), for a panel at the International Comparative Literature conference to be held in Tokyo that summer. The general theme of the conference was 'Imagination' – perfect, I thought, for this novel, which I had long wanted to write about because it was so obviously inspired by Surrealism, a subject in which I have a deep interest. Carter, like a number of other contemporary women writers I think of as feminist postmodernists, had a particular affinity with Surrealism. This was my chance to explore that affinity in some detail.

Here the plot thickens. It turned out that Carter wrote *The Infernal Desire Machines of Doctor Hoffman*, a novel whose title points insistently to European art and literature (from the *Tales* of E. T. A. Hoffman to the 'bachelor machines' of

Duchamp and the Surrealists), in Japan. It was in Tokyo, moreover, around 1970, that she first came upon two books about Surrealism and cinema that had a tremendous effect on her. Ado Kyrou, a 'true believer' in Surrealist theories of liberation through desire and through the exercise of the faculty of the imagination, wrote his books *Surréalisme et cinéma* and *Amour-érotisme et cinéma* during the listless 1950s, the last years of the Fourth Republic, in France.[1] A decade or so later, the Situationists and other revolutionaries of May 1968 reformulated some of the Surrealist theories into slogans on the walls of the Sorbonne and elsewhere: 'Power to the imagination!' 'I take my desires for reality because I believe in the reality of my desires.' By the time Carter discovered Kyrou's books in Tokyo, the 'events of May' had come and gone in Paris, but (in her words) 'extraordinary things were happening in Japan – they had their own version of 1968'. That, at least, is how she experienced it. Japan, in her eyes, was both a link to Europe and a country of absolute otherness – not only because she saw it as Other in relation to what she knew, but because she herself was seen, in the 'completely Japanese environment' in which she lived, as an unassimilable Other, a foreigner, '*Gaijin*'.[2]

The country that Roland Barthes, at just about the same time, was calling 'The Empire of Signs' because of its expansion of the notion of writing to non-verbal modes of communication, became, for Carter too, a place where the decoding of signs passed through vision rather than language: 'Since I kept trying to learn Japanese, and kept on failing to do so, I started trying to understand things by simply looking at them very, very carefully, an involuntary apprenticeship in the interpretation of signs.'[3]

The Infernal Desire Machines of Doctor Hoffman, I am going to suggest, is a novel *of* as well as *about* the Surrealist imagination, seen from the doubly distant perspective of an elsewhere and another time. 'The early 1970s, when Japan was just starting to boom', is how Carter described the time and the place (she wrote the novel in three months, in a Japanese fishing village on an island where she seems to have been the only European). A few years earlier, Guy Debord had diagnosed the 'boom' that Japan would soon adopt as the latest stage of world capitalism, the 'society of the spectacle'. Carter's novel stages, in a wonderfully inventive way, the question I ask more abstractly in the title of this essay: Is there a future for the totally free imagination espoused by Surrealism ('Only the word "liberty" still thrills me,' wrote Breton in the first *Surrealist Manifesto* in 1924) in a society ruled by images?

One last remark, by way of introduction. When I first decided to write an essay about *The Infernal Desire Machines of Doctor Hoffman*, and came up with a title, I had no inkling about the circumstances of the novel's composition. It was Angela Carter who informed me, after I told her on the telephone in London in May 1991 that I would be presenting a paper on *Doctor Hoffman* in Tokyo. 'Interesting coincidence. I wrote that novel in Japan,' she said, and proceeded to tell me about the two years she spent in Tokyo, her discovery of Kyrou's books, and the 'completely Japanese environment' of the island where she wrote *Doctor Hoffman*.[4] The Surrealists would call this coincidence 'objective chance'. I will be content to think of it as an auspicious start.

Postmodern Reflections

Since I have called Carter a feminist postmodernist, I shall follow the classificatory impulse for a moment and consider in what ways *The Infernal Desire Machines of Doctor Hoffman* is a postmodernist work. Brian McHale has proposed that despite the great variety of postmodernist novels, one major preoccupation they all share is with ontology, the nature of being: 'What is a world? What kinds of world are there . . .? What happens when different kinds of worlds are placed in confrontation, or when boundaries between worlds are violated?'[5] If McHale is right that such questions are implicit in all postmodernist fiction, then *Doctor Hoffman* is the very model of the genre, for it explicitly thematises those questions and uses them as major plot elements. Desiderio, the narrator-protagonist, is thrown into several different, incompatible kinds of world; and the story he tells is essentially about a conflict between two Masters, a war of possible worlds. On one side the Minister of Determination, whose totally rational world tolerates no slippages, no 'shadow between the word and the thing described'; on the other, the 'diabolical Dr Hoffman', who tries to do away with the very distinction between shadow and thing. In the Minister's world (which is what would generally be called the 'real' world) every object or person has a clear identity, vouchsafed by an unchanging name and a place in an elaborate logical and social hierarchy. Consistency rules and boundaries are strictly observed, especially the boundary between reality and dream, actuality and imagination. In Doctor Hoffman's world, it is just the opposite; his ruling principle is that 'everything it is possible to imagine can also exist'.[6] Thus peacocks can suddenly invade the audience at a performance of *The Magic Flute* ('It was [his] first disruptive coup,' recounts Desiderio, who was in the audience); rivers can run backwards, clocks can 'tell everybody whatever time they like', a man's hat can become his head, and 'in the vaulted architraves of railway stations, women in states of pearly heroic nudity, their hair elaborately coiffed in the stately chignons of the *fin de siècle*, might be seen parading beneath their parasols as serenely as if they had been in the

Bois de Boulogne . . .' (p. 19). The allusions to Dali's soft watches, Magritte's bowler hats, and Paul Delvaux's dream-like nudes are, of course, not accidental.

The battle between the Minister and the Doctor is, in Desiderio's words, a 'battle between an encyclopedist and a poet' (p. 24). But it might be just as true to say 'between a realist and a Surrealist', for as Desiderio's examples make clear, the Doctor-poet is a Surrealist image-maker. (Besides Dali, Magritte and Delvaux, elsewhere the novel evokes Ernst and Duchamp, among others.) In one sense, all of *Doctor Hoffman* can be read as a reflection on the opening pages of Breton's first *Surrealist Manifesto*, with its celebration of dream and the imagination and its indictment of 'real life' and the 'realist attitude' towards life. Equally relevant is the essay Breton wrote shortly before the Manifesto, the 'Introduction to the Discourse on the Paucity of Reality', which rhetorically asks: 'What prevents me from jamming the order of words, from attacking by that means the merely illusory existence of things?'[7] The notion of an 'alchemy of the word' goes back to Rimbaud, whom the Surrealists greatly admired. Doctor Hoffman's version of this notion is formulated as the 'Third theory of Phenomenal Dynamics: the difference between a symbol and an object is quantitative, not qualitative' (p. 96). If one imagines something – that is, desires something – with sufficient energy, it will exist.

If *Doctor Hoffman* is a postmodernist novel in its preoccupation with possible worlds or ontologies, it is postmodernist in another, somewhat different sense as well, which I can best elucidate by recalling what I wrote a few years ago about the 'postmodern moment':

> that moment of extreme (perhaps tragic, perhaps playful) self-consciousness when the present – our present – takes to

reflecting on its relation to the past and to the future primarily as a problem of repetition. How to create a future that will acknowledge and incorporate the past . . . without repeating it? How to look at the past with understanding, yet critically – in the etymological sense of criticism, which has to do with discrimination and choice *for* and *in* the present?"[8]

From this perspective, postmodernist fiction can be defined *formally* as a hyperselfconscious mode of writing that insistently points to literary and cultural antecedents or (as we say in the trade) intertexts; and *thematically* as a kind of fiction that reflects, implicitly or explicitly, on the historical and social present in its relation to the past and, if possible, the future. A double orientation – towards other texts, and towards the world – can be said to characterise all works of literature; or perhaps it represents two possible modes of reading. Still, I am suggesting that postmodernist fiction is distinguished by its high degree of formal self-consciousness *and* by its thematic preoccupation with present and past history. Linda Hutcheon has proposed the term 'historiographic metafiction' to define 'novels which are both intensely self-reflexive and yet paradoxically also lay claim to historical events and personages.'[9] I would simply emphasise that in order to be 'historical', events and personages don't necessarily have to appear in history books.

As far as my formal criterion is concerned – self-consciousness and intertextuality, the recognition of literary or artistic antecedents – *Doctor Hoffman* is a veritable collage of pre-existing genres and verbal or visual quotations. I have already mentioned a few evocations of Surrealist writing and painting, but there are literally dozens more – including, towards the end, the evocation by Doctor Hoffman himself of the Surrealist notion of 'objective chance' (p. 210).

In addition, the novel abounds in allusions to German Expressionist film, particularly *The Cabinet of Dr Caligari*, on which one whole chapter (Chapter 2, 'The Mansion of Midnight') and an important character (the 'peepshow proprietor', alias the Professor) are modelled. Moving backwards to the German Romantics, the *Tales* of E. T. A. Hoffman are not only alluded to in the novel's title, but provide one structural model for the overall story. This model, which one finds realised in many of the best-known tales of Hoffman, can be summed up as follows: a powerful father with magical powers keeps his beautiful but potentially deadly daughter (who is not necessarily human – she can be a doll, all the more alluring and deadly) tantalisingly out of the reach of a desiring young man, a situation that eventually leads to the death of the daughter (as in the tale titled 'Councillor Krespel'), or of the young man (as in 'The Sandman'). Carter's novel conforms to the first pattern, but adds a new twist: it is the young man himself who kills the daughter, as well as the father. (By a curious coincidence, Carter told me, Hoffman is also the name of the inventor of LSD, which led quite a few early reviewers to speak of the novel as a 'drug book'. Being a 'bookish person', she said, she was aware only of E. T. A., not of the LSD Hoffman, when she invented her visionary character.)

Besides the clearly designated intertexts in *Doctor Hoffman*, one finds, pell-mell, echoes of Proust ('I remember everything' is the opening sentence, and the beloved 'lost object' is named Albertina); de Sade (quoted directly, as well as parodied in the character of the Count, who 'rides the whirlwind of [his] desires' until he lands in a cannibal soup); *Gulliver's Travels* (one of the societies Desiderio discovers is a society of centaurs – who, being all too human, 'were not Houyhnhnms', he tells us), and any number of unspecified Gothic romances, tales of piratry, travel narratives, sci-fi thrillers, porn novels and picaresque adventures.

Such are the virtuoso, playful aspects of postmodernist collage. One could spend a long and pleasant time tracking down all the allusions and quotations, direct and indirect, and untangling the various generic threads. But it is equally pleasant simply to admire the web, even bask in it, without trying to untangle it. One extremely self-conscious textual moment I relish occurs in the beginning of Chapter 6. Desiderio, having temporarily thrown in his lot with that of the Count, has just spent a night with him in a brothel that evokes (with no small degree of parody) any number of pornographic novels, from de Sade's *Justine* to *The Story of O*. As they are about to embark on a new adventure (Chapter 6 bears the title 'The Coast of Africa'), Desiderio remarks:

> I had not the least idea what time or place the Count might take me to though, since his modes of travel were horseback, gig and tall-masted schooner, I guessed, wherever it was, it would be somewhere in the early nineteenth century.
> (p. 143)

Here the narrative, playing its mirror game (the technical term is *mise en abyme*), does not only 'duplicate' its own procedures, taking the reader in a single sentence from an unspecified future time (Desiderio's present) into the early nineteenth century and from a porn novel into a tale of adventure on the high seas; it also 'duplicates' the response of a reader who consents to being led along without much analysis ('I had not the least idea what time or place the Count might take me to') by the meanderings of the story and the author's luxuriant imagination.

Clearly, Carter takes extreme delight, as well as a kind of

swaggering pride, in her ability to play with and on a long, varied literary and artistic tradition. But where, one might ask, does this novel reflect on the historical and social present, and their relation to past and future? That reflection, I suggest, is to be found in the thematisation of Surrealist ideas about desire and the imagination on the one hand; and, on the other, in the descriptions of 'what it is to be a woman' in various societies. As we shall see, the two hands are not unrelated.

Laws of Desire

'My name is Desiderio,' says the narrator, by way of introduction. His name means 'desire' in Italian, although he lives in what appears to be a Latin American country where the official language is Portuguese and the indigenous Indian peoples speak their own Amerindian dialect. Desiderio-Desire is the child of a European prostitute and an unknown Indian father, a young man of mixed blood and mixed loyalties. He works for the Minister of Determination, but falls in love with the 'magician's daughter', Albertina Hoffman. He admires the Minister, a man as 'clear, hard, unified and harmonious as a string quartet', but defines himself as 'a man like an unmade bed' (p. 13). He refused to surrender to the 'flux of mirages' proposed by Doctor Hoffman, yet embarks with nary a backward glance on a journey that will turn out to be nothing if not full of mirages and miraculous visions. Although he lacks all the traditional heroic qualities (certainty, determination, ambition, aggression), he ends up a hero by ridding the city of its arch-enemy – and in the process also kills, to his eternal regret, the object of his desire, the woman he loves, his emotional double.

In short, Desiderio is ambivalence itself, a perfect emblem of the Romantic – but also, no doubt, the postmodern – subject. What further characterises him is a kind of paradoxically active passivity – for although he does nothing to initiate action, he is thrown into it; and once in it, he keeps going, as if his very passivity made it possible for adventure to seek him out. He has no fixed opinions, yet in the end he is forced to make an impossible choice: 'I might not want the Minister's world but I did not want the Doctor's world either. . . . I, of all men, had been given the casting vote between a barren yet harmonious calm and a fertile yet cacophonous tempest' (p. 207). He chooses the calm by killing Doctor Hoffman; yet his choice is hopelessly compromised by his regret at killing the Doctor's daughter as well. In a sense he had to kill her, for 'Oh, she was her father's daughter, no doubt about that!' (p. 13). But that does not prevent him from desiring her all the remaining days of his long life, or from dreaming about her every night. In the end, Doctor Hoffman, although defeated, has in a sense won: he has imposed the power and reality of dreams, if not on the whole city, at least on the 'hero' who killed him.

It is difficult to resist an allegorical reading of this novel. Auberon Waugh, one of its first reviewers, praised its success in combining 'allegory and Surrealism', something very few works had achieved (Waugh mentioned *Gulliver's Travels* and *Alice's Adventures in Wonderland*; I would add Leonora Carrington's *The Hearing Trumpet*, among recent works in English). Waugh then proceeded to define the Minister as personifying 'the forces of logic, reason, law and order, but also the excesses to which these properties are liable', while Doctor Hoffman 'represents poetry, and the liberation of the spirit but also anarchy and the "creative nihilism" of the rebel without a cause'.[10] In a more specifically historical mode, David Punter suggests that 'we can read the text [leading to Desiderio's rejection of Doctor Hoffman] as a series of figures for the defeat of the political aspirations of the 1960s, and in particular of the father-figures of liberation, Reich and Marcuse'.[11] Punter does not say so outright, but he seems to find Desiderio's choice itself a kind of failure: 'it is [Desiderio's] fate to will away pleasure for fear of the damage it might do to him and to others' (p. 214).

What Punter fails to mention is that the kind of pleasure offered to Desiderio by Doctor Hoffman is extremely drab: the Doctor, scientifically literalising the Surrealist dictum that desire makes the world go round, succeeds in channelling sexual energy to fuel the huge machines that bombard the city with mirages. To this end, he employs lovers who voluntarily spend all their time copulating in 'love pens', the energy they release being immediately collected and transformed into fuel. (As I have said, *Doctor Hoffman* is a novel 'of' as well as 'about' the Surrealist imagination!) Desiderio, desire itself, would be the prize energy producer if he consented to enter the love pen that awaits him and Albertina. Instead, appalled at the contradiction within a 'liberation philosophy' that depends on slavery (even if the slaves are willing love slaves), he turns and runs, killing both father and daughter.

Ricarda Smith, reading this ending, criticises Punter for what she considers his celebratory view of Marcuse (for she too sees Doctor Hoffman as an allegory of the 1960s philosopher). According to Smith, Carter is quite critical of Marcuse – indeed: 'contradicts Marcuse's optimistic view that . . . highly advanced productivity makes a "non-repressive civilization" possible'.[12] As for me, I find both Punter's and Smith's readings plausible. I am surprised, however, that neither mentions Surrealism, even though the character of Doctor Hoffman is, both textually and representationally, much more of a Surrealist than a Marcuse. Marcuse himself, in a crucial passage in *Eros and Civilization* where he argues for the social and liberating value of fantasy, can think of no better support for his argument than to quote a passage from the first *Surrealist Manifesto*, in French, ending with the sentence I have chosen as an epigraph: 'La seule imagination me rend compte de ce qui *peut être*.'[13]

To say that Carter 'contradicts Marcuse's optimism' – more exactly, the optimism Marcuse shared with the Surrealists about the liberating potential of fantasy and desire – is, I think, to miss an important point. For if it is indeed true that Doctor Hoffman is no hero, and that his method of liberation mocks its own proclaimed aims, it is not at all certain that he is an allegory of either Marcuse's philosophy or the Surrealists'. I would suggest that if he is an allegory of anything, it is of the technological appropriation (but I prefer the Gallicism *récupération*) of Surrealism and liberation philosophy – precisely that *récupération* which Marcuse himself, not at all optimistically, analysed as early as the 1961 preface to the second edition of *Eros and Civilization* (first published in 1955). Marcuse called this mode of *récupération* 'repressive desublimation' and saw in it, with something close to despair, the latest ruse of capitalism. He himself had hoped for something quite different: 'non-repressive sublimation', or the diffusion of the erotic impulse to all aspects of life, with an attendant decrease in aggression and release of the creative faculties. In his terms (but also in Surrealist terms), this would be the triumph of the Pleasure Principle over the Reality Principle: work itself would become a form of play. Instead, repressive desublimation turned this project on its head, and made even play – or love – into a form of work.

The 'methodical introduction of sexiness into business, politics, propaganda, etc.' is one example Marcuse cites of the way instrumental rationality encroaches on the realm of the erotic. Another example is the organisation of 'fun and leisure', which he identifies as simply the other face of repression, the social control of docile bodies. Marcuse's conclusion, in the 1961 preface to his book, is stark: 'The events of the last years refute all optimism. The immense capabilities of the advanced industrial society are increasingly mobilized against the utilization of its own resources for the pacification of human existence.' As he saw it, the very technologies that were to have made non-repressive sublimation possible by releasing human beings from alienated labour were being used to enslave them further:

> The modes of domination have changed: they have become increasingly technological, productive, and even beneficial; consequently, in the most advanced areas of industrial society, the people have been co-ordinated and reconciled with the system of domination to an unprecedented degree. (p. vii)

Reading Marcuse's preface today, one is struck by the way his analysis of the double-edged possibilities of technology dovetail with the even more pessimistic analyses of Guy Debord's *La Société du spectacle*, published six years later. For Debord, there is no question that the society of the spectacle is the product of a technology gone bad. One thing such technology makes possible is the reign of images, which Debord defines in a broad sense as the increasingly abstract relation of people to each other and to their environment. The opening lines of *La Société du spectacle* could have been written by Marcuse: 'All the life of societies in which modern conditions of production dominate presents itself as an immense accumulation of *spectacles*. Everything that was directly lived has distanced itself in a representation.'[14]

Like Marcuse, Debord and the Situationists were caustic in their critique of organised 'fun and leisure', especially as it was archetypally embodied in Club Med, founded in the mid 1960s.

If we now think of Doctor Hoffman's machines for projecting representations on the world, fuelled by the 'acrobats of desire' in their 'perpetual motion' of disciplined copulation, we may see in Carter's mad scientist the nightmarish synthesis of repressive desublimation and the society of the spectacle. The fact that this character was conceived in the country that would become the world's leading manufacturer of advanced electronic equipment takes on a particularly prescient, ironic cast.

Given the current interest in technology in both feminist and postmodernist circles, it is worth noting that Carter's position is not 'anti-technology'. Indeed, despite their pessimism, Debord's and Marcuse's critiques are not directed against technology either but, rather, against the uses to which it has been put. Contemporary celebrations of technology by postmodernist theorists – such as Donna Haraway's famous paean to the cyborg or, earlier, Jean-François Lyotard's hopeful pages about computer information networks – have generally not been much concerned with the ways technology, even a potentially revolutionary one, can *fail* to change the status quo.[15] Carter's novel, perhaps because it was written not long after the dissipation of the revolutionary euphoria produced in 1968, is closer in mood to the pessimism of Marcuse and Debord. But Carter's pessimism – or what one can take to be such – is not due to a disenchantment with technology; it is due, rather, to her sense (which I share, on the whole) that questions about technology cannot be divorced from questions about ideology and values.

And Surrealism, in all this? The first epigraph of the novel is a line of anagrammatic punning by the Surrealist poet Robert Desnos: 'Les lois de nos désirs sont les dés sans loisir' – literally: 'The laws of our desires are dice without leisure'. The laws of desire, of Desiderio, require ceaseless movement, the perpetual motion of 'dice without leisure'. But the movement of dice (note that *dés* can also be read as a short name for Desiderio) is, by definition, the opposite of the predictable and the mechanical. It is in order to maintain this movement – and hence the laws of desire, his laws – that Desiderio kills the would-be Master of desires – who, in true Master fashion, always remains unmoved – and his daughter.

It may be interesting to speculate on the relation of Surrealist ideas about desire to the 'desiring machines' dreamed up by Deleuze and Guattari in their *Anti-Oedipus*, published the same year as Carter's novel. At first glance, the *machines désirantes* may appear close to Doctor Hoffman's desire machines (such is the power of the signifier); but in fact they are far from them and close to Surrealism. For Deleuze and Guattari, as for the Surrealists, desire is 'in its essence revolutionary' and implies ceaseless movement – that is why their ideal subject is the bachelor, 'nomad and vagabond' (a kind of Desiderio, perhaps). The 'fixed subject' is the repressed subject. In their terms as well, Doctor Hoffman's love pens would have to be considered the very opposite of liberation, or revolution.[16]

What, then, is the fate of the Surrealist imagination in the society of the spectacle? Not good. At best, 'la révolution surréaliste' becomes a private passion, not a means to change the world. Desiderio, the public smiling man with a hero's statue in the town square, dreams every night of his lost Albertina, and writes his delirious memoirs in dedication to her. Meanwhile, life goes on as usual, dominated by the Minister's computers and clocks that all run on time.

'What It Is To Be a Woman'

If the 'Surrealist imagination' founders on the shoals of the society of the spectacle, then one of the reasons for this foundering is related not to technology or postmodern capitalism, but to sexual politics. Technology and capitalism change with the times – modern/postmodern, industrial/post-industrial, mechanical/digital. Sexual politics, by contrast, is timeless, transcultural, international – or so Carter implies, in my reading of her novel. Here is one place where the gap between technology and ideology becomes apparent: even the most revolutionary technological advances do not necessarily change the relations between men and women. Desiderio, in his various travels, observes a number of societies: the society of the Amerindian River People, that of the African tribe, and that of the Centaurs. In all these, especially in the last two, women are in a horrifyingly subordinate position. In the African tribe, women are raised to be soulless soldiers by having all feeling, including maternal feeling, literally excised out of them. Among the Centaurs, women do all the work while the men pray – and women are 'tattooed all over, even in their faces, in order to cause them more suffering, for [the Centaurs] believed women were born only to suffer' (p. 172).

This sexual politics of inequality does not characterise only the primitive or fantastic societies, it also characterises every other world that Desiderio visits or inhabits. The city he lived in, before the onslaught of Doctor Hoffman's images, was 'thickly, obtusely masculine' (p. 15), as is the Minister of Determination. But so, in its own way, is the insubstantial dream-world of Doctor Hoffman. The peep-show displays that Desiderio describes at several points are like Surrealist paintings, to be sure; but they are also unmistakably male voyeuristic fantasies (as Surrealist paintings often are), representing female orifices and body parts, and scenes of extreme sexual violence perpetrated on the bodies of women. One of them, bearing the suggestive title 'Everyone knows what the night is for', shows a three-dimensional model of a mutilated woman with a knife in her belly (p. 45). Its description evoked for me, by an immediate assocation, Duchamp's famous installation at the Philadelphia Museum of Art, *Etant donné* ('Given that'), which shows a similarly mutilated female figure; installed in its own dark room, *Etant donné* requires that the viewer glue an eye to a peephole in order to see the scene. Carter's peepshow as a whole may be an allusion to this work, which literally makes every viewer into a voyeur. Continuing the voyeur theme, the 'Erotic Traveller' chapter (Chapter 5) has Desiderio and the Count visit a Sadeian brothel, the 'House of Anonymity', which features live prostitutes staged in the most degraded and violated poses. In a sense, the violation spills over to the two men, who are dressed for the occasion in special costumes which mask their faces while leaving their genitals fully exposed: 'the garb grossly emphasized our manhoods while utterly denying our humanity' (p. 130).

Desiderio's own position in the novel is ambiguous. As a man, he generally enjoys the male privileges. (This is most emphasised in the episode with the Centaurs: Albertina is raped by every male in the group, and when she heals she is sent into the fields to work with the women; Desiderio, as befits a man, is allowed to study and roam, learning the Centaurs' customs and mythology.) At the same time, he clearly has an unusually sharp view of and sympathy for women's roles, and on at least one occasion he is made to find out 'what it is to be a woman' in a more violent way, when he is gang-raped by nine Moroccan acrobats in the travelling circus he accompanies disguised as the peepshow proprietor's nephew. This experience, he later tells us, allows him to understand what Albertina goes through when she is raped by the Centaurs, and to 'suffer with her' in the process. Finally, Desiderio is physically a mirror-image of Albertina, who herself takes the shape of a young man on several occasions. They are 'exactly the same height' (p. 136), and by the end of their adventures they look like twins: seeing himself in a mirror in Doctor Hoffman's castle, Desiderio remarks: 'Time and travel had changed me almost beyond my own recognition. Now I was entirely Albertina in the male aspect. That is why I know I was beautiful when I was a young man. Because I know I looked like Albertina' (p. 199).

Here, in the sexual ambiguities of the lovers, may lie the most politically radical aspect of *The Infernal Desire Machines of Doctor Hoffman*. But Carter did not develop those radical possibilities in this novel, as she was to do in her next, *The Passion of New Eve* (which, perhaps not by chance, accorded more attention to the figure of the mother than to that of the father) and in yet another way in the novel after that, *Nights at the Circus*.[17] The new twist brought by *Nights at the Circus* (in the meantime, Carter remarried and became a mother herself) is that the radical possibilities of fluid gender roles are given a happy ending. Similarly, the mood of her last published novel, *Wise Children*, is magnificently comic, with a self-consciously Shakespearian cast. In *Doctor Hoffman*, however, the ending is quite dark, if ironic: the social status quo is maintained and, despite the son's heroisation, the Father wins. It doesn't matter which Father, the Minister or Doctor Hoffman, for they both want to lay down the law – and even if it is not the same law, women's place remains identical in both. Albertina, like countless other daughters in literature (and life), loves her daddy above all other men, even to the point of self-sacrifice. Desiderio, like countless other males in Western literature and life, 'kills the thing he loves', and spends the rest of his days dreaming about her.

From all of which one may conclude that if the world is really to change, it will have to start by imagining 'what it is to be a woman' – and a man – differently. Differently from the Minister, differently from Doctor Hoffman, differently even from the Surrealists, whose imaginative faculties faltered on the threshold of sexual roles.

That, at least, was the necessary conclusion in 1972, when *The Infernal Desire Machines of Doctor Hoffman* was published and the women's movement in the United States and England was gathering steam. And in the mid '90s? I wish I could say that the problem has become historical – in other words, *passé* – in the United States, if not elsewhere. But time passes slowly in these parts. Although 'what it is to be a woman' is not the same now as it was then (some women today even get to teach Angela Carter and other feminist postmodernists at major universities, and obtain tenure), there is (as my mother used to say) plenty of room for improvement.[18]

Running with the Tigers

MARGARET ATWOOD

> The strong abuse, exploit and meatify the weak, says Sade. They must and will devour their natural prey. The primal condition of man cannot be modified in any way; it is eat or be eaten.
>
> (Angela Carter, *The Sadeian Woman* [p. 140])

> The tiger will never lie down with the lamb; he acknowledges no pact that is not reciprocal. The lamb must learn to run with the tigers.
>
> (Angela Carter, 'The Tiger's Bride', in *The Bloody Chamber* [p. 64])

What is a 'good' woman? What is a 'bad' one? Is goodness for women the same as goodness for men? Are women really 'like men', or are they fundamentally different, and if so, in what ways? And what are men 'like', anyway? These are questions that have been bedevilling the minds of men for at least two thousand years (and it is men, rather than women, who seem to have given this matter the most fretful attention). They also occupied Angela Carter a good deal, although the conclusions she reached – or rather, the patterns she played with and balanced against one another – were somewhat different from the more traditional predator–prey arrangements.

Although her interest in role-breaking and role-remaking

is evident from her first published work, her explorations of gender crossovers in relation to passivity and aggression were particularly intense in two books both published in 1979: her analysis of the writings of the Marquis de Sade, *The Sadeian Woman*, and her collection of revised fairy tales, *The Bloody Chamber*. It's fair to suppose that these two books represent two different approaches to the problem of the 'nature' of women and thus of men, one theoretical, one fictional; though in her work such divisions are less useful than in the work of others, since she blends myth-making into her theory and theorising into her myth.

The Sadeian Woman, her first work of non-fiction, appeared earlier in the year, but it's reasonable to assume that the writing, and certainly the thinking, overlapped. In both books, the distinctions drawn are not so much between male and female as between 'tigers' and 'lambs', carnivores and herbivores, those who are preyed upon and those who do the preying. In a world in which one has only these two choices, it is of course preferable to be a tiger, and it is to this that the Mad Marquis addressed himself.

Carter attacks the subject of de Sade in much the same way that de Sade himself may have attacked the chambermaids: with suavity, wit, no-holds-barred intelligence, panache, bravado, stiletto-like epigrams, and sudden disconcerting pounces. One of the things that really interests her is the reductionist nature of pornography as a form – the way it tends to leave out everything but the machinery – and where better to find this illustrated than in de Sade? Carter unwinds the Sadeian rhetorical ball of wool, undoing de Sade's knots and logical paradoxes, and what she finds at the centre of it is a sort of Siamese twin, both halves entirely constructed by men: the traditional-role female victim, Justine, and de Sade's 'new woman', Juliette, who is instead a victimiser.

For de Sade, women can escape sacrificial lambhood (the 'natural' condition of women, as exemplified by Justine and defined by men) only by adopting tigerhood (the role of the predatory aggressor, the 'natural' role of men, as exemplified by Juliette and also defined by men). In order to escape victimisation, women have to divest themselves of the trappings of conventional womanhood; they have to denature themselves, much as Lady Macbeth did, but minus the remorseful hand-scrubbings. Mercy, pity, peace and love, and especially chastity and motherhood, go out the window; in come ruthlessness, lasciviousness, the separation of sexual pleasure from procreation, and delight in the pain of others. Justine and Juliette, says Carter, 'do not cancel one another out; rather, they mutually reflect and complement one another, like a pair of mirrors' (p. 78). Carter quotes Apollinaire, who considered Justine to be '"woman as she has been until now, enslaved, miserable and less than human; her opposite, Juliette, represents the woman whose advent [de Sade] anticipated, a figure of whom minds have as yet no conception, who is rising out of mankind, who will have wings and who will renew the world"' (p. 79). Carter does not, however, buy this apocalyptic vision of a Winged-Victory Juliette as Redeemer (presumably associated, like Christ, with whips and bleeding hearts, though in reverse: she holds the whip rather than being subject to it, and the bleeding hearts are those of others). She comments:

> Seventy years ago, Apollinaire could equate Juliette with the New Woman; it is not so easy to do so today, although Juliette remains a model for women, in some ways. She is rationality personified and leaves no single cell of her brain unused. She will never obey the fallacious promptings of her heart. Her mind functions like a computer programmed

to produce two results for herself – financial profit and libidinal gratification. By the use of her reason, an intellectual apparatus women themselves are still inclined to undervalue, she rids herself of the more crippling aspects of femininity; but she is a New Woman in the mode of irony. (p. 79)

Some have interpreted Carter's analysis of Juliette as a seal of approval, but she by no means endorses the Juliette recipe. She sees Juliette's story as partly social satire, which it surely is – in a France ruled by tyranny and the exploitation of the poor by the rich, only the exploiters can prosper. Juliette, like Justine, she says, is 'a description of a type of female behaviour rather than a model of female behaviour . . . Justine is the thesis, Juliette is the antithesis; both are without hope and neither pays any heed to a future in which might lie a synthesis of their modes of behaviour, neither submissive nor aggressive, capable of both thought and feeling' (p. 79).

The Bloody Chamber may be read as a 'writing against' de Sade, a talking-back to him; and, above all, as an exploration of the possibilities for the kind of synthesis de Sade himself could never find because he wasn't even looking for it. Predator and prey, master and slave, are the only two categories – or roles, because in his world one person may play both, although alternately – that he can acknowledge; above all, for him sex between unequals cannot be mutually pleasurable, because pleasure belongs to the eater, not to the eaten. What Carter seems to be doing in *The Bloody Chamber* – among other things – is looking for ways in which the tiger and the lamb, or the tiger and lamb parts of the psyche, can reach some sort of accommodation.

The Bloody Chamber can be understood much better as an exploration of the narrative possibilities of de Sade's lamb-

and-tiger dichotomy than as a 'standard' work of early-seventies to-the-barricades feminism. There have, historically, been two main strands of feminist theory – that which maintained that women were fundamentally no different from men, and should therefore be allowed to do the same jobs and have the same rights as men; and that which postulated women as essentially other, but better: group-minded, sensitive and caring consensus-builders rather than aggressive, egotistical despoilers; birth-giving rather than death-dealing; gardeners rather than warriors; sufferers rather than inflicters of suffering; lambs rather than tigers. This latter strand of thinking has claimed special privileges for women on the grounds of their moral superiority, but it has been played several ways: women are more deserving than men, but because of the lamb-like nature of their superiority they also need more protection. This can be used to keep women isolated on their Victorian pedestals just as easily as it can be used to grant them special status and head-of-the-queue position in, say, job equity battles. (Women, being lambs, can't *seize* the head of the queue; they have to have it conferred upon them.)

It is Carter's contention that a certain amount of tigerish-ness may be necessary if women are to achieve an independent as opposed to a dependent existence; if they are to avoid – at the extreme end of passivity – becoming meat. They need, in their own self-interest, to assimilate at least some of Juliette's will-to-power. But their change from lamb to tiger need not be a divesting of all 'feminine' qualities, as it is for de Sade; also, although society may slant things so that women appear to be better candidates for meathood than men and men better candidates for meat-eating, the nature of men is not fixed by Carter as inevitably predatory, with females as their 'natural' prey. Lambhood and tigerish-ness may be found in either gender, and in the same individual at different times. In this respect, Carter's arrangements are much more subject to mutability than are de Sade's. He postulates the permanence and 'decreed' nature of virtue and vice: Juliette is born evil, Justine good, and so they remain. Carter, however, celebrates relativity and metamorphosis and 'the complexity of human relations'. 'The notion of a universality of human experience', she says, 'is a confidence trick and the notion of a universality of female experience is a clever confidence trick' (SW, p. 12). She sees all myths, including those of pornography and also recent feminist mother-goddess myths, as 'consolatory nonsenses' (SW, p. 5). But in *The Bloody Chamber* she proceeds to provide us with consolations of another kind, and she does so through the folk tale form, which is about as close to myth as you can get. In other words, to combat traditional myths about the nature of woman, she constructs other, more subversive ones.

The Bloody Chamber is arranged according to categories of meat-eater: three cat family stories at the beginning, followed by 'Puss-in-Boots' as a kind of comic coda; three wolf family stories at the end; and three ambiguous supernatural creatures – erl-king, snow-child, female vampire – in the middle.

The title story gives us two carnivores and two herbivores, one each of male and female. As a reworking of the Bluebeard story, it supplies a male protagonist who is about as close to de Sade's cannibal Minski as anything in Carter, complete with a Sadeian torture chamber and some appropriately gruesome dead wives. As befits a carnivore, the Marquis, with his tell-tale title, has a 'leonine' head, a mask-like face, and a soft, cat-like tread (p. 8). His cathood is like that of Borghese in *Juliette*, who is 'a glutton for pleasure, like a huge, cruel cat and cruel as a cat is sleepily cruel, by nature' (*SW*, p. 95). This monster's bride is thin, pale and virginal, exactly the kind of protected maiden de Sade delights in having his evil folk ravish, humiliate and kill. She is a 'good girl', like Justine, and like Justine she is the object of perverse male desires. About Justine, Carter comments:

> To be the object of desire is to be defined in the passive case.
>   To exist in the passive case is to die in the passive case – that is, to be killed. This is the moral of the fairy tale about the perfect woman. (*SW*, p. 77)

The man this passive and therefore doomed virginal girl comes to love – as opposed to fear and desire – is equally lamb-like, a sweet, blind piano tuner. These innocents would have been easy prey for the monstrous and sadistic voluptuary, were it not for the pallid heroine's adventurous, tough-minded mother, who has a background of man-eating tiger shooting in Indo-China, and who rides to the rescue – replacing the rescuing brothers of the Perrault version of 'Bluebeard' – and neatly shoots the surprised 'beast' with her dead husband's service revolver just as he is about to chop off the head of the helpless bride. The mother is not only a tiger-shooter: she herself partakes of tigerhood: 'You never saw such a wild thing as my mother, her hat seized by the winds and blown out to sea so that her hair was her white mane . . .' (*BC*, p. 39). It takes fire to fight fire, and tigers to fight tigers; and the tigers need not necessarily be male. That the passive heroine is not in fact killed off by her author is due in part to her loss of 'pure' perfection. She does not remain chaste, like Justine; her sexual initiation at the hands of the cat-man has left her not only with a blood-red ruby necklace round her neck, but with a blood-red brand on her forehead; a mark – to those who remember that other rewriter of folk tales, Hawthorne – of the imperfect and human stain of sexual passion.

For de Sade, energy of all kinds, including sexual energy, is desirable, since it gives one the power to be the tiger rather than the tiger-food; but it is 'real' – that is, male or master or tiger energy – only if it is used for destructive ends. Tigers do not create. For Carter, as for Blake, energy can be positive and creative, as well as negative and destructive. The answer to 'Did He who made the lamb make thee?' is obviously, for Carter, *yes*.

In her second cat family fable, Mr Lyon, who begins as a beast – in fact, *the* Beast of *Beauty and the Beast* – is changed by love from carnivore to herbivore. From a flesh-devouring savage animal who roars and runs on all fours, he devolves into plain Mr Lyon, walking quietly and on two feet, with his wife – no longer Beauty but Mrs Lyon – in his rather bourgeois garden. The love that changes – and in some ways diminishes – him is not only Beauty's love for him, a love which causes her to renounce the glittering, superficial social pleasures of the city to embrace a by now somewhat tatty dying animal; it is also his love for Beauty. Through it he loses his mythical dimensions – only sexual desire in isolation has a larger-than-life quality – but he gains his humanity.

The transformation is the other way round in the next story, 'The Tiger's Bride'. This too is a Beauty-and-the-Beast story, with the same virginal heroine, the same carnivorous hero, this time a cardsharp who covers his tiger's head with a mask and a wig, and wins Beauty from her father – who is quite ready to trade his daughter's virtue for his own gain – in a card game. All the Beast seems to want is to see her 'naked', which she at first refuses. Eventually, though, there are two disrobing scenes. The first is what the Beast and the father both had in mind when they made their deal: Beauty takes off her clothes as fulfilment of her father's contract, and the Beast is allowed to view her naked girl's body as an object. Deal concluded, she is free to leave the Beast's house; but she rebels at thus being a mere item of barter, and strips herself of all clothing – that of her former daughter-role, that of her present sex-object – down to her 'real' nakedness, that of herself as subject rather than object, watched only by her 'maid', a smiling mechanical similacrum of herself – the obedient shell her father has required her to be – who stands 'watching me peel down to the cold, white meat of contract, and, if she did not see me, then so much more like the market place, where the eyes that watch you take no account of your existence' (*BC*, p. 66). She intends not to sell, but to give herself; and not to give the 'cold, white meat' of the body detached from the self, but to give her 'existence'. When she reaches the Beast's den, she finds the trappings of his 'appearance' in disarray: mask and cloak and dressing-gown have been abandoned, and the Beast paces in his full tiger-shape in 'imprisonment between the gnawed and bloody bones'. The Beast is a prisoner, like de Sade's libertine as described by Carter: 'The passions he thought would free him from the cage of being become the very bars of the cage that traps him' (*SW*, p. 149). Herbivore meets carnivore, meat meets teeth, at the most basic and primitive level:

> He will gobble you up.
>   Nursery fears made flesh and sinew; earliest and most archaic of fears, fear of devourment. The beast and his carnivorous bed of bone and I, white, shaking, raw,

approaching him as if offering, in myself, the key to a
peaceable kingdom in which his appetite need not be my
extinction.

He went still as stone. He was far more frightened of me
than I was of him. (*BC*, p. 67)

This last sentence is surprising only to those who have not
read Carter's last word on de Sade's tragic libertine:

In his diabolic solitude, only the possibility of love could
awake the libertine to perfect, immaculate terror. It is in this
holy terror of love that we find, in both men and women
themselves, the source of all opposition to the emancipation
of women. (*SW*, p. 150)

Why? Presumably because love can occur only freely and
between equals, so those afraid of it will wish to preserve
the conditions of user and used. Equality in 'The Tiger's
Bride' is not achieved by the conversion of the tiger to Mr
Tyger. Instead, the woman is divested of her 'cold white
meat of contract', her status as object, and discovers herself
as animal, as beast-as-appetite, as energy rather than the
object of energy. The tiger licks off her skin, and underneath
it she is – behold! – a tiger herself.

'Puss-in-Boots', which follows, is a Rabelesian/Carter-
esque romp, a tribute to the playful kitten aspect of the cat
family. It is above all a hymn to here-and-now common
sensual pleasure, to ordinary human love, to slap-and-tickle
delight – not as an object to be won, achieved or stolen, nor
to be reserved by the rich and privileged for themselves, as
in de Sade, but available to all, tabby cats as well as young
lads and lasses. In spirit it anticipates *Wise Children*, with its
rollicking cockney narrative voice; it's *The Marriage of Figaro*
rather than *Don Giovanni*: it's no accident that the clever

valet Puss is himself named Figaro. It is, in a word, Carter
thumbing her nose at de Sade and telling him to lighten up.
Sex in 'Puss-in-Boots' is sensual, it's *fun*, which it never is
in de Sade, that 'great puritan' who will 'disinfect of
sensuality anything he can lay his hands on', who 'writes
about sexual relations in terms of butchery and meat' (*SW*,
p. 138), whose descriptions of orgasm are 'those of torture'
(*SW*, p. 149). Enough of the 'tragic style' of de Sade's
'eroticism', with its 'displays, its corteges, its sacrifices, its
masks and costumes' (*SW*, p. 149), its demon disguises, its
blood and murder, all the histrionic trappings of what de
Sade calls the 'hell-game' (*SW*, p. 148). Why take sex so
seriously, all the time?

But this story is – in the generally more Baroque context
of *The Bloody Chamber* – just a short entr'acte. It is followed
by three stories which are themselves in the tragic or
'butchery' style, more or less. First comes 'The Erl-King', in
which the erotic male woodland spirit – who also comes
equipped with a mane, who also is a heart-eater, a blood-
drinker – does a peel-off of his female human lover which
is reminiscent of 'The Tiger's Bride', but does not have such
happy results. Although he 'strips [her] to [her] last nakedness . . . then dresses [her] again in an embrace so lucid
and encompassing it might be made of water', he then
intends to imprison her – this 'perfect child of the meadows
of summer' (*BC*, p. 88) – in a pretty cage, like a Blakcian
lovebird. Instead he is killed by her. The return to a state of
nature isn't always good news for the human being: if she
becomes entirely a part of nature, her human self-consciousness will vanish and she will be bound to nature's cycle.
This girl does not want to be defined absolutely and for
ever by the Erl-King's seductive but obliterating sexuality.
In this match of inequalities it's her freedom against his,
and she chooses hers, afterwards opening 'all the cages' to

'let the birds free; they . . . change back into young girls, every one, each with the crimson imprint of his love-bite on their throats' (*BC*, p. 91).

'The Snow-Child' is a brief fable in which the Count's desire for a 'perfect' virginal girl-child as sexual object materialises as a snow-child (*pace* Hawthorne), much to the distaste of the Countess. The Count dresses the snow-child in the Countess's finery, and things are looking bad for the now-naked Countess (nakedness here is poverty, not essence), until she desires a rose. The snow-child picks the rose, but it pricks her and she bleeds; the blood kills her, since she is only an idea, an idea of virginal perfection, which cannot survive actual passion. The Count has sex with the dead body anyway (take that, *Playboy* magazine!) and is 'soon finished'. The snow-child melts, and the Countess has all her clothes again. But it is the rose that has become carnivorous: when the Countess touches it, 'it bites' (*BC*, p. 92).

Next comes 'The Lady of the House of Love', which reverses the gender polarities of the Lyon and Tiger stories. The carnivore here is a female vampire, a 'somnambulist', a sinister 'Sleeping Beauty', 'both death and the maiden', who drinks the blood of young men, hapless fools who wander in, miss the Gothic decor and baleful cobwebby and fungoid clues, and think they've stumbled across a no-consequences night of love. Like the Erl-King, she keeps a caged bird which does not sing; like Mr Lyon, she too longs for real human love, but she is subject to her own blood-sucking bird-of-prey nature. Like one of de Sade's creatures, she is 'a closed circuit' (*BC*, p. 93); and like a Sadeian villainess from *Juliette*, her knell is rung the first time she shows mercy. Like the Lady of Shalott, she is undone by a handsome – although rather thick – wandering 'hero', a virginal but strapping English bicycle tourist with 'the head of a lion', who is too rational to be afraid of her. In a reverse of the Sleeping Beauty thumb-pricking motif, where the princess's blood brings down the curse, she pricks her finger on a shard of glass from her own broken dark glasses, and sees her own blood for the first time. The young man, bringing 'the innocent remedies of the nursery' into her 'vile and murderous room', kisses her finger better for her: he drinks *her* blood. This exorcism, this turnaround, is too much for her: 'How can she bear the pain of becoming human?' Unlike Mr Lyon, she can't; for her it's her old mechanism, her old pattern, or nothing, and since she can no longer act out the predator-prey ritual, she simply dissolves; setting, however, her pet lark free.

In the morning, the hero is surprised by the tawdriness of his surroundings: 'how thin and cheap the satin, the catafalque not ebony at all but black-painted paper stretched on struts of wood, as in the theatre'. So much for de Sade's stage settings, his overblown trappings, when exposed to the common-sense light of day. All that's left of the vampire is – as in 'The Snow-Child' – a fanged rose. It is the rose of death, and it accompanies the young man to the trenches, in France; a somewhat Gothic ending, after all.

The collection concludes with three wolf stories. The first, 'The Werewolf', retells 'Red Riding Hood', only this time the wolf is not disguised as the grandmother, it *is* the grandmother. No self-sacrifice for 'the good child': she cuts off the wolf's paw, recognises that it and the grandmother's cut-off hand are the same, denounces the grandmother as a witch, and inherits her property. Moral: women can be werewolves too. Other moral: to be a 'good child' (*BC*, p. 108) does not mean you have to be a victim. In the demanding 'cold country', to be a good child is to be a competent child, to know how to recognise danger but to avoid being paralysed by fear, to know how to use your father's hunting knife to defend yourself against those who also hunt. 'Good' means 'good at'.

'The Company of Wolves' is a variation on 'The Tiger's Bride'. Again, the just-menstrual, virginal, innocent but tough Red Riding Hood makes her way through the forest. Again she meets a werewolf in disguise – this time not the grandmother but the proverbial hunter, festooned with dead birds: no vegetarian he, even in human form. As in the original story, girl and wolf make a bet about which one can get to Granny's house first, and also as in the original, wolf eats Granny. But the girl cannot be rescued from the wolf by the hunter, because the wolf *is* the hunter. So she has to rescue herself. She recognises her danger, but – like the girl in 'The Tiger's Bride' she does not show fear. Instead, she 'freely' gives the kiss she owes him by their wager, laughs at him when he says 'All the better to eat you with', because she 'knows she is nobody's meat', and climbs into bed with him. As with the tiger, it is the wolf who, in the face of gift as opposed to plunder, is – as befits a Sadeian libertine – more 'fearful'; in the morning the girl is 'sweet and sound', and the wolf has become 'tender' (*BC*, p. 118). As with all of Carter's would-be steaks and chops, this 'wise child' wins the herbivore–carnivore contest by refusing fear, by taking matters into her own hands, by refusing to allow herself to be defined as somebody's meat, and by 'freely' learning to – if not run with the tigers – at least lie down with them. Whether she has become more wolf-like or he has become more human is anybody's guess, but in this story each participant appears to retain his or her own nature. A consolatory nonsense, perhaps – don't try this technique on a street mugger – but at least a different consolatory nonsense, one that tries for the kind of synthesis Carter suggested in *The Sadeian Woman*: 'neither submissive nor aggressive'.

The last story, 'Wolf-Alice', is the most grotesque of the lot, featuring as it does a strange alliance between two misfits, a woman who was raised as a wolf and is therefore not fully human – she runs on all fours and howls rather than talking – and an undead ghoulish werewolf, who feeds on corpses and casts no reflection in mirrors. These characters are the carnivore in its least attractive mode. Wolf-Alice has none of the stately nobility of lion or tiger; she is human *manquée*, not beast-plus. As for the awful Duke, he isn't even beautiful, like the vampire of the House of Love. He is gaunt and filthy, a carrion-eater rather than a beast of prey. Like the Marquis in the first story, he too has a 'bloody chamber', but it's not an impressive one, merely extremely dirty.

The two establish a curious ménage in the Duke's mouldering mansion. Alice is sent there because the villagers can't deal with her animal ways, and the Duke lets her remain because she isn't afraid of him. Having been raised with flesh-eaters, and lacking human consciousness, she isn't upset by the sight of him in the kitchen with a man's leg slung over his shoulder: 'she, the serene, the inviolable one in her absolute and verminous innocence' (*BC*, p. 123). Her innocence is animal, pre-human, belonging to 'the Eden of our first beginnings where Eve and grunting Adam squat on a daisy bank'. In this setting, she would have been a 'wise child who leads them all'. As it is, she is mutilated.

Alice becomes a little less mutilated as she achieves a little more self-consciousness: she learns, for instance, to recognise her own reflection in a mirror, she learns how to deal with menstruation – a key item, in these blood-centred stories – and she learns how to put on clothes, the 'shrouds, nightdresses and burial clothes that had once wrapped items on the Duke's menu'. Dressed up in an old wedding gown belonging to a bride the Duke has eaten, she's prancing about in the graveyard when the Duke, surprised at one of his excavations, gets shot with a silver bullet by the bride's husband. This throws him into a state of 'aborted transformation', in which he is neither non-human nor human. Alice, wise child, to the rescue: she sees blood and a wound, and then, 'pitiful as her gaunt grey mother', she begins to lick, 'without hesitation, without disgust, with a quick, tender gravity, the blood and dirt from his cheeks and forehead'. As she licks, his reflection gradually appears in the mirror. She licks him into a new being, as the tiger does the tiger's bride; he becomes human through love, as does Mr Lyon. But it is not sexual love that so transforms him, this time; instead it is a different kind of love: instinctual, merciful, maternal.

There is a certain amount of parody in this story – Carter seems to be pushing the redemptive-love scenario just about as far as it will go – but it's a tribute to her skill that she gets away with it. She knows her motifs, and Wolf-Alice is in part a Frog Prince story – kiss the yucky thing, the really yucky thing, and it will get better; though the Duke, even when licked, is no prince. *You see* – she appears to be saying to the Marquis, or to both of them, the Bluebeard of her own first story and de Sade himself – *you didn't have to confine yourself to those mechanistic stage sets, those mechanical rituals. It wasn't just eat or be eaten. You could have been human!* 'Human', however, does not necessarily mean 'wonderful'. In Carter's world it is always, even at best, a little ambiguous. She does have a yen for tigerhood.

The fairy tale as a form continued to hold Carter's interest, as did the interplay between sex and love, freedom and bondage, prey and predation; and she continued to search for synthesis. The 'last acknowledged response to the

Grimms' that she wrote was yet another fairy tale, the very short but haunting 'Ashputtle: or, The Mother's Ghost', which is a new look at the Cinderella story; but by this time she appears to have turned away from a contemplation of the male–female Sadeian dialectic to a more intense exploration of the maternalism of 'Wolf-Alice'. (See the Introduction by Donald Haase to *The Reception of Grimm's Fairy Tales*, Wayne State, Detroit, 1993; p. 19; and the story itself, *ibid.*, p. 301.) In Carter's version, the Cinderella figure is a 'burned child', and the ashes that cover her are ashes of mourning for her dead mother. Her continued mourning renders her devoid of will, a passive cipher and thus she must play lamb to her new stepmother's tiger; she must be the victim and do the dirty work her stepmother used to do when the burned child's real mother was alive and the stepmother was the ashes-raker.

The mother – although dead – is given enough energy by her love for her child and her distress at its destitute state so that her ghost can come back – as in the original 'Ashputtle' – to bestow gifts on the child. First the mother works through the family cow, and gives the child enough milk so that she can grow, and 'she grew fat, she grew breasts, she grew up'. Then the daughter sees a man whom the stepmother fancies, and expresses a desire. It is the desire to steal the stepmother's boyfriend and have him for herself; in other words, it is a tigerish rather than a lamb-like desire, but simply by having it – by showing that she is turning away from the land of the dead and towards the land of the living – the girl enables the ghost of her mother to continue her sequence of gifts. First – as the cow – she gives the girl all of her milk so that she can wash herself, and her burn scabs come off. After this, the cow-mother tells the girl to wash herself next time. Then – having gone into the family cat – the mother's ghost combs the girl's ragged hair, to make her presentable, with an admonition to comb her own hair from now on. Finally the mother's ghost goes into a bird, who – in imitation of the supposed behaviour of the pelican – pecks its own breast and lets down a sheet of blood, which is partly menstrual in significance – the girl 'shouted out when it ran down her legs' – but which turns into a red silk dress. The bird tells the girl to make her own dress next time. Then the transformed, now beautiful girl walks off with the man, leaving the stepmother to rake the ashes again. It's noteworthy that the transactions in the story, the interchanges of energy and position, are all among women: the mother, the stepmother, and the girl. This time the man, no longer Duke or Marquis or tiger or lion or wolf, is merely an occasion for contest, a plot device.

The story has two endings: one for the girl, one for the mother's ghost. The man gives the girl 'a house and money. She did all right.' What the mother gets is a rest from mothering. '"Now I can go to sleep," said the mother's ghost. "Everything is all right, now."'

Carter always knows what she's doing with words, and the double ending turns on the double meaning of 'all right'. In the girl's case, it means merely 'okay', or 'not bad', or 'average'. The way the mother uses it, however – 'Everything is all right' – has a much stronger happy-ending connotation – all right as in 'solved', as in 'finished', and as opposed to 'something wrong' and 'something left undone'. From the mother's point of view, she has done her job: she has weaned her child away from her, as she would have done anyway had she remained alive, and helped her to achieve autonomous adulthood. That is the happiest ending she can imagine; that, and her own well-deserved 'sleep'.

From the narrator's point of view, the ending isn't a deliriously happy one, but neither is it an unhappy one. The girl has grown up, leaving behind the world of 'early childhood', which Carter characterised in *The Sadeian Woman* as 'a world of nightmare, impotence and fear' (*SW*, p. 148); in addition, she has got what she wanted. She has played both lamb and tiger, but at the end she is neither; she is instead a grown-up woman. If the result is only 'all right', it is also only human, part of that complexity, that mixed blessing, which Carter valued above the 'consolatory nonsense' of absolutist, reductionist myth, of 'spurious . . . archetype' (*SW*, p. 6).

And that, she implies, is not simply all we can – at best – expect, but also nothing we need despise.

'Mother is a Figure of Speech...'

··

NICOLE WARD JOUVE

> Mother is a figure of speech and has retired to a cave
> beyond consciousness . . .
>
> (Angela Carter, *The Passion of New Eve*)

'Silly old Bataille', Angela Carter said.

In her most devastatingly angelic, little-girl's voice.

1978. We were at one of Emma Tennant's *Bananas* launching parties. This particular *Bananas* issue had included 'The Immaculate Conception', one of the stories from *Le Spectre du gris*, which I had published with Editions des femmes. Later Virago would bring it out, Englished, as *Shades of Grey*.

She liked 'The Immaculate Conception', Angela Carter had said. She was generous to other women writers. Well, some. Why she was generous to me I wondered in later years, given her scathing dislike of the victim syndrome. Elizabeth Smart should have written *By Grand Central Station I Tore Off His Balls*, not *Sat Down and Wept*: that's what she exasperatedly suggested to Lorna Sage (Sage, 1992, p. 247). My story was about a woman who gets destroyed. Why hadn't Angela Carter hated it? Perhaps she enjoyed the tone, which was tough. Or the mock-Surrealist title. Or the destruction job, which was thorough.

She was writing a book on de Sade, she said. I gulped. As a young, foreign graduate student in Cambridge in the 1960s I had researched a thesis on the Satanic, Gothic and Byronic hero. The librarian had vetted me as a security risk (a French girl eerily homing in on the Frenchest of French stuff), then granted me access to the Divine Marquis: but I had to read him in a special quarter of the University Library. There sat I, week after week, in splendid isolation, in the penumbra of a palatial room, a quarantined bitch from abroad, the local scholarly population safe from rabies. I romped through the Apollinaire edition and old prints with wobbly first and last lines and 's's' that looked like 'f's', feeling for all the world like a freak spy who has wandered into a genteel script, or the *au pair* suspected of wanting to make off with the family silver when she only means to give it a good polish. I remember enjoying *Justine* and *Juliette* (they made me feel daring and free), and relishing the elegant eighteenth-century disquisitions of *La Philosophie dans le boudoir*.

Making access so difficult, Academia was treating me as my father had. As an adolescent I had stayed in on Sundays under cover of swotting, found the key to the forbidden books cupboard, and worked my furtive and excited way through *Les Liaisons dangereuses*. Sex was under lock and key. It went with the eighteenth century, a bloody, revolutionary age that wrote exquisitely precise understatements in limpid prose. Most forbidden of all, de Sade was the ultimate. The white goose that I was filled notebooks with extracts: about the savagery of nature, about wolves never eating one another. I now remember that in 'The Company of Wolves', Little Red Riding Hood's hunger matches the wolf's. Clever Angela. My own beast was an Alien. But I did jot down the bit about women's appetites being greater than men's. I liked that. *The 120 Days of Sodom*, however, speedily made me reach saturation point. I quit over its systematic tediousness. That finished de Sade off for me, and wasn't I glad it had when I saw Pasolini's *Salò*. With the arguable exception of *Foucault's Pendulum*, I don't think a book has ever so bored me.

Time passed. Things happened. Simone de Beauvoir's *Faut-il brûler Sade?* annoyed me in its sanity. I was perplexed by Roland Barthes's *Sade, Fourier, Loyola*. The indecency of equating the sadistic pornographer, the religious founder and the utopian Socialist! System-builders all three might be. The structuralist decision to consider 'nothing but' affronted me. And now here was this angelic-sounding Englishwoman, wading into it all as if nobody had been there before. Cool as a cucumber. I felt robbed. Who'd just waded into *my* bloody chamber? Dangerous stuff, I said. Reality may overtake fantasy. Look at de Sade. Look at Bataille, what he did with – to – Laure. . . .

'Silly old Bataille', she said.

To mistake fantasy for reality, she meant.

Lucky you, my good woman, I thought, who can so thoroughly distinguish between them.

I couldn't. Nor could I read her books. Understand anything about them, that is. In a strange way, the story of my relationship with her work is a story of misunderstandings and misreadings. The stuff was so close, I couldn't but relate to it. I was so different from her, I couldn't but be shocked, offended. It rubbed me up the wrong way. Just as well. I have noticed in nature films that tigers lovingly smooth and wet the felled leopard's hide with their tongues prior to tearing it with their fangs. Makes it easier to swallow. I write as a lone French leopard, still alive, thank you, still trying to find its way through the forest. I write out of fifteen years of misreadings. The only appropriate tribute, because it is precise. No soul-to-soul for Angela Carter. Explanation, exegesis or – worse – canonisation would lubricate the tiger's hide. She meant to stick in our gullets.

'Silly old Bataille', she said.
   'Silly old Nicole', I heard.

I   A History of Misreadings

Love was the first Carter novel I read. I found it baffling, and on balance I disliked it. The heroine – if that's the word – did seem too unfazed by the nasty things being done to her. She didn't even seem to mind being done in. The whole thing was cool – too cool in its Baroque and seedy precision; too socially accurate, with its black-nailed lank bovver-boys and decaying Beardsleyish decor, for the degentrified neo-*Story of O* I remember as *Love*. Maybe it's not at all like that and I've retrospectively made it up.

Then out came *The Sadeian Woman*. I wanted to hate it. I was in parts nonplussed, in others half persuaded. There was a strong point there. Threw me back to those days in the wainscoted room of the Cambridge University Library – why had *I* been there, if not for something very like what *The Sadeian Woman* was saying? *I* hadn't known how to explore it, let alone express it. One passage, however, tipped the balance against the book for me. Eugénie, the heroine from *La Philosophie dans le boudoir*, is being initiated, let loose, allowed to have her fantasies, by libertines. She has her mother raped by the libertines, impregnated with the pox, then sewn up. I had forgotten that bit. Carter talks about de Sade's creativity in thus allowing a daughter to be indulged in her most aggressive drives against the censoring mother. Liberating. At this the mother that I then was, the mother of an often angry fourteen-year-old daughter, felt affronted. Again that fucking business of fantasy and reality, I thought. All very well for that bitch to indulge herself. Unencumbered by a daughter of her own, she completely identifies with the daughter's point of view. What would she feel if she was at the receiving end – if she was the mother? Not quite so agreeable, is it?

I was determined to have another go. I knew that the intellectually snooty Editions du Seuil had bought *The Passion of New Eve*. I found a copy on York Station, Pan Books, with a black-booted, fishnet-stockinged blonde on the cover, complete with whip. Surprising what packaging does. You approach that book in a very different spirit now that it has a tasteful, intriguing, arty Virago Modern Classics cover: with such hallmarks of feminist gentility, who can help but have their critical antennae bristling? Mine weren't. I bad-temperedly toyed between displaying and concealing my s/m blonde from the frosty lady in tweeds who sat across from me at the BR table. It wasn't like having *chosen* to read porn. More like being caught with my hand in the till when I was putting money in, and all for the sake of bloody feminism. No doubt prospective glee at readers' discomfort played its part in getting Angela Carter to approve such a cover – or did she relish the drop on to the ledger of Inferior Culture? There is a question of class lurking about somewhere – the middle-class girl (Melanie or Little Red Riding Hood) leaving respectability behind, bonding into an exotic, sexy working class. The virgin and the gypsy. Sometimes porn is to erotica as lower class is to upper class. Be it circus, brothel or music hall, Carter always chose the lower class.

I wanted to shout at the lady in tweeds: 'This is LITERA-TURE, not porn, you know' – then I remembered how years before, when I was teaching Italian Literature, elderly Miss Easthwaite, who always wore a knitted bonnet and mittens, having trotted away with Moravia's *La Noia* in her canvas bag, trotted back the following week and asked, in her sweetest voice, 'I beg your pardon. But isn't it PORNOG-RAPHY?' Throughout *La Noia* an ageing painter makes love over every bit of ground that offers itself to an adolescent girl whose belly spasms at the moment of orgasm are so exquisite he can't leave off getting his tummy button glued to hers. He eventually dies on the steep staircase of his studio at a maximally spasmodic moment. I had ordered umpteen copies of the book for my class on the strength of Moravia's name, and was loath to be found out casting wickedness upon the waters at the expense of Hull Adult Education. 'Oh no, Miss Easthwaite,' I said, cheerfully, 'it is EROTICISM.' 'Oh, I see,' she said, 'but excuse me. Could you explain to me what is the difference?'

Weekend *Guardian*, January 1994. Pages of magazine devoted to Joan Collins. Married four times, the journalist explains: to a sadist, a neurotic, a junkie and a cad, in that order. She posed in thigh-high black boots for *Marie-Claire*. Page of main section given over to Camille Paglia's diary. She suffers from TV deprivation in Europe (not enough exposure) and also posed in black leather and studs for some other magazine. This is star-gazing of the most baffling kind, I reflect. Formations of Fantasy. Madonna & Co. Is it enough to be a glamorous toughie, or the mistress of the game, to join the New Left platform? If so, Juliette has won. Carter was a prophet, as always. Indeed, even Justine has ceased to be a victim today. She cuts off the

assaulting male's penis with a kitchen knife. No more sitting
down and weeping. The Bobbitt case makes it to the front
page all round the Western world. When, in the early
eighties, I wrote my study on the Yorkshire Ripper case, I
felt that I was boldly venturing into awesome territory
where angels feared to tread, and very few women had
trodden. Now the serial killer, including the female serial
killer, is almost as common as sliced bread. Nobody bats an
eyelid. Angels wear boots. The lambs have turned into
wolves. The early nineties certainly put my trouble with the
cover of *The Passion of New Eve* in historical perspective. If
this book survives long enough for anyone to come by this
essay in ten years time, who knows where we will be? For
in the meantime, Neo-Nazi movements grow. . . .

Anyway – there was I, almost fifteen years ago, on the
train, with *The Passion of New Eve*. The – bloodlessness? –
with which a ghastly series of Doomsday horrors were
being narrated fazed me. The ultimate in nihilistic cynicism,
I thought. Revenge on the decadent male with whose
unpalatable persona one remains saddled till the bleak end.
Having his tail surgically removed barely improves Evelyn.
Now he's become mythical Eve, the best you can say for
her is that s/he is at the receiving end of pain, where he
inflicted it. But whether the pain is hers or someone else's,
s/he does keep a near-psychopathic inability to feel it.
Empathy my eye. Unreality is the name of the game.
Bloodless was the right word. No blood flowed from any
wounding instruments – not the bungling abortionist's
needle when Evelyn's girlfriend Leilah gets messed up, nor
the emasculating knife that descends upon Evelyn. Zero's
Manson-like orgy of destruction, when his gang swoops on
Tristessa's mansion, left me feeling 'oh, well . . . having a

romp?' Feelings – love, nostalgia – so much hot air. Puppets all. Sawdust and celluloid. But there was no denying the clear, cold grace of the writing.

Then two things happened. An American student in one of my classes, reading aloud an extract (Mother about to perform surgery on Evelyn), and reading it in an easygoing, unfazed, deadpan way, got the whole class (myself included) in hysterics of laughter:

> Oh, the dreadful symbolism of that knife! To be castrated with a phallic symbol! (But what else, says Mother, could do the trick?) (*PNE*, p. 70)

All right: I had missed the point. Then my fifteen-year-old son, seeing the whip and fishnet stockings on the cover, made off with the book. At thirteen he had pinched my *New French Feminisms* and passed it round the gym locker room at his comprehensive: boys looking for the spicy bits must have received quite an education. My son found *The Passion of New Eve* terribly clever. It defeated every pornographic expectation from its male readers, he thought. Goes to show how sophisticated these youngsters can be, damn them. He went on to read every Carter novel and story he could lay his hands on. I followed suit. Reported his reaction to Angela Carter the next time we met, thinking she would be pleased. 'But of course', she said. Damn her. Was I the only daft one? But I had by that time become a sort of convert.

I didn't dare own how thoroughly *I* had misread her. But I've always been struck since then by the ease with which young people 'get it'. Get her. Something about the spirit of the time, her being ahead, in tune, getting the whiff of things to come. Which she did. Playfulness. Speed.

Everything up – not for grabs, but for suspension, deflation, metamorphosis.

I hadn't much liked *The Infernal Desire Machines*, nor *Fireworks*. *The Bloody Chamber* was the first Carter book I actually enjoyed. Perhaps it was the territory – Perrault, the Grimm Brothers, folk, Gothic. Always loved the stuff. And for the first time I picked up the extraordinary, deft array of literary and cultural references, the rewriting and weaving-in of other writers. Fireworks indeed. In the first, the Bluebeard story that gives its name to the collection, I recognised a canny reader of Colette. It shimmered with skilfully modified bits from the *Claudine* novels, from *My Apprenticeships*, *My Mother's House* – and put to impertinent use a wonderfully intimate knowledge of the art and life of *fin-de-siècle* French Decadence. 'The Tiger's Bride' pleased me. Not just because of the way it reverses 'The Bloody Chamber', the story of poor young girl married to rich, lordly, hairy older stranger. Though she's cast in an archetypal patriarchal script, sold to pay her father's gambling debts, made to strip down to 'white meat' by the pandering valet, the bride is not afraid of the Tiger. He's a Tiger, not a Marquis, as in 'The Bloody Chamber'. She holds 'the key to the peaceable kingdom in which his appetite need not be my extinction' (p. 88), not the key to bloody murder. When the Tiger fails to smell fear on her, he purrs. The walls of his castle crumble. A happy as well as a witty Fall of the House of Usher – ushers, panderers, familial prostitution, valet, gone. The Tiger was as much the prisoner of the pornographic spell as the girl. Her fearlessness frees them both. As he begins to lick her white skin, it falls away, and there appears in its place shining fur. 'Nascent patina.' It made me think of the wet fur of a new-born colt. Of the glowing dark fur of sea lions as they hoist themselves out of the water, shaking themselves. When they've dried themselves on the rocks, their fur is thick, the colour of golden sand. Their ecstasy is equal whether they're diving and shooting through the waves, rolling about, jumping, or blissfully spread on a rock, belly up, so that the air can cool their fin-pit. 'My ear-rings thawed and I was shaking water out of my beautiful fur.'

Yes, that's it, I thought. That is the state. The active state of pleasure in which you become stripped not just of old clothes, habits, but of the old skin. There is a lot of territory to cross to get to that state, and it seemed to me that this was what Angela Carter had done: gone through the pornographic spectrum in order to come out at the other end. Unnervingly and irreverently explored the alienating figures of Romance, the rebellious Heathcliff-type hero (Jewel in *Heroes and Villains*), then the Wild Older Man (de Sade, Bluebeard, Mr Rochester, Colette's first husband, Willy) and disposed of them. Out with demon lover and patriarch. In with gentle boys, piano tuners, students wheeling their bicycles into vampiric castles and being jolly nice about it. And if Mr Wild Older Man still strolls in, he's been mellowed by a cocktail of alcohol, Joycean literacy, Scott Fitzgerald desperation, and a certain trouble with potency: he's Irish, alias the Ross O'Flaherty of *Wise Children*, and he imparts prodigious skills of metaphor to his young, un-coy mistress.

Fear had to be conquered. Nothing sacred. Fear it is that makes predators of our wolves and tigers. 'If Little Red Riding Hood had laughed at the wolf and passed on, the wolf could never have eaten her', said Colette (Colette, 1948–50, p. 50). 'The tiger will never lie down with the lamb; he acknowledges no pact that is not reciprocal. The lamb must learn to run with the tigers' (*BC*, p. 84). Girl's fearlessness delivers man from his beastliness.

Or am I being sentimental? Pulling Angela Carter in a

direction she wouldn't acknowledge. *She'd* never write about a *real* sea lion, now, would she? So busy transforming every little thing into artifice. 'Feux d'artifice' is the French for fireworks. She won't even allow earth to be earthy – or rather, to symbolise what is genuine, and can, through symbolisation, become a means to power. In *Wise Children*, the casketful of authentic Stratford-upon-Avon earth that Shakespearian actor Melchior Hazard takes to Hollywood, to sprinkle on the American cast of *A Midsummer's Night Dream*, is meant to imaginatively reclaim, colonise, American soil. Sacred relics upon which you build the new churches, the films. But what happens? When Melchior's illegitimate children look for the casket, it turns out that the cat's been using it as a shit-box all the long train voyage from New York to LA. And beyond. So what do the girls do? They replace it with a bit of local loam, as in the story of Bid Dan's ashes that have been lost by the little girl to whom they had been entrusted when the men made a beeline for the pub, and she refills the jar with ashes from the grate, and the men returning from the pub have a good cry and say: What a small thing we are, and all that's left of us is a handful of ashes and a few burnt eggshells. Hey presto! as Carter would say. Nobody the wiser.

I am of the earth-loving persuasion. Though I was bred in a provincial city flat in the South of France, I love the country, trees, rocks, sea. Carter is city through and through. No time for twilights, identifying birds or plants by name. I – though your genuine exile, living in a country other than the one I was born in, or perhaps because of that – have put down roots in a variety of places. Over sea, one ocean. They tug at me, bewilder me. Carter, moored in the one place, London, is an imaginative wanderer, a lover of the picaresque. The high road is her way. Only in her last novel do characters claim roots: Brixton. It's taken me half a century to shed my Romanticism, and I still love myths, symbols, religions, silence, solitude. Angela Carter was, as she said herself, in the demystifying business. Her books swarm with characters, brim with unhampered, unromantic promiscuity. You say 'soul' to me, and I like it. You say 'soul' to her, and she throws up. Invite her characters to a party, and they perk up. Take me to a wood, and I revive.

I write all this because recognising her for what she is as precisely as I can, and identifying the reasons for my distance from her, is my way of not absorbing her, refusing to kill her off. I had rather be wrong, or unsubtle, than play an academic game of theorisation and explanation that would enable the tiger that she was to be tamed, shorn of its claws. The most violent and shocking things – hard-core porn, serial murder – have in recent years become fashionable, under pretext of the innocuousness of fantasy, the right to public knowledge, or the supposed seriousness of looking into our fascination with crime. But the very jadedness which so much exposure and play provoke almost makes psychotics of us all. We no longer feel, we play, as if the 'real' violence media circuses invite us to play with thereby ceased to *be* violence, and did nobody any harm. The charge in Carter, the gunpowder that's in every one of her rockets, is her subversion of the images, the processes of alienation themselves. She won't cease to play – not because she won't feel, but because she wants to reveal the power at work in the game shows. She pulls the plug. Meets fire with fire – or rather, the sacralised with wit.

It is, it now strikes me, a gross mistake to read the antics of the day's idols as Carter's prophecies come to pass. The Joan Collinses and Camille Paglias, red in lipstick and nail polish, only seem to be the flesh-and-blood fulfilment of what *The Sadeian Woman* praised in Juliette. They do have in common with Carter's Lady Purple, Daisy Duck or Tristessa that they serve to embody media fantasies. But Carter's puppets and divas are man-made. Her writing, its antics and self-deflating rhetoric, exposes, unpicks the fabrication process: never promotes the illusion. It shows the divas to be the ideological products of light and celluloid, issued from the mirror chambers of a narcissistic, *male* imaginary. New Eve in the mirror is ex-Evelyn's dream girl. His dream diva, Tristessa, is a man in drag. My adolescent son was right. *The Passion of New Eve* is almost as carefully geared to a male readership as Genet's *The Blacks* is to a white audience. In *Wise Children* Saskia, the carnivorous Delia Smith of a TV show, in her highbrow, successful-career-woman version of domesticity, is the very picture of preda-tory alienation. If the powers that be love you, that means they are using you. Ask who produces and who consumes, whose interest you serve. Angela Carter was that thing she said Sade failed to be: a moral pornographer. She refused to promote any vested power, patriarchal or other. She wouldn't let herself be bought, play anybody's game, be taken in. It would be a disaster if her present vogue turned into fashionableness. Which is why my own distance, and one-time dislike, are so useful.

At the 'Shape and Tone' at a York lowbrow gym: 'Did you see that piece about Joan Collins in the *Express*?' 'Well, if I had her money. . . . She's got a special teacher that makes her work out two bloody hours every morning.' 'If she had to pack up for three every morning. . . .' 'We would all have her figure, girls, if we had her money. Wouldn't we now?' 'Course we would.' All about Mammon. In *Wise Children*, Dora finds out that Mammon is what Hollywood amounts to. Yet the fascination is so acute, the flirting with its glamour so compulsive.

But there is more.

The story that most delighted me when I first read *The*

Bloody Chamber was 'Puss-in-Boots'. The romping Cavalier's voice – Rabelaisian in its relish, its physicality – eighteenth-century interloping Figaro with its gift of the gab and *roué* pirouettes: the original tale demystified in terms of class and period, yet the childish pleasure at animal antics found anew. I thought there was a great future in that voice, the sheer *jouissance* (there goes a big word) of the verbal inventiveness. In the ensuing years, it seemed to me, food and sex and class and materiality became combined with a phenomenal gift of the gab in ways that made me think of Joyce, Dickens. . . . Suddenly Carnival was there. Queen Carnival. Belching, farting, drinking, dyeing, flying, dancing, fucking, in the train of Puss-in-Boots there came Fevvers, from *Nights at the Circus*, then Dora and Nora among the multitudinous twins of *Wise Children*. The Bloody Chamber had been crossed. The initiation rites, menstruation and all, gone through. The beasts, the tigers and the wolves had been encountered, mated with. Body was there. Dare I say – feelings? It wasn't deconstruction any more. If it was still postmodernism (if the word hadn't been around, someone would have had to invent it for Angela Carter) it had a considerable amount of gut.

Dare I go further? Let postmodernists shout 'Off with her head!' Reading *Wise Children*, I had to admit that I empathised with the *values* of the twin sisters. Do credit to a good Christian, of the 'By their fruits ye shall know them' variety. Much too much sex of the exclusively non-marital kind for an institutional Christian, yes, but let him who is without sin. . . . Dora and Nora, now, remain uncorrupted by Mammon, impervious to snobbery or fame; restore husbands to their distraught spouses, renouncing in the process a girl's best friend, a diamond as large as the Ritz. They take in the old, the orphaned, the abandoned and the handicapped, be they stepmums or cats; have hearts as big

as houses, an endlessly innocent capacity for delight. . . .
'Except ye . . . become as little children. . . .' Warmed the
cockles of my heart, it did.

Another misreading? Am I still wanting life, and people,
and your GENUINE article, earth? Never learn, will I?

She and I, like chalk and cheese.

Chalk is the genuine thing. Comes from cliffs.

But you can eat cheese.

When I sent Angela Carter my book on Colette, she sent
back a Christmas card with fat puddings on it. Inside it said:
'Read it at one gulp. Mmmm.'

II Fantasy and Separation

What has all this to do with the mother?

She's been the story under the story. I knew it years ago,
when I was repelled by Carter's endorsement of the sexual
punishment meted out to Eugénie's mother in *La Philosophie
dans le boudoir*. Felt that it was purely the daughter's point
of view.

What about the mother? I want to ask again.

There is a link between my difficulties about fantasy and
my insistence on the mother. People who are able to
distinguish clearly between reality and fantasy, psychoanalysis tells us, are people who are grown up. They have
separated off from the mother. They are differentiated.
Individuated. Mature.

This is so according to Freudian patterns: maturation
occurs when the Oedipus complex has been successfully
overcome. It is also so according to Jungian patterns. Jung
pleads for a separation between the image of the mother,

sung and celebrated in all times and languages, and the 'human being called mother whom chance made the bearer of that experience' (quoted in Humbert, 1983, p. 59). When we have arrived at a knowledge of this, we no longer bring the enormous weight of meaning, of 'heaven and hell', to bear upon those 'weak and fallible beings' who were given us as mothers. You could say that it is because she is truly detached from the mother, because she can distinguish between the real and the imaginary mother, that Angela Carter has no compunction about attacking the *archetype*: Mother has nothing to do with mother.

'Poor old Bataille.' Poor old Nicole, who did not know the boundaries between fantasy and reality. But Angela Carter kept everything separated. She was the *moral* Pornographer, using Pornography to make her reader think, instead of indulge, or want to imitate. She kept herself, her life, anyone remotely resembling her family, lovers or friends, out of her books. None of her novels is autobiographical, not in any visible way. She was individuated. Even fantasy, in her hands, is not allowed to be a lure, an indulgence. For there are types of fantasy which give form to our secret dreads, our censored wish to violence: like Mary Shelley's *Frankenstein*. If such fantasy is subversive, it is only because it dares what the decencies of realism forbid. Yet it upholds the decencies. The unreal guarantees the real. *Unheimlich*, the uncanny – literally the un-homely – maintains home, the *heimlich*. And fantasy (as in horror) can be self-indulgence. Safe fear, which serves to make danger or destructiveness, inside or outside us, unreal. The fantasised solution mothers us. It protects us from having to seek active solutions in the real world. But in the work of Angela Carter, fantasy if always at one remove. The reader neither enjoys Evelyn's wickedness nor gets a kick out of Mother's castrating knife. There is no narrative safety, no cosy resolution, be it bliss or apocalypse. The very appeal of pornography, of fantasy, of dream, is being deconstructed. Exposed as so much machinery. Well individuated indeed. The very coolness with which Angela Carter looks on at the horrors done to Eugénie's mother, and sees them as fantasy, is a sign of her detachment. Her advanced state of maturity.

This convinces my brain, but not my gut. Writing is not only what is intended, what is proffered. The very fact of returning again and again to a particular theme, or trope, is significant. Would anyone spend so long in the houses of pornography, unless they were fascinated by them? Would the mother be so severely under attack, unless there was deep anger against her somewhere? In Carter's work the patriarch is repeatedly shown to be shallow, his power mechanical or not so great after all. But the fiercest rebellion is against the mother, what she stands for. At least up to the last two novels.

III   The Fiction of Maternity

At the end of *Portrait of the Artist as a Young Man*, Joyce's Stephen Dedalus leaves Ireland to go into exile. He quite self-consciously leaves the mother behind. She's winded, jaded, 'forever mending' Stephen's 'second-hand clothes'. The mother is a lot of things: Mother Country, Irish nationalism, myths of origins and identity, biology, realism. She also stems from the character's 'real' mother. At the beginning of *Portrait*, the child Stephen associates the mother's good-night kiss with the wet mud into which he has been, that day, thrown by bullies at school. The word 'kiss' is made to connote moistness, nausea.

There's a story called 'Clay' in *Dubliners*. Sweet, elderly, spinsterly, naive, know-your-place Marie visits her nephew and family for Christmas. The children play: blindfold her, lead her to touch, and guess at, a cold wet substance that remains unnamed except in the title. Clay – or shit? The nephew is angry, and tells the children off. Then waxes sentimental at an old song: tears prevent him from finding the corkscrew.

Marie. . . . Mother. . . . Mud, clay, earth. . . . No casketful of Irish earth in Joyce's luggage (and no cat either, one presumes). The mother's had it, she's jaded. All she can do is tamper with a worn-out past. From the mother Stephen turns to the father: 'Old father, old artificer, stand me now and ever in good stead.' Last words of *Portrait*.

When written-from-exile *Ulysses* picks up on Dublin, the mother is dead. Guilt haunts Stephen. He wanders in search of an adoptive, an artificial father. Bloom is a very unpatriarchal father figure. Called Bloom, for a start. Peaceable, uncompetitive. Content to watch the 'limp father of thousands' float in the bath water like a languid flower, he combines the 'old artificer's' gift of playful language with an infant's corporeality. Very oral and anal, Mr Bloom. Consciousness lies comfortably amid digestive processes. He enjoys kidneys, shitting, the descent of wine down his gullet, the rise of desire. . . . Lusting, wanking. . . . Perhaps rooted in Molly Bloom's gracious willingness to wallow all day in bed, brimming with juices. Never mind her afternoon visitor, Blazes Boylan. Wearing the horns is a small price to pay for the knowledge that Gea, Great Earth Mother, is there, prone, non-stop, free-associating, 'Yes' incarnate. Bloom it is, however, who enables Stephen to find father and home rolled into one.

In a disquisition oft-quoted, most prominently in recent feminist years by Gilbert and Gubar, Stephen, meditating on Hamlet, says:

> Fatherhood, in the sense of conscious begetting, is
> unknown to man. It is a mystical estate, an apostolic
> succession, from only begetter to only begotten. On that
> mystery and not on the madonna which the cunning Italian
> intellect flung to the mob of Europe the church is founded
> and founded irremovably because founded, like the world,
> macro- and microcosm, upon the void. . . . *Amor matris* . . .
> may be the only true thing in life. Paternity may be a legal
> fiction. (Joyce, 1971, p. 207)

Paternity is a fiction. A creative fiction. It is the fiction that enables fiction to be regenerated, endlessly to self-generate. With the fiction of paternity does freedom come. It makes everything possible: multiple bastardy, adopting and inventing fathers, freeing the individual talent from tradition, from the anxiety of influence. Thanks to that fiction you can take off, leave them all behind: the ideologies, Irish folk, nationalism, the Celtic twilight, the Catholic Church, being a macho man, the romances of the last Romantics, Yeats's wild swans. You're freed from reverence. You can twist and shake and mix and warp language, wrench up sound from thing, let sound take the lead. Kiss connotes mud. You can let puns and rhetoric do the wake. Finn-again.

Isn't the boy who buries the articulated swan in Angela Carter's *The Magic Toyshop* called Finn? The novel's patriarch, Uncle Philip, has used a huge puppet of a swan to pretend-rape Melanie, in a staged replay of the myth of Leda and the Swan. Only a puppet, neither animal nor god, Carter answers Yeats's 'Leda and the Swan'. Rape of mortal woman has nothing to do with political violence. The trope is a patriarchal power trip. Uncle Philip's swan has neither knowledge nor power. He is all cardboard, and creaking machinery. Only Melanie's fear makes him overwhelming.

Joycean Finn is her ally in this demotion of the myth. And her lover. There's a long way from that to seventy-five-year-old Dora finally making it with wandering, self-exiling, conjuring red-haired centenarian 'Joycean' Uncle Peregrine in *Wise Children*. But again Joyce surfaces there. If at the last, by means of Dora, Carter wanted to consummate her lifelong passion for Nuncle Joyce on Daddy Shakespeare's bed, she would have been a fool to deny herself. As it is, they go at it so vigorously that they almost bring down the chandelier on the whole theatrical show downstairs.

There is a paradox. Father figures and patriarchal power (if I dare to use the word) are attacked, deconstructed, shown to be hollow or vulnerable in Angela Carter, whether as de Sade or Uncle Philip or Bluebeard or Melchior. But in her choice of artifice, her relentless demolitions of myths, stereotypes, images, then carnivalisation of the whole show, Carter is Joyce's illegitimate, self-doubling niece. She severs the cords between words and things, words and beliefs, images and power. In so far as archetypally, as image or as language, the mother stands for bodily writing, oneness with 'reality', lack of differentiation, Carter could be said to have chosen the way of the father, not the mother. I find it significant that she should have written one of her rare autobiographical pieces on 'Sugar Daddy', not on her mother. It is a beautiful and loving piece. The brief evocations of the mother are ominous: 'he always thought he could buy us off with treats and so he could and that is why my brother and I don't sulk, much. Whereas [my mother] – ' (in Owen, 1983, p. 22). 'If I am short-tempered, volatile as he is, there is enough of my mother's troubled soul in me to render his very transparency, his psychic good health, endlessly mysterious. He is my father and I love him as Cordelia did, "according to my natural bond".' She does object, she quickly adds, to the notion of a 'natural bond' but whether it is cultural or not, that bond is strong. 'And I do think my father gives me far more joy than Cordelia ever got from Lear' (ibid., p. 30).

Her books attack archetypal and traditional images of the mother. Biology or motherly love my eye. Down, indeed, with all bonds in flesh. Virginia Woolf had written of the need for the woman who will be an artist to kill the Angel in the House. Carter goes one better: to the end of the daughter's anger. She advocates the savage punishment meted out by de Sade to Eugénie's mother. Mothers or grandmothers, in her fiction, are speedily and neatly disposed of (e.g. wolf eats grandmother). Or they contradict all motherly representations: the girl's mother in *The Bloody Chamber* is a tiger-shooting, horse-riding, pistol-wielding heroine who takes over from damsel-saving Western cowboys and the brothers of the Perrault tale, bumping off Baddie Bluebeard in the nick of time. As for Mother in *The Passion of New Eve*, though outwardly she conforms to the Matriarchal Goddess pattern of the Mary Daly or pre-Minoan variety (she's black, archaic-looking and sports tiers of breasts), though she behaves like a Freudian little boy's worst fantasy, she's also a cosmetic surgeon and mad futurist dictator. *Nights at the Circus* Fevvers is brought up by a brothelful of adoptive mothers, with matter-of-fact cockney Lizzie as faithful attendant and fairy godmother. Even the vestigial physiological mother of Nora and Dora in *Wise Children*, 'Pretty Kitty', the seduced foundling who dies in childbirth, turns out at the end to have (possibly) been a fiction invented by 'Grandma' Chance to mask her own production of the twins, at fifty. No other writer I can think of has so repeatedly and passionately jousted against what feminists call 'biological essentialism'. If Simone de Beauvoir and countless others are right, and it is woman's biology, her being the 'sex that gives life', which 'destines' her for second place, then Carter's systematic and endlessly inventive attacks on images of motherhood, her divorcing 'biology' from mothering, are so many blows for women's freedom. In her last two books, Lizzie and the Hazard girls, none of them biological mothers, do some excellent mothering: you could add that Carter has re-created the part of motherhood that could be salvaged. 'Mother is as mother does', Nora remarks: Grandma Chance, whether she was their biological mother or not, has made the girls feel safe as houses.

In *The Passion of New Eve* Angela Carter hunted the archetype down to extinction. Having vainly travelled through underground conduits in a parody of mythical journeys to the Underworld, Eve finds that 'Mother is a figure of speech, and has retired to a cave beyond consciousness' (p. 184). You cannot ever access mother's body. What you *can* invent is mothering. In come Lizzie, Grandma *Chance*, Dora and Nora: the septuagenarian twins beat today's quinquagenarian technological reproduction mothers at the anti-ageism game, becoming as they do the new twins' father and mother. Both.

Feminine Mr Bloom was, after all, father and mother combined.

Why did I say, then, that Carter chooses Joyce's way of the father? She may choose artifice, but she goes one better than Joyce, beyond the fiction of paternity: she promotes the fiction of maternity. Denying the imaginary mother's body, the Gea–Tellus metaphor, making mother's body absent, a figure of speech, and the narrative a process of endless invention, she frees Molly Bloom. No need for Molly to stay in bed, to be the 'real' body whose presence guarantees the show, assures the boys, the fictional daddy and son, Stephen and Bloom, that homecoming is possible. If the Child is father of the Man, Dora asks in *Wise Children*, who, then, is mother of the woman? Well, in Carter's 'The Bloody Chamber' she comes charging in and delivers you from the Sadeian aristocratic husband. As Lizzie in *Nights at the Circus*, she has a magic clock in her handbag, and also delivers you from the fantasies of an evil aristocratic libertine. As outsize Fevvers, the ultimate male fantasy, large as Ghea–Tellus and self-proclaimed *intacta*, she is a trapezist, she can fly: she is a confidence trickster. Carter substitutes backstage for back into the archetype. She finds ropes and pulleys, props, make-up, dye, sequins, where others saw gods, virgin mothers, stars, angels.

And so – what am I going on about? Not the way of the father – beyond both father and mother. Subverting both, combining both, demoting both. All that's left is the act. The performance: conjuring or doing.

All about freedom. A form of feminist existentialism.

Daring to imagine and endorse the daughter's anger against the mother, her wish to sadistically punish her, delivers the possibility of a new, cheerful, active, duty-free form of mothering. In *Wise Children* it comes as Naturism, the non-nuclear family, and fun all round. Skirting as close to incest as you might wish: getting laid by your father's twin brother, as Dora does by Uncle Peregrine (who, moreover, has always been thought to be her dad), is not a bad way of flouting the taboo. Bataille, who claimed that Eroticism could be found only through defying taboos, might have approved.

I argued above that it was Angela Carter's imaginative courage in traversing the pornographic scene that delivered the sexual delight of *The Bloody Chamber*, and the later novels. She couldn't have done it without having precisely that ability to separate fantasy from reality which – I also argued above – is made possible by separation from the mother. No need to cling, to feel endangered by what comes to you, from outside you. Lamb can lie down with wolf. Mother's body can be lost – indeed, sent down the drain: no need to go looking for it, to make caves into its substitutes. Mother can be absent: child will play. Mature adult can be as parodic with words and forms as she pleases. Reinvent mothering if need be.

'Old father, old artificer, stand me now and ever in good stead.'

I hear a weird echo of the last sentence of Joyce's *Portrait* in the last sentence of Carter's *Passion*:

'Ocean, ocean, mother of mysteries, bear me to the place of birth' (p. 191).

Does it mean that the mother, *in extremis*, is allowed back in? Or that, as ocean (traditionally male, as against feminine sea), she is just what you travel on – not the place, but a guide to the place, where birth can happen?

IV Writing and the Mother

Can the mother write? Tillie Olsen and Adrienne Rich asked in the seventies. Does woman, 'alienated from [her] real body and [her] real spirit by the institution – not the fact – of motherhood' (Rich, 1977, pp. 38–9), need violently to detach from motherhood? If she wants to create, must she be 'Kali, Medea, the sow that devours her farrow' (ibid., p. 32)? Does she need to become pure mind or, on the contrary, to reclaim her body from all institutions? Have women, by being reduced to their mothering function, been alienated from their own bodies, their desire, their pleasure, and should they strive to find them? 'Our skin is alive with

signals; our lives and deaths are inseparable from the release
or blockage of our thinking bodies' (ibid., p. 284).

Is motherhood the root cause of the trouble? Women,
Nancy Chodorow argues, 'tend to remain bound up in
preoedipal issues in relation to their own mothers'. Mothering 'involves a double identification for women, both as
mother *and* as child'. This makes women find motherhood
a satisfying way of expressing 'their mothering capacities'
(Chodorow, 1978, pp. 204–5). The girl – the daughter – has
the tricky role of needing both to identify with her mother
in order to become a mother herself, and to become 'sufficiently differentiated to grow up and experience herself as
a separate individual' (ibid., p. 177). As for the mother,
once a mother, how does she perform the balancing act?
Finding a way out of alienation seems just possible for the
daughter: is it impossible for the mother? Does this mean
that mothering ought to be separated off from motherhood?

Debates have raged over the last twenty years. Some
women writers – Olsen, Morrison in *Beloved*, Christa Wolf
in *Cassandra*, Michèle Roberts in her last two novels –
explore motherhood from the inside. Others identify it as
the enemy. Carter is in that camp. She never writes from
the vantage point of the mother. Always that of the daughter. In Woolf's *To the Lighthouse*, the adoptive daughter, Lily
Briscoe, has to refuse both mothering and motherhood in
order to create in painting. Yet her attachment to, love for,
grief at the disappearance of, Mrs Ramsay made her relation
to the mother part and parcel of the creative act. Androgyny, perhaps? But Carter rebuts, demotes and negates the
mother:

> If the daughter is a mocking memory to the mother – 'As I
> am, so you once were' – then the mother is a horrid
> warning to her daughter. 'As I am, so you will be.' Mother

seeks to ensure the continuance of her own repression. . . .
(Carter, 1979, p. 124)

The goddess is dead.
And, with the imaginary construct of the goddess, dies
the notion of eternity, whose place on earth was the womb.
(ibid., p. 110)

Carter does not only kill the Angel in the House, she goes
for the genitals of the creative archetype. Where Jung said
that each of us has to come to terms with the Mother in us,
Carter answers: 'nothing but a figure of speech'. Wind and
piffle. In the face of the theorists – Jacqueline Rose, for
instance (1986, p. 36) – she denounces the misleading
romance in assimilating the maternal body with the unrepressed. She exposes the 'relation between the theoretical
occulting of femininity by maternity and the engulfment of
the daughter by the mother' (Gallop, 1982, p. 114).

But what if, instead of being emancipatory, the down-
grading and refusal of motherhood was the ultimate in
phallocracy, the perpetuation of women's subjection? What
if the counter-view – to be found in some so-called French
Feminisms – was right? According to that view, the pre-
oedipal – the early symbiosis with the mother, undifferen-
tiation from her body, said to be a longer stage for the little
girl – is a source of power, not impairment. Women's
celebrated longer immersion in the pre-oedipal, which
Freud saw as archaic, as unknown to 'us' as 'the pre-
Minoan civilization before the civilization of Greece'
('Female Sexuality', 1931), is their strength. Or can be. It
means, in early Cixous, that the mother's body is imaginatively available, a source of writing. Fantasy here, interestingly, is not the realm of words as detached from reality but
the suppressed, the unconscious:

Let's look not at syntax but at fantasy, at the unconscious:
all the feminine texts I've read are very close to the voice,
very close to the flesh of language, much more so than
masculine texts. . . . There's *tactility* in the feminine text,
there's touch, and this touch passes through the ear.
Writing in the feminine is passing on what is cut out by
the Symbolic, the voice of the mother, passing on what is
most archaic. ('Castration or Decapitation', *Signs*, no. 7, Fall
1981).

Julia Kristeva's concept of the semiotic – as the irruption of
drives that have to do with the archaic body, closeness with
the mother's body, desire for incest with the mother – has
been much discussed and much used, and goes in the same
direction as Cixous. Neither Kristeva nor Cixous argues that
there ever could be language that would be all semiotic, or
feminine: the archaic would be only babble. Any language
is an interplay between the symbolic and the semiotic, even
if (like the language of science, or the law) it seems to leave
no room for the semiotic. But poetic, revolutionary or
'feminine' writing makes for a high incidence of unconscious impulses. It unleashes the repressed. It allows the
semiotic to erupt rather than keeping it at bay.

In her early work Irigaray also argues that what gets
repeatedly censored in women is the mother's body.
Women can profitably search for 'the imaginary and the
symbolic of intrauterine life and of the first bodily encounter
with the mother' (Irigaray, 1991, p. 39): through eroticism,
through writing. They can thus be redeemed from the
'darkness', the 'madness' in which they have been abandoned. For these French writers, different as they may be,
mother is most definitely *not* a 'figure of speech'. She is not
to be left to the 'cave beyond consciousness'. Indeed, to
refuse to explore the 'dark continent of the dark continent'

(as Irigaray calls it) – that is, the mother–daughter relationship – is to perpetuate an ancient repression, refuse one's own womanhood. Is this what Carter does, at least up to *Nights at the Circus*? Does she, in her rejection of the mother, produce another form of suppression?

My feeling is that she does. That she needed to do it, because she had such accounts to settle with the mother. (Things do change in *Nights at the Circus* and *Wise Children* – largely, I would venture, because of the experience of motherhood. But I will not draw that in: Carter kept her life too carefully away from her writing for me to want to trespass. 'Look! Don't touch!' Fevvers signals. If Carter rejected the 'femininity' of touch in favour of the eye, of display, of the confidence trick, I should take her at – face value? 'There is nothing like confidence' is the last phrase, Fevvers's, in *Nights at the Circus*.) My feeling also is that both *The Passion of New Eve* and *The Sadeian Woman* lend themselves so readily to being read as counter-tracts to French theory of the seventies – Lacan, Cixous in particular (Keenan, 1992) – that it is almost certain she knew exactly what she was doing. I once introduced Angela Carter to Hélène Cixous in London – they were doing a *mano a mano* – and Carter professed terror at the encounter. I now wonder whether her terror had something to do with coming face to face with what she had attacked.

Yet reflecting on seventies and eighties debates on *écriture féminine*, having felt initially certain that none of it could be found in Carter, I now wonder. . . .

Up to and excepting *Wise Children*, Carter's language is all wild sex and mind, with nothing in between. Breasts? Good Lord no. Guts – They creep in, in the later period. You couldn't have all that Rabelaisian stuff without, could you? No heart, but nominally. Nor womb, except surgically: technology and artifice. It occurs to me now that Joyce, who goes for the thingness of names, the materiality of language, who lets words mutate and beget of their own accord, allows in much more of the mother's body than Carter (and that is why he can be Cixous's nuncle as well as Carter's – they are after very different parts of him). Not that Carter doesn't have a wonderful ear. She can alliterate as well as the next person. But one word does not lead to another. One word can move without the other. Plot is continuously being invented. It does not proceed out of an internal necessity. Images do not grow out of their own momentum. Symbols (caves or colours) are not allowed to signify, except ironically, like the brand of the key on the bride's forehead at the end of 'The Bloody Chamber'. The Bloody Chamber itself is full of machinery: not the Red Deeps. Textuality is not allowed the initiative. Wit – mind – is in charge.

In all these senses, Carter does not write 'feminine' texts. No 'tactility', as Cixous puts it; no voice of the mother, no 'innermost touch'. No 'giving': 'Look, but don't touch!' (Fevvers). 'You can look if you pay': what Carter says Colette's texts are saying. No 'endlessness' (Cixous, 1981). No '"other meaning" always in the process of weaving itself, of embracing itself with words, but also of getting rid of words in order not to become fixed, congealed in them' (Irigaray, 1985, p. 29). Quite the reverse. Carter has a gift for the cryptic, the lapidary, the frozen. 'He had made himself the shrine of his own desires, had made of himself the only woman he could have loved!' (Eve about Tristessa, 1982, pp. 128–9).

Yet to my surprise, as I think more about it, in other ways she does. Cixous also describes a feminine text as 'wandering', full of excess, unpredictable, disturbing. This fits the bill. Irigaray advises the woman writer to accept being inside and doing mimicry, but as masquerade. This more than fits the bill: it seems to be a blueprint for what Carter does. As does Kristeva's plea for plurality, her endorsement of carnivalesque modes as *Polylogue*. . . .

Are they the modes of the daughter? Could they be those of the mother?

V   The Mother's Desire

The revolutionary gesture, for Irigaray, would not be to vent one's anger against the mother, nor to make her gallop to the rescue, wielding a (phallic?) pistol, but to allow the mother to be sexed: 'if mothers could be women, there would be a whole mode of a relationship of desiring speech between daughter and mother, son and mother' (Irigaray, 1991, p. 52).

Desire between daughter and mother, son and mother. I can't think of any examples in Carter's novels, though there's plenty of desire. Younger woman and older man, daughter and surrogate father, yes. Cousin and cousin, yes. Man–woman and woman–man, yes. All from the vantage point of the daughter. Mother's desire: no. In *Wise Children*, Saskia, an older woman who has an affair with her nephew, is much frowned upon. A baddie through and through. Not much sympathy, either, for Lady Margarine's infatuation for her brat of a son. Grandma is, *in extremis*, discovered to have had it off with Father Melchior, and desired to marry Uncle Peregrine. Dora is perfectly reconciled to Lady A, now Centenarian Wheelchair, having taken a tumble with Peregrine. But these sexed mothers are in the wings. The narrative never goes over to them. No daughter ever desires a mother, let alone a return to the archaic body. No mother is seen as desiring. Though at the very last, the trope appears. Shortly before her death, Carter made a TV film about the Christian story. Its Western iconography was presented as God's Family Album. God had taken the snapshots. The story ended cruelly with Michelangelo's *Pietà*, her beloved son's corpse in her arms. Was History, Carter's voice asked, fuelled by the Father's jealousy of the love between mother and son? 'O Ii-sis . . . und Osi-iris'. . . . We were getting close to myth. . . .

And yet, to be fair, I see, rereading *The Sadeian Woman*, that de Sade is criticised specifically for lacking the courage to admit that the maternal function could be 'corrupted into the experience of sexual pleasure and so be set free' (p. 128). Eugénie may dare to attack her mother: she remains a prisoner of the father's authority. Yet in her own fiction – except *in extremis*, as I said, when Grandma Chance is discovered on page 223 of *Wise Children* to be both mother *and* sexed – Carter never explores that freedom she blamed de Sade for not allowing. But perhaps having done it *in extremis* is enough? It makes me sad to reflect that in her presentation of the dead son in the mother's arms, in Michelangelo's *Pietà*, Carter was displacing what she knew was coming: the death of the mother herself. And the son's *Pietà*.

VI

I think that myths are great stories. Inexhaustible sources. If they are lies, it is only in so far as they are stories, or as we freeze them into gendered meanings.

The more cultures we look at, the more infinite the permutations of the mother. And the father.

The idea that I live in a postmodern world does nothing for me. I do not believe that technology is women's great ally, as Carter has claimed, nor that artificial reproduction is going to liberate me (helpful as contraception is). Freedom will come from getting to a state of balance between inner and outer. Self and shadow. Me and world.

I see our relation to the mother as our attempt to navigate between our need for closeness and our need for independence. The father is consciousness, and what structures the need. The mother is our tussle with reality, the reason why we endlessly attempt to make sense of the world. Desire for the mother fuels us. The father compels us, and enables us, to let go. The mother is earth, water. Materiality, feeling. The father is air, fire. Thought, inspiration, light. The mother is what enables me to think my relation with the earth. The father, with the sky. I don't care twopence about binaries. Or hierarchies. One doesn't move without the other. There is no model of creation that humans have invented, artistic or otherwise, which is not in some way bisexual. Even 'gender trouble' feminists most opposed to maternal thinking keep talking about the *matrix* of a position. One may object to the institutional use to which our doubleness, and sexual complementariness, are put. To motherhood being the means to the subjection of women. It doesn't mean that the baby should be thrown out with the bath water. If there is creation, the mother is there somewhere. If I wish to exterminate her, tear her to pieces, it's because she's there. If I am here, it's because she's been there.

There is such a thing as the unconscious. There is an unconscious in any creative text. I haven't gone looking for it much in Carter, except as a tussle with the mother that changes with time and experience, but there is much that could be said about the unconscious in her texts.

Where does this leave me?

I have spent years, through dreams, analysis of dreams, wide-ranging reading and looking at paintings, through relationships, through writing: looking for the mother. It's been a great surprise to me that I should need to go on such a quest. I always thought I had more problems with the father. But it wasn't so. It's been an even greater surprise to discover, and begin to accept, that I wasn't going to find her. Not because she was a figure of speech. Nor because she has retreated to a cave beyond consciousness. We can go to the caves beyond consciousness. Where id was, there ego can be. But the quest for mother seems to lead me to acceptance of her absence. I do not know whether this is what they call separation. By chance, I come across this, from Michèle Roberts, whom I would have thought would be at the antipodes of Angela Carter, in *The Wild Girl*:

> So this . . . was the Mother, of whom I had so
> complaisantly sung before I knew her properly. . . . She
> was an absence – with no division between night and
> day. . . . I crawled . . . believing this to be the moment of
> my death. (Roberts, 1984, no. 1, pp. 115–6)

How bizarre, I thought, hearing an echo of the end of *The Passion of New Eve*, that the wish to destroy the fiction of maternity, and the wish to find the mother, should end at the same point! But is it the same point? And is it an ending?

Reflecting on the course I have travelled, writing out what has been in my mind for so long – some of it, at any rate, since I have travelled alongside Angela Carter for so many years – I find this:

It is no accident that the books of hers that I have been able to love should be the late ones. They are the books in which Carter begins to negotiate a different relation to the mother. One of accident – Grandma *Chance*. Of metonymy: the old crone by the seaside Eve finds at the end of her passion is just there, singing, the forerunner of other strange figures to come in later books. It is also a relation of acceptance.

In *Wise Children* Dora recognises the limits of what she does. The narrator is no longer taking on the world, and subverting it. Dora quotes Jane Austen: 'Let other pens dwell on guilt and misery.' She acknowledges the limits of carnival. The war was 'no carnival, not the hostilities. No carnival' (p. 163). As World War I killed Mrs Ramsay the mother, in the 'Time Passes' section of *To the Lighthouse*, so does World War II kill Grandma Chance, as time is swiftly passed over. The Time of Shakespeare's *The Winter's Tale* hovers here also: but it is their decision to clear Grandma Chance's room of its possessions, and paint it white for a nursery, that propels the old sisters back into life, just as it is the two old cleaning women, Mrs Bates and Mrs McNabb, in Woolf, who begin to revive the house.

No doubt knowledge of Carter's ensuing death makes me sentimentalise this book, but let that be – I'll stand by that. I sense that Carter, feeling the end coming, jumped with both feet over tragedy, and landed in Shakespeare's late plays. Infra dig, backstage, and on the wrong side of the blankets, of course. There are joyful, as ever subversive, resolutions: resurrections, long-lost daughters and sons finally recognised by long-lost or denying fathers or recognising undetected mothers. Dora does register, though, that it is other people's tragedies that make our comedies.

Jungians (and Winnicottians?) say that out of maturation, the internalisation of mother and father in us, the child can at last be born. And play. How strange, I think, that Carter, having spent her writing career so resolutely subverting fathers and mothers, should end it with the birth, and adoption, of wise children by playful parents. . . . Jung talks of the *divine child*. Carter answers: wise, not divine; and plural. Carnivalesque to the last.

But here I touch her.

And want to play.

New New World Dreams:
Angela Carter and Science Fiction

....

ROZ KAVENEY

Distinctions have to be made, but they often reveal contradictions and complexities; the moment you draw an edge between two adjacent ideas, it blurs back into vagueness.

Angela Carter was at no time a science-fiction writer, but she wrote several stories for one of the major British science-fiction magazines, and rather regretted never having published in the most important of the others. Angela Carter was not a science-fiction writer, but she made free use of tropes deriving from science fiction; she was not a science-fiction writer, but she was Guest of Honour at SF conventions and taught writing to a number of young and later influential figures in the SF world. She was one of the crucial influences on a whole generation of British SF writers, yet she was never a writer of science fiction.

It is necessary to make this point repeatedly, because this essay is not trying to claim her work for the genre; that would be to impose on it a set of restraints which would be fundamental betrayals of the freedom, the openness of discourse, which was one of the crucial descriptions of her fiction. There is a history in science-fiction studies of ill-judged attempts to annex to the genre writers whose relationship with it was more tenuous than identity; this is not one of those attempts.

Angela Carter had very little interest in the hardware of

science-fiction and genre fantasy; it is not clear how much of the older material she ever bothered to read. She never specifically said that rockets and blasters, or swords and the controlled magic of sorcerers, were rather tedious boy's games, but she managed, in general, to give that impression. What she liked in science fiction was the freedom it gave its practitioners rather than the dictates of tradition and the market that went with those freedoms – the freedom to play with causality and to regard character in a way less linked to Leavisite moral fictions or a bourgeois myth of identity which is three-dimensional and self-determined.

Carter was keen on expressing the mutability of individuality; *The Passion of New Eve* (1977) *The Infernal Desire Machines of Doctor Hoffman* (1972) and *Heroes and Villains* (1969) all address this more or less directly – the changes through which their protagonists are put are remorseless, one might almost say sadistic in their intensity. One need hardly point out that these are the three novels in which Carter most clearly uses the tropes of SF and genre fantasy. Meanwhile, the two novels in which the protagonists are entirely centred on who they are are novels whose protagonists are performers; In *Nights at the Circus* Fevvers's identity is, of course, founded on a particularly complex double-bluff of pretending to be a fake version of what she is already. Even here, though, the process of education through which her reporter lover is put to make him a fit juvenile lead has a strong relationship with the plots of the earlier novels.

Character is always provisional, whether you are a socialist, a feminist, or a postmodernist; Carter was all three. For a number of reasons – sometimes to do with the limited or skewed talents of some of its practitioners, sometimes to do with a conscious pursuit of the idea as hero, sometimes out of deliberate wilfulness – character in science fiction has often been up for grabs. (One of the principal bones of contention in recent years between Movement cyberpunks like Bruce Sterling and William Gibson on the one hand and New Humanists like Kim Stanley Robinson has been this very question, with Sterling accusing Robinson of attempting to water down the integrity of the genre by re-establishing in it the entirely untenable bourgeois notion of the individual. Robinson has in turn responded with novels almost aggressively inhabited by three-dimensional characters in which the vision of social forces interacting with character is tragically powerful; *Red Mars* and its sequels are among the best work the genre has ever produced. Much of the rest of the best SF is, of course, entirely otherwise.)

While the British New Wave SF of the sixties regularly mocked the older pulp tradition for its thinness of fictional texture generally, of which two-dimensional characterisation was often a symptom, intensity of characterisation was never necessarily part of its own project. J. G. Ballard, for example, deals almost entirely in archetypes, in stern British and American administrators trying to cope with the hearts of darkness into which apocalyptic events plunge them; Michael Moorcock's *Jerry Cornelius* novels started as a jokey transposition of his earlier Sword and Sorcery material into techno-thriller terms, and became a far more complex game in which the unchanging masks of the characters in his commedia dell'arte stock company were used to demonstrate the unchanging pursuit of class and establishment interests, or for a formalist harlequinade of sexual contentions.

Carter regularly expressed her admiration for New Wave SF and for two of the three major writers who came out of it, Ballard and Moorcock. Unlike a lot of critics, she did not regard their genre roots as an embarrassing past folly – on the contrary, when she reviewed Ballard's *Empire of the Sun* she specifically mocked in advance the people who would suddenly notice his major status in this mainstream work[1] when they could have spotted it as early as *The Atrocity Exhibition* or his various novels of apocalypse. Similarly, when she praised Moorcock's *Mother London*, it was as much as anything else the sheer fecundity of Moorcock that she admired, a fecundity[2] which included his potboiling but often excellent fantasy trilogies as much as the more careful work[3] for which he won awards.

Carter also expressed admiration for the work of less well-known New Wave figures like John Sladek, whose *Candide*-like picaresques about a robot – *Roderick* and *Roderick at Random* – are too little known.[4] This was not merely generosity of response, though it was that as well; it was an expression of the view that there were people who were doing something with narrative parallel to what she wanted to do. The New Wave were guerrillas of interior landscapes, like the Surrealists, but not as obsessed with putting women in their proper place; they were, in brief, on her side. The relationship between the New Wave and sections of the experimentalist mainstream was, in any case, rather close; Hilary Bailey was at different times co-editor of *New Worlds* and of *Bananas*. Carter later expressed regret that she had written only for the latter, not for the former, and wrote for *Interzone*, the principal British SF magazine of later years, during its earlier phase when a collective, of which I was one, tried to ride the horses of genre and experimentalism simultaneously.

SF, then, is something of a coalition of overlapping interest groups; Carter's work was not necessarily going to appeal to those whose main interest was making propaganda for technological improvememt, or recycling power fantasies of the saving of the world or the destruction of seventeen species of stroppy alien. Much of that readership, though, whatever attracted it to the genre in the first place, has stayed in place because of a fascination with the painted stage that the obsessions of the creators of the genre have built; SF and genre fantasy have their admirably formalist aspect, where iconic material is shuffled in pleasing patterns, with something new added from time to time as an improving spice.

The formalist aspects of Carter's work – the extent to which she combined stock motifs and made of them a collage that was entirely her own – was bound to appeal; sections of the SF readership discovered in the course of the 1970s and 1980s that they had been talking postmodernism all their lives and not noticing it, and Carter was a part of that moment (along with such writers as Russell Hoban, Alastair Gray and Ian Sinclair[5]). What Carter did not possess, did not want and did not need was the strong sense of historical personal involvement with all the wonderful gaudy nonsense of space opera, time travel, and the rest of it; she was selective in her fascinations.

The iconic material she was prepared to use herself was for the most part that whch could be most easily reconciled with her passion for Surrealism or her political preoccupations. Fictional apocalypses are prettier than the real kind, and in Carter's work there is often a passion for ruins. Sometimes the parallels between Carter and the work of genre writers are not so much mutual influences or borrowings as arriving at the same solutions to similar problems; Carter used, and enjoyed using, a whole armament of slick plot tricks like the scam around Fevvers's identity – not because of the parallels with a variety of similar devices surrounding mutants and monsters in pulp SF and horror, but because it really was an old trick which might just work.

An important part of Carter's quiver of fictional devices

was setting up a stock narrative gambit and then confounding or subverting it. Much of the time this was combined with elements of bawdy, slipping into a mode which one can call carnivalesque without necessarily meaning by that exactly what Bakhtin did; equally, this process was often ideological in tendency, and what was being subverted was specifically bourgeois or patriarchal ideology. The fairy-tale versions of *The Bloody Chamber* and later are all good examples of this; 'In Pantoland' indicates that Carter saw this less as postmodernism than as a continuation of the McGillian class humour of the British past. It should never be forgotten that SF was only one of the sources from which she occasionally took the things she needed. When she does handle SF material directly, it is likely to be in this way, continually criticising, by refusals of standard closures, the implicit ideology of the conventions of that to which she is also paying homage. *Heroes and Villains* is a version of the post-apocalyptic novels of the fifties, in which an older sort of decline-of-civilisation novel which goes back to Mary Shelley's *The Last Man* (1826) or Richard Jefferies's *After London* (1885) is blended with specific fears that it is our own civilisation whose distorted tatters will be handed down among radioactive ruins. The Cold War fifties were a golden age for novels about the aftermath of atomic war and other collapses, both inside and outside the SF world; one can oversimplify this issue, but English examples tended to be about return to a safer pastoral existence, 'back, beyond our father's land'; while American examples tended to be far more about a continuation of legitimacy – Walter Miller's *A Canticle for Leibowitz* (1960), with its monks making illuminated copies of electronic schematics, is the obvious prototype.

It is almost beside the point whether Carter had actually read much of this material, or absorbed it as the air which one then breathed; *Heroes and Villains* is a book which participates in these debates. Where many such novels would have set up the opposition between the Professors and the Soldier caste who either serve or rule them according to one's perspective, or that between both and the barbarously vulnerable Barbarians, as a satirical comic inferno, Carter treats the opposition in far more literary terms. Where mutants in, say, John Wyndham's *The Chrysalids* (1955) are an encoded description of a variety of pariah elites, including both the obvious minorities and, by implication, the minority enlightened enough to read fictions of this kind, Carter uses her mutants as decor or for touches of entirely literary pathos. Fantasies of the decline of civilisation, she argues through this novel, can usefully be viewed as related both to pastoral and to clergy. The ruins and overgrown paths among which her characters wander are a speaking, a moralised, landscape in which even the city exists almost entirely as a place made up of decorative streets and buildings rather than as the moral community for which it normally stands in her work; the shifts of loyalty and perspective which dominate the narrative are as complex as – perhaps explicitly echo – those in Sir Philip Sidney's *Arcadia*.

Carter is also paralleling the post-apocalyptic visions of Surrealists such as Ernst, whose paintings found their way, by one of those coincidences which is no coincidence at all, on to the jacket covers of the equally apocalyptic novels of Ballard – *The Crystal World*, for example. She is interested in the literary effect of glittering vistas, rather than in the stock genre fantasies of historical decline and renaissance; if she is preaching a moral lesson, it has to do with something other than fantasies of resurgent empire-building.

The strutting rascals among whom her heroine throws her lot are doomed by their own nature and by history, and the dying fall with which the novel ends, the offstage slaughter of Marianne's Barbarian lover Jewel, is a troubled hint of what is to come. The Soldiers and Professors are seen as an essentially sterile culture – Marianne's father is writing a book on the archaeology of social theory which no one will ever read. It might almost be Casaubon's *Key to All Mythologies*. This sterility is the very opposite of Miller's monks in *Canticle for Leibowitz*, his mockery of whom is gentle and, in a sense, incidental; it should be remembered that Miller's Catholic triumphalism sees the Church as an *effective* guardian of knowledge and hierarchy.

Carter's feminist anarchism is ruthless in its debunking. Where Sidney was programmatically preaching the virtues of civilisation and politeness as against the rabble whom his noble heroes mutilate, Carter's sense is that civilisation is as sterile in its way as the Barbarians are in theirs – that the only hope lies with Marianne or with Mrs Green, Jewel's matriarch foster mother, to become whose equivalent Marianne aspires at the end of the novel.

Some critics have seen the sometimes violent sexuality of this novel as essentially retrograde and involved in rape fantasies; they are, I think, ignoring the whole for the part. Marianne is drawn to the glamour of Jewel and the lost, roaring boys of whom he is the leader, but the glamour wears thin. The novel starts with her being in disgrace for knocking down the son of the Professor of Mathematics who, in a game, spends so much time boasting that he, as warrior, is about to kill her, as Barbarian, that he becomes vulnerable to her; it ends with Marianne surviving her lover and finding a new sense of herself as matriarch – 'I'll be the tiger lady and rule them with a rod of iron'. She is also, of course, identifying with the child whom the shaman Donally tried to tattoo into tigerhood and killed in the process; Marianne will not die, but triumph. To state this baldly, and make it as convincing as Carter does, is to refuse the details of power fantasy while instilling its force; even in 1969, the tactics of Carter's later, explicitly feminist work were well in hand.

This is a Marianne who will rule by her own wit rather than by inheritance or marriage; her lover is dead, and the two elder mage figures who have instructed her have gone as well. Her name has always implicitly reminded us of Miranda in *The Tempest*. Jewel was as much Caliban rapist as ingénu wooer, and neither her father nor Donally is a particularly credible or creditable Prospero; all she is left with as companion is Mrs Green, perhaps a little too sensible to be Sycorax, and the last thing Donally's tortured familiar does in the novel is lapse, after describing Jewel's death, into silence. There are parallels with *The Tempest* here, parallels evoked in order to refuse them; with them, of course, she refused the parallels to *The Tempest* from which *Forbidden Planet*, that most famous of 1950s Hollywood SF movies, constructed itself.

Save only for this: Jewel, like so many other male characters in Carter's work, is clearly a Creature from the Id.

Heroes and Villains takes place after, and therefore outside, time; her second apocalyptic novel, *The Passion of New Eve*, is far more a novel of its time, both in its sense of sexual dissent and its sense of the troubles that Amerika was brewing up for itself. It shares with Ballard that sense of the American deserts as places of dark and menacing Romance; this is a savage America, whose fall is a Great Burning.[6] The slight romanticisation of guerrilla violence has its links with the apocalyptic strain of William Burroughs, also a man with a desert fixation; and the use of that sort of urban legend which masquerades as scabrous insider gossip – the iconic Hollywood goddess who is really a drag queen – overlaps with Burroughs as well.

In the earlier chapters of the novel, Evelyn is hardly literally an innocent; he is, however, an innocent in that he is an Englishman in the United States. There is a long tradition of British novels, from Dickens through Waugh to Lodge and Bradbury, which treat the Englishmen in America as a Candide-like punching bag for the awfulness of transatlantic cousins; it is typical of Carter to use a trope most associated with precisely that sort of toothless blokeish satire she loathed for such entirely different purposes. It is necessary that Evelyn be in some ways an innocent so that he can become a tabula rasa on which Eve, the new self he becomes, can be written. It is also necessary that he be treated as innocent because he is being set up and must enter freely of his own accord (leaving a little of the happiness he brings?) – even the black militants, in the middle of their war with the white state, hear his cut-glass vowels and let him go. Above all, it is necessary that he be an innocent to begin with so that Eve, stripped of his original sins of masculinity and its carelessnesses and sel-fishnesses, can be doubly innocent. She is the sacrificial lamb, stripped of sin so that she can be victimised by everybody else's; she is also the innocent simply because it is to her that things and environments proceed to happen. When Eve ceased to be a man, she ceased to be an agent in her own story – other women may actively pursue their own desires and needs, but the most she ever manages is to escape from one mess into another. Novels modelled on Candide describe processes of education; this is what they have in common with picaresque novels, novels about rogues, and why both tend towards that episodic structure named after the latter.

The book's essentially picareque structure, in which Eve/Evelyn moves from one set of skewed social circumstances to another, has a certain amount in common with a whole generation of writers of what Brian W. Aldiss called 'comic infernos', satirical extrapolations of current trends, like Frederik Pohl and C. M. Kornbluth. The difference between this sort of thing and Swift, from whom it fairly clearly derives, is one of technique – or, to be more precise, it is the technique of the third book of *Gulliver's Travels* rather than that of the other three; we are not taken through an endless proliferation of details – strange societies are merely sketched in for our benefit, and we become imaginative tourists there rather than inhabitants. The decaying New York of the early chapters is a matter of generalisations and telling details rather than a clear and precise landscape; it is the backdrop to Evelyn's instruction in the alchemy which is to be the pervading science of the novel, and the betrayal of Leilah which is to have been his great sin. The deranged fundamentalist child soldiers who kill Tristessa are the sort of telling satirical conceit which would have been less effective at greater length – they are a comic inferno device, used for other purposes – as a way of denying Eve the happiness which is almost within her grasp, and educating her about the realities of life.

Zero is a more complex piece of satire, and arguably a less generic one. The sort of survivalism he represents, particularly in its gross violence and misogyny, has become – largely since 1977, when the novel was written – a particularly unpleasant feature of one strain of SF. It is not especially likely that Carter was aware of such earlier examples of it as Heinlein's *Farnham's Freehold*, let alone of the actual survivalist movements with which this particular, unpleasing sub-genre is complexly involved. Zero is an unholy cross between the macho littérateur and Charles Manson, on whose domestic manners Zero's treatment of his harem is presumably based. And Manson, of course, found congenial reflection of his ideas in the actions of the messiah of a previous Heinlein novel, *Stranger in a Strange Land*. The relationship between Carter and genre SF is not always a matter of her having read or thought about specific books; it is that she was interested in those aspects of the culture where ideas from SF were liable to make their mark.

Life in Zero's ménage is a nightmare representation of male desire and the sort of complicity in one's own oppression, identification with the oppressor, which some people refer to as the Stockholm Syndrome. If this is in some ways the most memorable section of the book, it is because it is the point at which satirical extrapolation of the political most aptly overlaps with the carefully delineated personal. What stops Carter ever looking like a radical feminist, rather than a radical and a feminist, is a sense of irony and perspective, and the complexity that lends her. Zero's passionate hatred of lesbianism goes along with a desire for a harem that involves turning a blind eye to what goes on in his harem at night. Eve's desperate fear that Zero might perceive her as a former man leads to an over-acting of the feminine that makes him worry that she is lesbian.

The further irony, of course, is, that Zero's ultimate fear fantasy is of the Hollywood star Tristessa, whom he believes to be a supernatural super-dyke whose celluloid glance has sterlised him. Tristessa is the perfect mimic of endured female suffering, and a man; it is Eve's preparedness to escape endured situations as soon as she can which is, perhaps, for Carter the indication of the reality of her transformation. There are interesting parallels between all this and the essay in *Nothing Sacred*, 'Lorenzo the Closet-Queen' in which Carter argues that D. H. Lawrence's fetishistic obsession with descriptions of women's clothes is a sort of transferred transvestism; Carter's world-view is one in which the remarks of the voguers in *Paris is Burning* that three-piece suits are drag as much as sequin frocks is almost a truism.

The Passion of New Eve is a novel which might have been expected to end in a utopian vision of sexual equality or transcendence that would parallel, or redeem, the various sexual hells it has shown us earlier. Carter refuses standard literary and generic closures; she is not one for telling us what to do or what to believe – the moment of happiness between Eve and Tristessa, brutally terminated by the boy soldiers, is, it turns out, about as good as it gets. Eve meets Leilah again, and they get on; she crawls into caves in an attempt to find Leilah's mother, her own ideologically motivated surgeon, and the ensuing Night Journey is some sort of return to the mother, but not a very satisfactory one. Since it is not clear whether or not Eve is pregnant, it is not clear whether the 'place of birth' to which she refers to herself as journeying in the last line is the place where she will be born yet again, or the place where she will give birth, or both. This is a novel of open discourse, in which we ultimately have to devise our understanding for ourselves.

Carter's occasional uses of SF material, and her constant use of material in which genre fantasy tries to claim a proprietary interest, made her one of the non-genre figures that fans and writers from the notoriously inward-looking SF genres tended to read. Her habit of revisionist engagement, in her fiction as much as in her reviews and polemics, with orthodoxies she found offensively bourgeois, sexist or reactionary, was congenial to such readers, used as they were to the sort of polemical echoing standard in SF, and to a lesser extent in other fantasy genres.[7] She was, simply, a writer who – many such readers felt – was on their side, and who to some extent talked their language; in conversation, and on panels, she was interested in, and interesting

about, SF ways of handling story material however different
her own preoccupations.

This in turn meant that she was available as an influence
on the SF and fantasy of the last two decades. Perhaps the
most obvious influence is that of *The Bloody Chamber*, which
set the tone for a whole sub-literature of revisionist fairy
tales, but has been especially influential on two of the best-
selling fantasists in the literature. There are other obvious
influences on Terry Pratchett, for example – Wodehouse
being his master in matters of farce plotting – but the
particular stroppy attitude to the clichés of fantasy and
other literatures which has made Pratchett so successful at
the very least parallels Carter. Comic conceits such as the
one in *Witches Abroad*, where story is seen as a force of the
universe, like gravity, compelling events to fit various
narrative patterns, such as the story of Cinderella, have a
close family relationship with conceits like those in late
Carter stories like 'The Ghost Ships' and 'In Pantoland'.
Postmodernism is the air both writers breathe, and Pratchett
is perhaps the only comic fantasist who has seen the comic
potential of Vladimir Propp's theory of folk tale as assem-
blage of modules – his light commercial comedies share
with Carter's more serious work a sense of the importance
of mediating, balancing with each other, the enquiries of
the intellect and the certainties of common sense. It is
perhaps also from Carter that Pratchett acquired his taste
for writing about tough old women of overpowering presence and good sense; there is more in common between
Pratchett's witches and the ex-showgirl narrator of *Wise
Children* than one might at first glance suppose.

Tanith Lee is perhaps better known in the USA than in
Britain, in spite of being a British author; it is noticeable that
her tales have started to appear in anthologies of fairy tales
such as Lurie's and Zipes's without quite the acknowledge-

ment on the part of those editors of her solid roots in the publishing category and social milieu of genre SF and fantasy. Lee was productively influenced by *The Bloody Chamber*, an influence which is still working its way out in her work – the *Dark Dance* sequence shares with Carter a sense of South London, portrayed with a vividness that transforms the mundane into the mythicised, as well as of distinctly perverse sexual and dynastic relationships. Lee's own first book of revisionist fairy tales, *Red as Blood*, is perhaps rather too pat in the way it takes Carter's technique of re-examination and uses it for slick commercial magazine fiction; yet at its best she had learned from Carter how to combine with the twists of reinterpreted plot stylistic gambits that twine around them. The title story, for example, takes a slick insight – Snow White has skin white as snow, hair black as night, and lips red as blood, and tends to hang out in a coffin; therefore she is a vampire, QED – and works the conceit through in a diction which might seem sentimentalised decadence, until we realise that what is on offer in the closing sequence is a Wildean pastiche in which the awakening Prince is a redeeming Christ. Later tales in this vein, like the much-anthologised 'Bite me Not, or Fleur de Fur', become ever stranger and more convoluted in their combination of elements – *The Masque of the Red Death* and semi-intelligent vampire angels, in that particular case. Lee lacks Carter's controlling good sense, but has her own interesting extremist sensibility. What can be argued fairly strongly is that the revisionist feminist approach to stock material which is part of Carter's legacy, though not hers alone, came at a point at which Lee was at some risk of never escaping the role of hack crown princess of heroic fantasy which early success had forced on her; and that the growing integrity of her later work owes much to Carter's example. Carter's example also demonstrated how

a perverse sensibility could be united with formalist ele-
gance, rather than left to flop all over the page in native
freedom; Lee's work became tighter and terser than the
wish-fulfilment dynastic fantasies with which she had her
early success.

The Carter heroine, sensible, sassy and resourceful, came
along at the right time to help young SF and fantasy writers
think about the difficult and necessary task of establishing
strong female protagonists in a form that had traditionally
provided its power fantasies in a distinctly gender-biased
fashion. Marianne and Fevvers – often combined with their
cousins of the heart, Moorcock's tough aviatrixes and
adventuresses – have given rise to an extensive group of
homages and thefts. The heroines of a whole group of more
recent British writers – Colin Greenland, Geoff Ryman,
Mary Gentle, Neil Gaiman – would not have been the same
had they not admired, and taken notes from Carter. John
Clute has argued, his tone mingled with serious concern at
the drift towards sentimentalisation of the implied voice,
that these heroines – these Temporal Adventuresses – are,
for good and ill, one of the particular resonances of the
British SF of the late 1980s and early 1990s. Whatever the
indulgence of authors somewhat in love with their heroines,
this is a valuable corrective in genres whose ruthless examination of orthodoxies too often in the past, in the matter of
sex and gender, left a lot of stones quite aggressively
unturned. The other thing which has to be said about her
effect on this group is simply that she set an example of
how cliché could be avoided, of taking genre material and –
not only for polemical purposes – making it new. Far more
widely than through direct contact as teacher, fellow-
panellist or acquaintance. Carter was for a lot of English
writers in the SF/fantasy field – particularly women and
other members of out-groups – an example of what the

writer's career could be, of the possibility of combining seriousness with play, of the seriousness *of* play.

At a panel to discuss her legacy specially arranged for the Easter Convention immediately following her death, it was noticeable how many of those present were unable to speak for their sorrow; some of the most voluble people in a field noted for loud and annoying authors were inarticulate with sobs. While people were saddened when, say, Philip K. Dick or Fritz Leiber died, there was nothing like this public manifestation of personal grief, even in the SF community. This grief had its origins partly in Carter's physical presence at the edges of the social world SF is when it is not being a literary genre. She was, on occasion, directly involved in teaching creative writing to people from the SF world. Three of the original *Interzone* collective – including its current editor, David Pringle – were part of a group whom she and John Sladek taught at Lumb Bank in 1979. Simon Ounsley, another *Interzone* collective member, recalls how he produced a comic fantasy novel of less than excellent execution and Carter, having endlessly corrected its many weaknesses, none the less agreed, on the last night, to read aloud six pages of it, and no more.

> 'I chose the best bit, of course, and Carter read it – no, better, *performed* it – with astonishing vigour. It was as though she were reading from her favourite book, not from some scrappy unfinished novel she couldn't abide. People sat around laughing. And in all the right places Carter extracted every ounce of wit and irony from the threadbare lines.
>
> 'And then, when she had got through the six pages, she stopped, in mid-sentence, just as she had promised. People groaned. They did not exactly implore her to go on, but they did ask politely.
>
> '"No," she declared emphatically, "I shall not read

another word of this utter rubbish!" and she flung the manuscript down upon the table in front of her. . . .

'I was grinning all over my face. Somehow Carter's declaration had come as the perfect end. . . . It was almost as if she had become one of the characters in the novel. Melodramatic. Larger than life. It had been a generous performance.'

Terry Pratchett says of Carter: 'She had an intelligence that radiated for twenty-five metres around her', and 'a way of looking which made you feel that whatever you were going to say next had better be interesting.' All the conversations I have had with people in the SF world who knew her include that slight sense of the dangerous; Carter was a fabulously likable person, but never an easy one. Her relationship with the SF world was in some ways a difficult one, and an unreadiness to suffer fools gladly was sometimes to her advantage in those dealings. Irritation at and involvement with a world are no more incompatible than the deep affection and slight sense of terror Angela Carter inspired in most of the people in the SF world who knew her.

The Dangerous Edge[1]

ELAINE JORDAN

> And through all the nine years which followed I did
> nothing but wander here and there in the world, trying to
> be spectator rather than actor in all the comedies which
> were being played there; and reflecting particularly in each
> matter on what might render it doubtful and give occasion
> for error, I rooted out from my mind, during this time, all
> the errors which had introduced themselves into it hitherto
> . . . . trying to discover the falseness or uncertainty of the
> propositions I examined, not with weak guesses, but with
> clear and assured reasonings, I found none so doubtful that
> I could not draw from it some sufficiently certain
> conclusion, even if this might not be other than that the
> proposition contained nothing certain.
>
> (René Descartes, *Discourse on Method*)

> The habit of sardonic contemplation is the hardest habit of
> all to break.
>
> (Angela Carter, *The Infernal Desire Machines of Doctor
> Hoffman*)

'Our interest's on the dangerous edge of things': infested
with citations from an English literary education, I've
always liked this one from Browning's 'Bishop Blougram's
Apology'. Angela Carter's writing, which I encountered in
the late 1970s with *The Passion of New Eve* and *The Sadeian
Woman*, worked a risky edge, political and literary. This is

why it continues to give pleasure and provocation. It's an enterprise and achievement of its own kind, individually and historically marked, of sharp, luxuriant skill, which is of major significance both in late-twentieth-century writing and to feminism (I mean enterprise in the heroic as much as the commercial sense). The awkward place in which I find myself as an admirer – caught between the dictates of censors and less-than-liberal libertarians – is also a place in which feminism finds itself.

Judith Butler's *Gender Trouble* has had considerable influence in disseminating theoretical arguments which deconstruct the opposition between what is 'natural' and what is 'artificial', which is embedded in our language and ways of thought, but not universal. These arguments are already implicit and explored in Carter's writing over three decades. Copying is what we do, in language, culturally, and in unconscious identifications; but copies, or impersonations, are not identical to originals, and the originals cannot be finally traced and end-stopped. This is both corrupting and hopeful, conservative and transgressive, creative. Recently Butler said, of the conservatism and subversiveness within feminism, that although the kind of feminism represented by Catharine MacKinnon should not be demonised, nor her intellectual strength denied, she

> has become so powerful as the public spokesperson for feminism internationally, that feminism is going to have to start producing some powerful alternatives to what she's saying and doing. . . . [T]he paradigm of victimisation, the over-emphasis on pornography, the cultural insensitivity . . . has to be countered by strong feminist positions.[2]

Angela Carter's essays and fictions always did counter these tendencies, with which feminism has recently been too much identified, without ignoring the abuses that give rise to them. Her vital criticism of feminism from the inside is one reason why the assessment of her work by John Bayley, written within a month or so of her death, is so obtuse, if not worse:

> Indeed if there is a common factor in the elusive category of the postmodern novel it is political correctness: whatever spirited arabesques and feats of descriptive imagination Carter may perform she always comes to rest in the right ideological position. . . . 'Every woman's tragedy is that after a certain age she looks like a female impersonator' [*Wise Children*]. One of Carter's chief talents has been to help create a new kind of persona for real women to copy. The Carter girl of the Eighties, with her sound principles, earthy humor, and warm heart, has become a recognizable type: in a sense all too recognizable, for if you are not like that by nature you have to work hard at maintaining the pose. . . . Carter's achievement shows how a certain style of good writing has politicized itself today, constituting itself as the literary wing of militant orthodoxy.[3]

Bayley takes a look at the talent, then asks 'would her fictions invite a second reading or does the vitality die in the performance?'. It's clear that he thinks the second death is unavoidable, or wants to make it so. His review, rather obsessively concerned with *Love* at the expense of later work, sets up yet again his personal authority as a well-tempered critic, but the put-down of Carter is vicious, in its partial incomprehension as well as its intent to deprecate as soon as possible any 'inflation' of her reputation, and readership. A new Addison here, who would damn with faint praise and teach the rest to sneer.[4]

It's a nasty piece of work to deal with. 'Talent' and, elsewhere, 'brand' set my teeth on edge, but to explain why

I think these terms of advertising management and market-ing expertise demean Angela Carter's achievement, I'd have to negotiate the fact that as a worker in the market she would not have pretended superiority to the rest of us, working too long in this condition, while critical of the conditions – who wouldn't be? And what can I do to resist Bayley's assessment of her as exemplary of 'the literary wing of militant orthodoxy', when my first impulse to write about her work was in opposition to some Marx-ish and radical feminist critiques, which argued that far from being politically correct, she reinscribed patriarchy, no less?[5]

In *Women in the House of Fiction*, Lorna Sage notes Carter's reservations about the influential 'Madwoman in the Attic' style of feminist literary critique, whereby madness (dis-ability? deviance? ineffectual anger?) can be seen as 'subver-sion'.[6] In a similar spirit Mandy Merck, in *Perversions*, questions feminist melodrama – for example, Gloria Stei-nem's reduction of Marilyn Monroe's beauty and achieve-ments to an exemplary suffering in which all can share: 'suffering, in melodrama, is itself evidence of merit'.[7] You could compare the degraded cult of Diana, the Sad Princess of romance, not the classical stern hunter with her own laws. Carter's analysis of Justine the good girl, in *The Sadeian Woman* (pp. 54–7), was a foundation for my feminism: like the bolt of lightning which finally puts de Sade's Justine out of her virtuous misery, it surprised me out of some self-defeating attitudes, especially the habit of wanting to be the innocent and well-intentioned party by established stan-dards, not the active initiator of anything for other reasons, or reasons of one's own. Justine in *The Sadeian Woman*, like Mignon in *Nights at the Circus*, is associated with 'Marilyn Monroe' as a cult figure, one which includes a self-mocking attitude to the comedy of sexual norms (see 'The Blonde as Clown', *The Sadeian Woman*, pp. 63–71).

Carter suggests that the virtue of the Justine figure is defined negatively, by not-enjoying; and her protest is passive, a constant hope that there will be someone to rescue her (*The Sadeian Woman*, p. 54). To say this doesn't undermine resistance to the actual victimisation of women, or to the more general and covert cultural elements which sustain it. It does resist a feminism which overemphasises an identity for women as victims who must always appeal to a higher authority, the law, the state. 'The lion will never lie down with the lamb. . . . The lamb must learn to run with the tigers' (*The Bloody Chamber*, p. 63). In Carter's beast fables, lions, tigers and wolves are often much better than men, a judgement on them.

In *Sex Exposed* Lynne Segal laments the identification of feminism with hostility to pornography, and of heterosexuality with rape or 'sleeping with the enemy', which has meant that feminist discussion of sexual desire has been increasingly left to lesbians, and debates about sadomasochism.[8] It's easier to complain about penetrative sex and the hard man than about anxious failures of the phallic ideal, which might make up as large a part of complaints against men (and masculine complaints) if it weren't so dodgy even to mention it. Mandy Merck's final essay in *Perversions* discusses the Sex Wars between feminists, and 'the disciplinary implications of a community ethic which regulates sexual conduct in the name of politics', whether conservatively or subversively. She concludes ironically that to fuse our political and sexual imaginaries is a mistake, but that it's impossible to keep them apart.[9] Feminist campaigns against pornography and sexual violence must, in trying to change laws, seek alliance with lawmaking power, but the transgressive force of active female sexuality can become a new imperative: give up the vanilla and lavender and really, girl, try harder to impersonate a macho slut.

To counteract victimhood as the ruling paradigm for feminism, I'd like here to try on the figure of feminine lawgiving, embodied, as Bayley suggests, in Carter's writing. *La loi* is feminine in French anyway: to take up this identification would be to 'come out' about the will to impose of both puritan and libertine feminists, who generally prefer to think of themselves as oppositional rather than as lawmakers. Since much hostility to feminism is to women laying down the law (directly, or indirectly by complaining), this speculative attempt would be a tactic of 'mimicry' such as Luce Irigaray proposed: acting out the ascribed identity so as to expose it as playing out a role which could be changed, to call into question the system in which it plays its part.[10] It also draws on Merck's ambivalent, minatory suggestion that daughters, like poets, might become legislators. She takes up Jacques Lacan's perverse reading of Kant – 'that the law is not founded on the good, but the good is founded on the law'.[11] Though oppositional discourses usually assume (somewhere, at some point) that there is a good way of being or doing things which is repressed by authority, social laws and institutions, it may be that it is those 'bad' laws which incite ideas of the good, including pleasure.

Here Merck appeals to Lacan's 'Kant avec Sade' (*Ecrits* II, Editions du Seuil, Paris 1971), an essay cited in the bibliography of Carter's *The Sadeian Woman*, which Merck also uses substantially in her final essay on feminist Sex Wars. That the force of law can be thought of not simply as repression but as a pleasure, and that this is what allows the pleasures of transgression, is part of Carter's argument:

> Although Sade's sexual practices would hardly be punished so severely today (and it was punishment that inflamed his sexual imagination to the grossest extent) his sexual

imagination would always be of a nature to violate any law
of any society that retained the notions of crime and
punishment. This would be especially true of those societies
which most rigorously practice punitive justice. . . . For
these legal crimes to be described by an honest pervert, or a
moral pornographer, as 'pleasure' is to let the cat out of the
bag; if Sade is to be castigated for tastes he exercised only in
the privacy of his mind or with a few well-paid auxiliaries,
then the hanging judge, the birching magistrate, the
military torturer with his hoods and his electrodes, the
flogging schoolmaster, the brutal husband must also be
acknowledged as perverts to whom, in our own criminal
folly, we have given a licence to practice upon the general
public. (p. 33)

The most flagrant abuses by authorised perverts may seem,
sometimes and in some places, to have been abolished, but
Carter points also towards vicarious pleasures, ambivalent
reponses to the reporting of horrific crimes and their trials.
If we've any sense, we know that fascination with detection
and judgement in all its detailed repetition of horrible facts
is as appalling as it is appalled; a high proportion of the
readers of True Crime magazines, soft porn, are women.
We know that the punishments of ministers and judges are
not necessarily practised only in an official capacity: the
grammar of 'of' works both ways here, as these things do:
it's a real partnership. To judge, and to wish, will, and
enjoy punishment, are complex satisfactions. The good
may be founded on the law, rather than the law on what is
good; pleasure as one of our good things rests, like piety
and horror, on cultural laws and the fantasies that sustain
them. Fictional writing can dislocate old laws, old structures
of meaning and feeling; can articulate new imaginaries, new
symbolic orders, new laws, in a region which is not real,
but one of possibility.[12] It is something like this that I have

in mind in thinking of a 'feminine' lawgiving, rather than the singular monumental abstraction, *La Loi*.

II

Angela Carter's shorter fictions – revisions of fairy tales and myths, and screen versions such as *The Magic Toyshop* and *The Company of Wolves* – don't lose the magic of the original stories in imagining ways of unlocking their constraints. It is always more complex than a simple inversion or the addition of a feminist tag to the lore, the laws, of traditional materials. The enchantment, the passion, the intensely thought working of this, is what I find great about her writing; but she is also great in rethinking the fables of Enlightened modernity, Cartesian distance from the body, its actions and desires, for example; the world-traveller's addiction to 'sardonic contemplation'. She, and her narrators, are entrammelled, caught up in it all. It's easier to see what she's about in the more condensed, obviously 'revisionary' forms than in the longer 'speculative' fictions which I want to discuss here: *Heroes and Villains* (1969), *The Infernal Desire Machines of Doctor Hoffman* (1972), *The Passion of New Eve* (1977) and *Nights at the Circus* (1984). She planned a trilogy beginning with *Hoffman*, but whether *Heroes and Villains* is the lead-in that gave her the idea, or *Nights at the Circus* the more optimistic and benign conclusion, I don't know. I do think these four novels should be read as a sequence. Earlier works – *Shadow Dance* (1966) and *Several Perceptions* (1968) – prefigure her concern with sensual subjectivity caught in visual images and cultural relics, but are still fundamentally stories of a crucial change in some young person's life. They are closer to standard realist fictions of experience, development and choice, and this may also be true of *Love* (1971) and *The Magic Toyshop* (1967), though it startles me that the latter came so early; it seems nearer than other early work to *The Bloody Chamber* and *Nights at the Circus* in its will to demythologise, and its kindness. *Wise Children* follows on from *Nights at the Circus* but is, I think, distinct from the sequence I want to consider – a postscript, maybe, drily critical also but more celebratory, not so ambitiously speculative.

III

Replying to a letter of mine about attacks on her work by some feminists, Angela Carter wrote that the title story in *The Bloody Chamber* is 'a deliberate *homage* to Colette': 'I wanted a lush fin-de-siècle decor for the story, and a style that . . . utilises the heightened diction of the novelette, to half-seduce the reader into this wicked, glamorous, fatal world.' She went on (in a long parenthesis, prickly as well as apologetic) to draw attention to *Heroes and Villains*:

> If you *teach* 'Heroes and Villains', that is, and havn't been put off by that distinctly ideologically dodgy rape scene, which I put into the novel in the first place for reasons of pure sensationalism and which I can't defend on any other grounds except that 'H and V' is *supposed* to share a vocabulary with the fiction of repression, i.e. 'The sheikh' – this isn't defending it, it's explaining it. Note, however, that it doesn't make Marianne feel degraded – it makes her absolutely *furious*. And, in common with all the rape-fantasies to which some women used to admit, the aggressor is a man of compulsive allure and unnatural beauty. A 'demon lover' who absolves the woman of all

responsibility for her own desire, so she can continue to maintain her white state of purity.

[All quotations from letters are transcribed *sic* from MS.]

Then a further parenthesis, in critical self-revision character-istically combined with assertive confidence: 'Marianne isn't in the least interested in being pure, which is probably why she feels furious, rather than soiled – but she *is* very much a stranger to her own desire, which is why her desire finds its embodiment as a stranger.' This suggests that Marianne's rape by Jewel can be read as an allegory of her fantasies (let me reiterate, regrettable as it is to have to be so cautious: the facts about rapes have nothing to do with *women's* rape fantasies, except in so far as representations of rape are culturally available at all levels; everything that is culturally available is Carter's territory). It is only their estrangement which Marianne and Jewel have in common: 'He was as complete a stranger as she could have wished to meet and her only companion' (*Heroes and Villains*, pp. 21–2). They are both symbolic or allegorical figures, not 'realistic characters'; and in this story it is she who is the subject, he the object of her fantastic desire, the young chief and sacrificial 'Unfortunate Lover' of the book's epigraph.

Desire and alienation are explored in Carter's series of speculative fictions, which combine (as she said de Sade's did) the picaresque, moral critique, and nightmare: the lamb running with the tigers, but hers are more benign tigers, more like Blake's Tyger than de Sade's privileged libertines (see the tiger-groom of 'The Tiger's Bride' in *The Bloody Chamber*). The lambs are more fierce. The idea of alienated desire implies that there is a real true desire with which you could be intimately and ultimately at home. In this there is common ground with Pat Califia, the author of *Macho Sluts*: 'Sm [lesbian/gay sadomasochist culture] seems to have some fundamental faith in the rightness of desire: Pat Califia says that sexual desire is "impeccably honest".'[13] On the contrary, our own desire must be strange to us, what we don't know about: we know that we enjoy, and how, but not the source; we'd lose it if it were less strange. Carter's critical journeying through scenarios of captivated desire does start off, I think, in search of the real true thing; though her point about Marianne is that she disavows her own sexuality entirely. Through her speculative fictions Carter comes round to mocking modern Romantic fantasies of the restoration of unity and wholeness in the fulfilment of desire (as in the ludicrous hallooing of 'Reintegrate the primal form!' in *The Passion of New Eve*, p. 64). When we privilege an end to alienation we participate in the plot of Christianity and its secular heirs, Romantic, philosophical and political – the belief that what was lost in the past can be redeemed and restored. But Carter's writing doesn't give up on the romance, the hopefulness, of desire.[14]

She finds that there is no end to the construction of gender and sexuality, as masquerade, as mimicry and as creative affirmation that can take us by surprise.[15] The abyss between desire and its satisfactions, and between the thinkable and the thing thought of, is crucial to the persistence of desire and thought. In *Heroes and Villains* Donally, a displaced intellectual, deliberately regresses to a sort of shaman to construct a social mythology for the Barbarians, Jewel's tribe. As it turns out, both the Enlightened positivist 'Minister of Determination' and his antagonist, the poet-physicist Doctor of modernist relativity in *The Infernal Desire Machines of Doctor Hoffman* and also, in *The Passion of New Eve*, Mother – a more than double-breasted scientist of myth and reproductive technology – all have, fundamentally, the same project: to close the gap between concepts or fantasies and sense perceptions, between actuality and the abstractly or imaginatively conceivable – to integrate the primal or ultimate form, as it were. Their success would overcome alienation, and make the order they impose the only reality there is. The same would be true of Carter's pre-modern societies: the River People and Centaurs in *Hoffman*, the Finno–Ugrians and their shaman in *Nights at the Circus*. The importance of her speculative fictions is in this persistent exposure of modernity and its primitivist desires – that what can reasonably be conceived can happily be realised or, conversely, that an original unity of belief, value and experience can be restored. These fictions are good companions, hopeful but disabused, in a changing world where claims to universality struggle with different particular claims; in which Carter's feminism is exemplary but not exclusive. In the end, when Fevvers in *Nights at the Circus* gets her heart's desire, her experienced but new-hatched man in bed, it's still important that the question 'is she fact or is she fiction?' remains open.

IV

Like much of Carter's early fiction, *Heroes and Villains* is full of the romance of roughie-toughie manhood. What is the good of pretending that some women don't respond to this, or of censuring them for it? 'They left the print of the heels of their boots on my heart', says the sentimental but practical Mrs Green, explaining why she chose to live with the Barbarians rather than the Professors (p. 65). Marianne's experience as heroine is one of captivity, rape, and forced marriage designed by Donally: the unpacking of her crumbling wedding gown Gothically evokes the whole institution of 'something old, something new' in engulfing satin and tulle: 'The bodice crackled and snapped' (p. 69). The tactile fantasia as she tries it on is much nastier than the rape, and *that* has a lot to do with the expectations she's been taught – 'Will you rape me and sew a cat up inside me?' is one of her first questions when she and the Barbarian chieftain Jewel mutually rescue each other from her home in the compound of the Professors (her escape is into captivity, but it's still an escape).

When their marriage is performed he has a horrified flash of recognition – he 'the sign of an idea of a hero . . . she . . . the sign of a memory of a bride' – which isn't explained immediately. This is partly because he has recognised her as the sister of a boy he killed in the raid on the Professors. Her indifference to her brother and to vengeance shocks his punitive but passionately affectionate familial and fraternal feelings. Given that Carter is repeating and revising Enlightenment hypotheses about the origins of society, which we cannot imagine except from our social perspective, Jewel here displaces Rousseau's image of the natural man as an isolated individual, in the *Discourse on the Origins of Inequality* (for Rousseau, familial and sexual relationships are social, not natural or original). Until Donally and Marianne get on to him, Jewel is part of the family, albeit *The* Family as far as the tribe is concerned. It is, *contra* Rousseau, the civilised Marianne who is the true isolate. Jewel's moment of shock prefigures the end. Although he and Marianne do have a time of reciprocal passion, it is clear that their relationship has always been a power struggle between his primitive beauty, and communal belonging, and her detached observation of him, as of her brother's death. Near the end she says to him bitterly:

> 'You are the most remarkable thing I ever saw in my life. Not even in pictures had I seen anything like you, nor read your description in books, you with your jewels, paints,

furs, knives and guns, like a phallic and diabolic version of
female beauties of former periods. What I'd like best would
be to keep you in preserving fluid in a huge jar on the
mantelpiece of my peaceful room, where I could look at you
and imagine you. And that's the best place for you, you
walking masterpiece of art, since the good Doctor educated
you so far above your station you might as well be an
exhibit for intellectuals to marvel at as anything else. You,
you're nothing but the furious invention of my virgin
nights.' (p. 137)

Supremely conscious, she knows and says that he cannot
go and live with the Professors because he would become
an object of research, like the Hurons and Iroquois, but she
has brought the professorial gaze with her. The possibility
of 'a reciprocal pact of tenderness' (*The Sadeian Woman*, p. 8)
flickers and fades: 'to neither did it seem possible, nor even
desirable, that the evidence of their senses was correct and
each capable of finding in the other some clue to survival in
this inimical world' (p. 148):

> When she perceived she and her Jewel were, in some way,
> related to one another she was filled with pain for her idea
> of her own autonomy might, in fact, be not the truth but a
> passionately held conviction. However, might not such a
> conviction serve her as well as a proven certainty? (p. 132)

Marianne's well-preserved autonomy, and her consuming
fantasy of the *homme fatal*, the Unfortunate Lover 'drest/In
his own Blood',[16] have been the regulating law of *Heroes and
Villains*. By the end, pregnant with Jewel's heir, she is all set
to become the solitary Machiavellian Tiger Lady, ruling the
tribe through the power of their fear of her. Of course the
power of passionately held conviction could work for reciprocal relations as well as for autonomy, or for some articula-

tion of the two, and this seems to be what the narrative voice is suggesting, full of regret and maybe a bit of hope. The rape is one moment in this scenario, in which Marianne is not, on the whole, an innocent victim. Neither is Jewel, but he is the candidate for the sacrificial role, and it is he, the emergent primitive, who is destroyed. The narrator is not an innocent either: the fascination with Jewel as beautiful Barbarian is a revenge for the erotic objectification of women.[17]

In *The Infernal Desire Machines of Doctor Hoffman*, the detached observer, stranger to his desire, is male, Desiderio; a role serially taken up by the unwilling transsexual Evelyn/Eve in *The Passion of New Eve*, and by the journalist Jack Walser in *Nights at the Circus* (Fevvers, who shares the narration there, and Dora Chance in *Wise Children*, are interested, not obtusely detached, narrators, though this is not to suggest any pure virtue in the female narrator). None of them is a role model; they play parts in fictions which provoke speculation, in a more open way than the symbolic or allegoric, or the realistic, all of which suggest some prefixed meaning.

It is Desiderio who narrates his quest, his goal to eliminate Doctor Hoffman, through a series of discrete episodes in each of which, like Gulliver, he compromises his objectivity, taking on some of the desires and beliefs of the communities he encounters (Jack Walser, too, sets out to perform a character assassination, on Fevvers, but unlike Desiderio he is himself radically transformed as an object and subject of desire). The Doctor is the Merchant of Shadows, the producer of cultural representations which control desire and perception. A later version of this figure is the Shakespearian actor in Hollywood, Melchior Hazard in *Wise Children* – in his ambition, at least:

> acquiring control of the major public dreaming facility in the whole world. Shakespeare's revenge for the War of

Independence. Once Melchior was in charge of the fabulous
machine, he would bestride the globe.[18]

This series of fictions has a strong interest in the fantastic
power of the silver screen, exemplified most obviously in
the obsessive Amerika of *The Passion of New Eve*, with its
allusions to *Metropolis*, Greta Garbo, *Sunset Boulevard*, the
swimming pool of frozen tears, and so on [19] – an originary
fund of image and narrative which ironically displaces the
primitive origins assumed by John Locke's 'In the beginning
all the world was *America*', the epigraph to *The Passion of New
Eve*. The artificiality of the adventures and escapes of 'Eve
on the run' allegorises the business of making up stories,
which in their turn displace Hollywood sentiments about
the pleasurable suffering of femininity, and the naturalness
of heterosexual romance. As in *The Passion of New Eve*,
there's already a good deal of consciously self-conscious
theorising in *Hoffman* about Time, Desire and Representation. Carter parodies her serious will to theorise, doing it
and cheerfully inviting questions. The fictions of natural
man produced by the Enlightenment, by Rousseau and
Locke, were retrospective, artificial supports to theories of
social, political, ethical life; like Descartes's scepticism, they
served to dislocate the old and establish something new.
Like Freud, Hoffman's early colleague Mendoza had a
theory of the retrospective organisation of remembered
time. However true that is of personal memory traces and
the writing of history, it is not quite true of fictional
narrative: the events we read (going more or less straight
ahead as we do so, like Desiderio in action and narration)
are organised by decisions about where they're going. The
flagrant exposure of this is typical of Carter's writing: her
narrator gives us a preview: 'this is going to happen, and
now I'll show you blow by blow'.

The fiction is that it has all already happened to Desiderio, and he is recounting it, but often (as with Márquez's *One Hundred Years of Solitude*) we may feel that the writer has just suddenly had a wonderful idea about what could happen here. So fictional decisions about the past and the future have much the same status, back-formed but also baptismal, innovatory. The narrative of *Hoffman* both remembers and prepares for the earthquake, one of those cataclysms which do happen but which in fiction look like an arbitrary escape route, cancelling the old and demanding confrontation with new conditions: imagining the latter with courage is the law regulating Carter's fictions, since the conditions of the world are not simply what we make up. Doctor Hoffman provides his agents with a bag of woefully stereotyped samples from which all desires can be generated (pp. 42–9, 58–60, 107–8), and the enemy agent Desiderio scrupulously tries to list them, but scrambles the samples in doing so. This scrambling then produces further events of the narrative (e.g. the trampling by wild horses, p. 107), accidental interventions in a 'universal' pattern – but anyway: 'I lost the . . . list in the earthquake which, according to Mendoza's theory, was already organizing the events which preceded it with the formal rhetoric of tragedy' (p. 107). Desiderio and his boss the Minister, and Doctor Hoffman, have depended on there being a single rule, a straightforward line of enquiry, or a universal set of patterns.

Mendoza's theories also supposed an orgasmic explosion of Time (his early erotic experiments with the Doctor were devoted to this theory). Carter subverts the forward projection of Desiderio's mission, to discover and eliminate the Doctor and his secrets: this is not simply a rational project, or the retrospect of a trauma or a bright idea, but already written in the fragmented body parts and romantic fantasies

of the peepshow (pp. 44–6, 58–60) which Desiderio has
forensically described and which, in his ignorance of his
own desires, go on to dictate the rest of the story – the
polychromatic orgasm of past, present and future which
Mendoza had promised. Desiderio's purposive line of action
(as conventional to adventure stories as Marianne's captivity
is to Gothic romance) had an unconscious set of dictating
principles, which he didn't know but which are clearly
displayed on the surface of the text, in the pornographic
and romantic samples. His particular object of desire, and
other self, is embodied in Albertina, the Doctor's daughter.
She forms, fragments and re-forms, as his guide in different
episodes, while Desiderio is preoccupied with whatever
belief system is the order of the day. Often he fails to
recognise her, and finally he kills her, though there's
nothing especially personal or passionate about this.

The narrative of *Hoffman* is produced from the fragmented
and unrecognised elements of Desiderio's desire as much
as from his deliberate – if sceptical – service of rationality,
and of traditional narrative. He makes up his story according
to his desire, but doesn't know this. Like Marianne, he
succeeds in a rationally designed purpose, and produces as
a side-effect 'the dreary shapes of an eternal November of
the heart' (p. 221). He does kill the Doctor, and Albertina
too – so his desire lives on, in the perpetually lost object
that motivates his dreams and his narrative.[20]

V

'Primitive communities', like 'basic instincts,' have often
figured as not-alienated: the what-once-was that cannot yet-
be-retrieved, the broken middle of modern post-Romantic
fantasy and theory, the Lost World, future utopia. For the

pre-modern communities that Angela Carter evokes – the River People and Centaurs in *Hoffman*, the Finno-Ugrians in *Nights at the Circus* – the autonomous self split between conscious rationality and unconscious desire (Marianne, Desiderio) just doesn't figure as a problem. Their oral traditions, however, maintained by shamans, mythographers and theologians, have a purpose in common with her modern scientific and cultural educators. 'Mother' in *The Passion of New Eve*, like Donally in *Heroes and Villains*, exposes this: both work on the borderline between technology and the deliberate construction of communal myths. They all want to make belief, value and reality the same, and the same for all.

Desiderio in *Hoffman* has a spell of captivation by the sadistic all-consuming world of the Count, de Sade and Dracula in one, which proffers, like *The Sadeian Woman*, a mockery of pornography and prostitution. Men turn into silly pricks in the House of Anonymity, the fantastic objects sold them into carcases, meat: they are absolutely fantasies, and absolutely flesh, nothing in between.[21] After this scenario, Desiderio and Albertina wander into the compulsions of a world ruled by masochistic religion. The Centaurs' myths and rituals are meant to atone for their sinfulness; in counterpoint to the Count's individual will, it's the human, not the horse, part of them that they find disgusting. The Centaurs tattoo the human bits of their skin (as Donally tattoos Jewel, as the Wild Boys in *The Passion of New Eve* are tattooed with the beliefs to which they are committed), and plan to do the same to Desiderio and Albertina, and to shoe them with iron before redeeming these (almost) wholly human beings, and their contaminated selves, by turning them loose to the sacred herds of wild horses.[22]

The Centaurs' lives are 'engrossed in weaving and embroidering the rich fabric of the world in which they lived'. 'This gave the women a certain dignity that would otherwise have been denied them for every one of the most insignificant household tasks . . . was performed as if in a divine theatre' (pp. 182–3) – as in George Herbert's 'Who sweeps a room, as for thy laws,/Makes that, and th'action, fine'. This is the seventeenth-century rhetoric which Charles Taylor, in *Sources of the Self: The Making of Modern Identity*, sees as part of a new modern value for everyday life, failing to note how this is gendered, and serves to deprecate more revolutionary sorts of activity for the handmaidens who might prophesy, preach, and dream dreams, but sweep floors instead.[23] Fantasies are part of the construction of whole cultures, as of persons, 'using the tools of ritual to shore up the very walls of the world' (p. 186). Desiderio is modern, unlike the Centaurs – 'I only wanted to find a master, the Minister, the Count, the bay, so that I could lean on him at first and then, after a while, jeer' (p. 190) – but in this scenario he begins to adopt their historical certitude, like that of the Wild Boys in *The Passion of New Eve* or the Finno-Ugrians in *Nights at the Circus* (the single-issue, solipsistic communities through which Eve travels in *The Passion of New Eve* are akin to the pre-modern communities).

Albertina – a feminine companion at this point, though often she is androgynous, and unrecognised – is more interested in 'the problem of the reality status of the centaurs', convinced that 'though every male in the village had obtained carnal knowledge of her, the beasts were still only emanations of her own desires' (p. 186). Desiderio, more passively, accepts this too: 'If we were the victims of unleashed, unknown desires, then die we must, for as long as those desires existed, we would finish by killing one another' (p. 191). Wild horses will tear them apart. His insight does not transform him, however, but only prefigures his killing of Albertina, and the consequent persistence of his idealised desire for her, lighting up the November of the heart in which he lives on, dreaming and writing.

Although Albertina is, as Elisabeth Bronfen has said, the emanation of Desiderio's desire, and depends for her existence on the story he tells (except in so far as she is composed of cultural allusions – to Baudelaire, Proust and so on: a black swan, de Sade's valet, a 'bouquet of burning bone'), it is she, as a womanly other self, who critically evaluates what is going on in 'Nebulous Time' and intervenes to work their rescue, in a way which shows the other side of her belief in the power of her own desires. Grotesque and absurd as the Sadeian Count was, his faith in the power of his desiring will is one element that can resist captivation by the Doctor's simulacra (stronger than Desiderio's scepticism, it is comparable to Marianne's passionate conviction of her autonomy in *Heroes and Villians*), and this is the model for the rescue that Albertina summons up by concentrating her desire for escape on one point like a burning-glass (p. 97; pp. 192–3; an image from de Sade quoted by de Beauvoir: 'Must We Burn Sade?', p. 42.). Albertina's concentration brings an *event* into the hapless nebulous time of myth. Towards the end of *The Passion of New Eve* Lilith/ Leilah also figures in the transformation of 'myth' into 'historical events'. Both Albertina and Leilah metamorphose into crisply practical guerrilla leaders at this point, though with a difference which depends on the different relation of Desiderio and Eve to them. The new Eve acknowledges the necessity of Leilah's transformation from whore-victim to militant in an uncertain struggle, while keeping open yet another imaginative horizon; whereas in the earlier *Hoffman* Desiderio is really turned off by *this* Albertina, who is one of a more unstable set of projections: his own.

Carter constantly allegorises scenarios of captivation and resistance, trying to see how what is represented by such figures as Will, Desire and Reason might negotiate between the cultural myths that generate desire and the historical conditions and events that underlie, undermine or transform them. This is a different genre from 'authentic history', as she mockingly insists in *Nights at the Circus*. Any effects would be in readers' responses. The collision of the claims of myth and history, which is staged here in *Hoffman* – as at the end of *The Passion of New Eve*, in 'Elegy for a Freelance' (in *Fireworks*, 1974, between *Hoffman* and *Eve*), and in *Nights at the Circus* ('turn of the century', 'revolution', the 'New Woman') – could be understood as a Bakhtinian dialogue between discourses which figure urgently in modern and postmodern claims and demands, with feminism representing a particular set of these; pervading and pervaded by other particular struggles.

VI

Carter's speculative fictions work through specific linguistic play which is allusive, parodic and creative as well as ironic, and – my concern here – through the structuring of narrative scenarios which may captivate the reader but also challenge preconceptions and demand alertness. Judgements of her work have often been made from limited perspectives which ignore the extent to which she entwines the local with the global, and sees universality as something to be challenged when it's assumed as given, and constructively struggled for when it's not: an imagined world in which values follow the same laws, and one in which they're endlessly different, incommensurable, come to much the same hopeless and coercive totality in the end. Carter reimagines modern dreams of the primitive, or the estranged Other, and replays the European inheritance of critical thinking from the Enlightenment on, the good gifts and the curses of modernisation (empowerment, and exclusion; international support for basic rights, and colonialism, for example). This work is sustained: responsive but not random fun. Often her seriousness in rethinking imaginary enchantments can be seen only retrospectively, which is one reason why these central fictions require further readings, and especially reading in sequence. She traces a substantial part of twentieth-century cultural and political experience and theory with scepticism and commitment, delighted irony and a sense of fair play: as she once characterised Bugs Bunny in a midday radio programme I happened to hear: 'an undeceived rabbit, streetwise in the best sense, expecting the worst and hoping for the best'. Acting up Gramsci, and like Blake, she literalises one of the root meanings of 'fantasy' – to make visible, to show, in imaginative vision and critical witness. Her sensitive, exuberant, enlivening skill in effects of writing also celebrates – not uncritically – the projection of fantasies on the screen, whose various forms and transmissions cross the difference between public and private (she became equally interested in the auditory imagination and effects of radio; and how good it would have been to have had her libretto of Virginia Woolf's *Orlando* realised at Glyndebourne).

The law articulating her work is feminist, and addresses particularly – though not exclusively – the interests and desires of heterosexual women, which are, as Lynne Segal suggests, compromised and inhibited by some forces within feminism; and are also, I guess, what John Bayley doesn't like to have discussed too flagrantly. In the Postscript to *The Sadeian Woman* Carter quotes Emma Goldman: the idea that sex is merely dual, and that 'man and woman represent two antagonistic worlds', is absurd and must be done away with. (Nevertheless, people do live this dualism and will say, seriously: 'They are a different species'; I don't dismiss the experience that leads to such bitter judgements, though I don't see much hope in thinking that way.) I have also wanted to think about the range of feminine regulation, and women laying down the law (or interfering with it), in Carter's fiction. In the case of Desiderio, this 'feminine law' is an aspect of himself, of his motivation, to which he is a stranger, so that his desire, like Marianne's in *Heroes and Villains*, may infinitely enhance, or degrade, its object, but precludes any reciprocal tenderness towards one who also desires him, the seductive but dogmatic Albertina. As with Marianne and Jewel, this would need more negotiation than either party is capable of; Jewel and Albertina remain impassioned fantasies. In *The Passion of New Eve*, 'woman-power' is shown in Tristessa's transvestite conversion of himself into his fantasy of a beautiful and glamorously suffering woman, one that has imposed on a generation of film-goers (he is the complementary case to Evelyn's surgical, but also media-assisted, transformation); and in the way Tristessa's destroyer, the grotesquely phallic alternative artist Zero, standing on one leg and psychotically anxious about dykes, is maintained by the toothless girls who believe in him. This chiasmus, this curious crossover between the impositions of the woman-identified and woman-hating man, is preceded and underpinned by Mother's transformation of herself into a many-breasted myth, goddess-priest and doctor of medical technology, in order to impose her inversion of phallic power on her vestal virgins, on Eve, and later on the world.

From all this Eve escapes, as a not at all proper or natural woman, wary and adventurous, wonderful. We should not take these laws too absolutely, necessary as they are to cultural fiction and fantasy, to articulating how things should or might be, what we can hope and what we can't be doing with, and shouldn't have to do with. *The Passion of New Eve* is open in its conclusion. In a letter, Angela Carter called it:

> my favourite of my novels because it is so ambitious, so serious and so helplessly flawed – flawed, I guess, partly because I started off writing the novel thinking I was interested in myth with a capital M., [deletion] you know what I mean, and ending up realising that Myth bored me stiff which is why Mother has a nervous breakdown when the revolution starts.

The Passion of New Eve is my favourite too. The flaw, the critically creative change of mind, is one key to the 'trilogy', Carter's exploration of the uncertainties of cultural and political captivation, resistance, and enjoyment. At the end a black woman, Leilah/Lilith, enters 'historical time' in guerrilla conflict and solidarity with other groups, but there is still also an unfinished Eve, setting out, with Leilah's help, to sea and an open future. Leilah and Eve are not exclusive identities, and though the ways they take are different, these are not mutually exclusive options either. I guess this is the kind of thing John Bayley reads as 'militant orthodoxy'; I read it as much more openly questioning. We could imagine, if we want continuity, that the child Eve is pregnant with (not by herself, according to Mother's parthogenetic plan, but from her passion for the almost-transsexual Tristessa) turns up on Lizzie's doorstep in *Nights at the Circus* and becomes – not quite the New Woman, but the great big tricky performance artiste Fevvers. With her, Platonic transcendence of the merely sensually human becomes the common pleasure of pantomime.[24]

VII

Not quite The New Woman: *Nights at the Circus*, like *Wise Children*, offers a range of possible roles and identifications, which define actual persons as much as the images on their skins will, in the course of time, suit and fit Carter's tattooed figures (the images themselves will change, especially on the younger ones). The possibility of revolt against the internal tattoos of ideology and naturalised, familiar myths is what Carter goes on trying on. Defending what a woman may be like 'by nature' is Bayley's cause, in reviewing her work, arguing against the powers of impersonation. The distinction between nature and culture is itself culturally specific, and has never been easy to make. Bayley's distinction militates against resistance to habit and internal inscription, and against change, which is risky but happens, and is to be intelligently thought on. In *Heroes and Villains* the narrative stance was critical of Marianne's analytic autonomy, which estranged her from her desire, but likewise of Donally's project to inscribe communal myths of power on the individual and social body. To put them inextricably together, the concept and the body, is the naturalising and totalising ambition of all Carter's modern and pre-modern shamans, scientists and aesthetic educators, weaving the fabric of the world, shoring up its walls.

The disease, diagnosis and cure, in Carter's new myths of modernity and its dreams, are a hair's-breadth apart – except that her fictionality and whole way of writing insist that we must know that a space must be kept for uncertainty and recreation. Her ultimate detached observer is Jack Walser in *Nights at the Circus*, who is taken apart and reconstituted as the anxious and tender – but not too tender – heterosexual lover. The end of Carter's trilogy leaves us not with the recovery of a lost object of desire according to the laws of previous times, but with the need to go on resisting scenarios that enthral and frustrate; and to go on making up stories that others can, happily, join in.

In the Alchemist's Cave:
Radio Plays

••

GUIDO ALMANSI

Some so-called 'minimalist' writers – for instance, those of the American school – operate within a small range of human material, making minute variations on a set of hypotheses about life and experience. At a much higher level, other 'minimalist' writers operate within a small range of stylistic material, making minute variations in language and writing. They aim at a maximal effect through minimal interference. Wherever possible, they reproduce uncontroversial fragments of reality and language, leaving their personal stylistic mark, as it were, in the corners, on the margins, in the folds of the mnemonic narration or in a given linguistic texture. Take Samuel Beckett, for instance: he smuggles his extremist ideology of nihilism into a narration of events which are banal and commonplace taken one by one, but become exceptional as a whole, expressed in a language made of elementary syntactic forms. In other words, his literature consists of a few facts barely described and scarcely narrated in an outstandingly private language, which tends to silence, to what cannot be expressed. A language which fatally stops halfway between sender and receiver.

It we have at least two types of 'minimalist' writer, there must also exist, at the level of both experience and linguistic utterance, 'maximalist' writers. Writers who narrate ample stories on a grand scale, with a rich and highly imaginative language, without qualms or shame. Angela Carter partakes of the glory and the drawbacks of the 'maximalist' creed, both in the vastness of her subject matter and in the exuberant vivacity of her writing. A great writer and a great critic, V. S. Pritchett, used to say that he swallowed Dickens whole, at the risk of indigestion. I swallow Angela Carter whole, and then I rush to buy Alka Seltzer. The 'minimalist' *nouvelle cuisine* alone cannot satisfy my appetite for fiction. I need a 'maximalist' writer who tries to tell us many things, perhaps too many things, with grandiose happenings to amuse me, extreme emotions to stir my feelings, glorious obscenities to scandalise me, brilliant and malicious expressions to astonish me. Entirely the contrary of the American 'minimalist' writers, whom Angela Carter once defined as 'rich kids jerking off'.[1] She was irritated by the fact that the richest, most powerful middle class in the world could produce only these little smug parables of anguish. What she aspired to (and her readers as well) was exactly the opposite: meatiness of subject, breadth of interests, Baroqueness of fantasy, intensity of imagination, a touch of exuberance in the writing. And big, open-ended parables of horror. (What else?)

But perhaps these random observations leave out the most imperious characteristic of her writing: the intensity of sensual life, the subtlety and acuity of Carter's sensorial feelers, her specific curiosity about the functioning and range of our five senses. Angela Carter is a great sensualist of contemporary literature, a writer who knows how to evoke *carnally* the reality of smells and tastes and colours, transcribing them with such visionary realism that a stinking smell – the smell of excreta in a circus, for instance – hits the reader like a stench in a dream. An old woman in *Wise Children* (1991) 'always put on so much Rachel powder she puffed out a fine cloud if you patted her' (p. 27). How could you surpass the evocation of a granny powdering herself through the physical detail of this little cloud? The aspiring actress who has just been seducing the great Shakespearian actor (also in *Wise Children*) clings to him 'like skin round sausage (p. 153): a sentence of breathtaking vitality.

Angela Carter's style has this continuous felicity when she describes things happening in our bodies, with the five senses, or during an erotic performance. Take the love scene in the sleeping car (again in *Wise Children*): 'Once he'd got it in her, they never moved, they let the train do all the work. CHOO-choo-choo-choo. The engine would get up steam, the pistons go faster, faster, faster until: WHEEEEEEEEEeeeeeeeee . . .' (p. 118). This scene reminds us of the expressive energy of onomatopoeic devices in another extraordinary 'maximalist' writer, Henry Miller. As a deeply convinced feminist, Angela Carter probably despised Miller. But he should be read for what he really is, a Baroque 'maximalist' following – from the other shore, as it were – the great lesson of American transcendentalism, and not as a pornographer. The quotation comes from *Tropic of Cancer*: Macha, a pseudo-countess, has come from Russia with her bags of treatments against venereal diseases, and ends up dossing with Henry and his menagerie of friends. At one point, she tells them: 'In Russia it often happens that a man sleeps with a woman without touching her. They can go on that way for weeks and weeks and never think of anything about it. Until paff! once he touches her . . . paff! paff! After that it's paff, paff, paff!'[2] Who needs articulate language when sheer sounds do so well? In spite of innumerable differences in subject matter and cultural interests, both Henry Miller and Angela Carter are fundamentally 'carnalist' writers who attempt to let the flesh speak directly, in a short circuit that bypasses the winding lanes of language.

Let us take another example: her description of a character, the *tiger*, both in *Nights at the Circus* and in the short story 'Lizzie and the Tiger' in *American Ghosts and Old World Wonders*[3] (Angela Carter is extremely good on tigers, as on all wild animals). In *Nights at the Circus*:

> The tiger ran into the ring, hot on the scent of Sybil.
> It came out of the corridor like orange quicksilver, or a rarer liquid metal, a quickgold. It did not so much run as flow, a questing sluice of brown and yellow, a hot and molten death. It prowled and growled around the remains of the chimps' classroom, snuffing up its immense, flaring nostrils the delicious air of freedom fragrant with the scent of meat on the hoof. (p. 111)

In *American Ghosts* (pp. 13–16) the tiger is described through the astonished eyes of a child, Lizzie Borden, killer of her father and stepmother,[4] a historical character to whom Angela Carter returned twice.[5] 'Nothing could be . . . more beautiful than its walk.' It was the most beautiful thing she had ever seen, but also the most beautiful thing in the world in absolute terms, 'a miracle of dynamic suspension' (p. 14).

> The tiger walked up and down; it walked up and down like Satan walking about the world and it burned. It burned so brightly,[6] she was scorched . . . the quick, loping stride of the caged tiger; its eyes like yellow coins of a foreign currency; its round, innocent, toy-like ears; the stiff whiskers sticking out with an artificial look; the red mouth from which the bright noise came. It walked up and down on straw strewn with bloody bones. (p. 13)

This is a tiger seen through the worried eye of a visitor at the circus, plus the mythical tiger seen by a child, plus the one seen with the aggressivity of a huntsman, plus the one seen by those who contemplate both the tiger-tiger outside and the tiger-emblem in themselves, at the bottom of their own souls – meditating, like oriental mystics, on the 'tigerness' of human beings and the 'humanity' of tigers:

> All its motion was slung from the marvellous haunches it
> held so high you could have rolled a marble down its back,
> if it would have let you, and the marble would have run
> down on an oblique angle until it rolled over the domed
> forehead on the floor. (pp. 13–14)

The beast is a diabolical and wild divinity ('Satan' [p. 13]), hence not so very far away from a human being, who is also diabolical and wild. Once she has met the tiger, Lizzie is doomed; but the method is above all sensorial, in spite of the reference to 'Satan walking about the world'.[7] In the vision-prophecy of Angela Carter, it is as if the great tiger had sown the germ of the idea of massacre in the mind of the little girl. Tigers, and other beasts, are at home in both the metropolitan and the fairy-tale narratives of Angela Carter. They are animals seen both in their zoological character and in the psychological reality of their effect on the human observer.

'The eye sees what the heart knows', said Blake, quoted by Angela Carter. The heart already knows the tiger before the eye tells it. Even tears, often the exclusive territory of sentimentalism, are rescued by her in their substance and smuggled into the area of the five senses: 'When you look at children crying, they cry as though it's perfectly natural. The way they cry as an immediate response to something! We stop doing that, we learn that it is not natural to cry. It's a precious body fluid like any other.'[8] Wisdom and knowledge abide mainly in the body. 'La profondeur est dans la peau', said Paul Valéry, and the most secretive message lies out in the open, as in Poe's 'Purloined Letter', and is exposed by our limbs.

It would seem logical, therefore, that the writer should exploit all the five senses in order to express what she knows and what she wants to say about the world. Theatre would therefore seem to be particularly suitable to Carter's style and interests, even more so than the novel and the short story. But though she dedicated a novel to the theatre world (*Wise Children*), to my knowledge, she has hardly written *for* the theatre. On the contrary, either because of the casual circumstances of her life, or out of her deep vocation, Angela Carter devoted a good deal of her energies to radio plays, where, by necessity, four-fifths of the five senses are sacrificed. There are no smells, no touches, no tastes, no sights, in radio drama: only hearing, with an intensive exploitation of the sole sense located in the ear. What Angela Carter succeeds in doing with such limited sensorial means (in particular in the four radio plays collected in the volume with the title *Come Unto These Yellow Sands*[9]) seems to me extraordinary.

In her brilliant introduction to this volume, Carter takes the opposite view to the one I have just expounded. Radio (which she calls 'wireless', in homage to her youth: she was a child of radio, just as our children belong to the television era) is not a limitation of the five senses but a multiplication of the narrative possibilities. 'Writing for radio involves a kind of three-dimensional story-telling', she writes, with characteristic enthusiasm (p. 7). What is lost at a visual level is amply compensated, because the resources of radio blur linearity of narrative, 'so that a great number of things can happen at the same time,' (ibid.), exploiting 'that magical

and enigmatic margin, that space of the invisible [so important in Angela Carter's nocturnal world], which must be
filled in by the imagination of the listener' (ibid.). In the
alchemist's cave her imagination makes of a radio studio,
with all the possibilities offered by a repertoire of sound
effects, Angela Carter seems delirious with joy. You can
have everything: 'Aural hallucinations to invoke a sea-coast,
a pub, a blasted heath beyond the means of any film maker'
(ibid.). Suppose the blasted heath is not what you need?
OK: what kind of wind do you want? 'Summer, winter,
spring winds, a gale, a breeze, wind in trees, in bushes,
over water. Every wind in the world is stored away in the
sound archives. . . . An Oriental market? Near East or Far
East? At dawn, at noon, at dusk? If a Near Eastern market,
with or without the muezzin?' (p. 8)

Let us catalogue the sounds evoked in the first few
minutes of her magnificent radio play *Puss-in-Boots* (pp.
117–58): an invisible heckler; mewing; fish removed from
the pan; harp chords; electronic birdsong; organ music;
church acoustics; the noise of a congregation leaving church;
bolts being locked; fugue of locking-up noises; scratching of
pen nib; breathing; the rattle of climbing equipment;
screaming; whimpering; gibbering; footsteps upstairs; a cat
maiming a rat, or tearing it, or gobbling it up; sounds of
bedsprings when something momentous happens on top. In
twenty pages of the written text, all these archival resources
are summoned up. And the combination of various sound
effects has hilarious results, such as the noise of the hero
and the heroine copulating (first on the bed, then on the
floor: different noises [pp. 146, 155]) accompanied by hunting horns (to intimate the cuckolding of the old husband)
and battering on doors (the old governess's attempt to enter
the room) (p. 146). Or the most vehement and clamorous
coitions, accompanied, appropriately, by Tchaikovsky's

1812 Overture (where the orchestration, as is well known, requires the rumbling sounds of artillery) (p. 157).

Puss-in-Boots[10] is the most joyous of her radio plays; it displays all the shamelessness verging on obscenity, the vigorous bawdry and robust vulgarity, of Angela Carter. The old fairy tale is readjusted according to the code of the first canvases of the commedia dell'arte (merry copulations of a young unmarried couple; cuckolded old husband; servants enjoying themselves; punishment of the old hag). Angela Carter states that Puss is Harlequin and his mistress, the she-cat Tabita – or Tabs – is Columbine; the two ancient figures (husband and old hag) are also stock characters in that kind of play (p. 11). She privileges vulgar characters who can be vulgarly exhibited. Take Fevvers, the winged trapeze artiste in *Nights at the Circus*. Her changing room is the quintessence of smells and feminine squalor (especially for a male reader).[11] When she eats, hers is a wild beast's repast (pp. 22, 53). When she yawns 'with prodigious energy, [she opens] up a crimson maw the size of that of a basking shark, suddenly and hugely, taking in enough air to lift a Montgolfier' (p. 52); when she opens her great eyes with a seductive aim, there is 'such a swish of lashes that the pages of [the journalist's] notebook rustle in the breeze' (p. 48); when she laughs, 'the echo of her sussultations spread in the world in a magnetic wave' (pp. 294–5). Her gestures are carnal, vulgar, sensual and aggressive, all things which give men a great fright. 'Go for the ballocks, if needs must' (p. 182), suggests her governess. And Carter herself often aims in that direction.

We are dealing with a vulgarian with an explicit and explosive style of writing who, fortunately, is not at all ashamed of her virtuosity in vulgarity, or afraid of shocking the reader, especially if he is male (women are more resilient, according to her view of the world). Take her

macabre zest for excreta of all kinds (see *Nights at the Circus*);
the enthusiastic description of every variety of sexual performance (In *Wise Children*, Daisy 'had left . . . lipstick on
every pair of underpants further up the hierarchy than
assistant director on the way to the top';[12] and Melchior
'lent his mouth here, his arsehole there, to see if that would
do the trick' (ibid., p. 24); her way of stretching her
description of erotic activities to the limits of extreme old
age (in *Wise Children* a centenarian make love to his seventy-
five-year-old niece – who may, in fact, be his natural
daughter [p. 219]); her balancing act on the verge of the
most extreme bad taste: for instance when a corpse, stuffed
with garlic in order to be protected from attack by vampires,
is gastronomically described as a 'cadavre provençal'.[13] Or
in *Puss-in-Boots*, when the hero, to make sure that the old
man is dead, starts fondling his wife's bosom in order to
ascertain his lack of reactions;[14] or afterwards, when the
adulterous lovers decide to copulate on the floor next to the
bed occupied by the corpse (p. 155). In Carter's radio plays,
as in her novels and short stories, everything happens in a
constant equation between human and animal levels.

With *The Company of Wolves* (pp. 55–82)[15] and *Vampirella*[16]
the reader of Angela Carter is back in more familiar ground:
the folkloric material of fairy tales and superstitious legends;
the Gothic atmosphere of haunted castles, wolves and
werewolves, stories of vampires, and all the paraphernalia
which, during the great period of success of Gothic literature, had lowered the genre to the level of feuilletons and
sensational and unpromising stories, and which Angela
Carter renewed with zest and sympathy. In their radio
versions, however, these stories mainly allow her to explore
with greater freedom phenomena which 'need not necessarily be confined to the representation of things as they
are',[17] or as we imagine them.

The metamorphosis from man to wolf (in *The Company of Wolves* p. 67), which is much more effective on radio than in any film, goes beyond the visual imagination of both reader and listener. The tiny remark of Little Red Riding Hood's granny in the *Company of Wolves* – some wolves are hairy on the *inside* (p. 60) – implies a necessary 'suspension of disbelief' in the listener if he or she is momentarily to accept the existence of lycanthropes. In the meantime, Angela Carter enjoys following with her 'thoughts microphone' the vagaries of the secret intuitions which haunt living people, dead people and dead-alive beings, such as the Count in *Vampirella*, while mundane conversations are interchanged between the other characters. This is 'the subjective interpretation' of the world, mentioned by the author herself in her preface (p. 8). By orchestrating the familiar sounds of the wolf – once upon a time a very familiar character, but now almost entirely relegated to the realm of legend – the writer succeeds in hurling her listeners into a universe where the fear of wolves was a concrete, daily reality for rural populations, and was not much more remote for urban populations. The surrealism of these sound tricks enables her to smuggle in the most incongruous aspects of her script – for instance, the passages in highly convoluted language given to Red Riding Hood. The little girl is explicit and plausible when she claims her right to decide over her own body (rather than being food for wolves or lycanthropes: 'I'm meat to no man' p. 80), but the authorial voice interferes with some of her statements, such as: 'I stand and move within an invisible pentacle, untouched, invincible, immaculate . . . the clock inside me, that will strike once a month, not yet . . . wound . . . up (p. 61). I would find these words intolerably incongruous in a written narration,[18] but they become natural in the radio context, where they converge to our ear from a void, a nothingness, from a community of speakers to a community of listeners. Red Riding Hood blazes like firelight for the lycanthrope – 'Am I too bright for you, sir?' (p. 80) – in the same way as the tiger blazes for Lizzie Borden and scorches her.[19] The radio allows this to-ing and fro-ing between the 'realistic' character, the little child, curious yet frightened of her adventure, and the 'symbolic' character who seduces the wolf-man.

Vampirella, says Carter, was her first radio drama, and it was born as such. The noise of a pencil idly running along the top of a radiator reminded her of long, pointed fingernails running along the bars of a birdcage.[20] Now, what kind of person might have such fingernails, and at the same time possess a birdcage? Clearly a lady vampire, who would be as bored (and as *blasé*) as the writer herself at that moment. Hence the story, which incongruously couples a young British cyclist exploring Transylvania (where he encounters more magical and frightening experiences than in his preceding misadventures as a soldier along the North Western Frontier) and the last descendant of the vile stock of Vlad the Impaler, condemned to her vampiric destiny but saved from her lot by a chaste kiss that restores her to mortality. But a fate harsher than any encounter with the vampires is waiting for the young man: we are on the eve of the 1914 Sarajevo assassination, and the main character must join his regiment in order to go to war. There the Count, defeated in the specific story as told by Carter, triumphs in the universal story as told by God. The battle of the Somme is 'the perennial resurrection' of Dracula (p. 116).

The story is well made and ingenious, and also historically fascinating because of the link between vampirism and war. Yet I personally prefer its narrative version in 'The Lady of the House of Love'.[21] In *The Bloody Chamber* Angela

Carter cancels the very conventional Count, father of Vampirella, who behaves like a perfect vampire with his history of stakes driven into the heart, his compulsion to renew his misadventures between life and death and new life and new death through innumerable resurrections, his ghostly chucklings and infernal evocations of murderous ancestors. Besides, the short story omits all the radio play's scenes of cannibalism, necrophilia and necrophagy, which the writer so enjoys – for instance, when she claims that an act of coition with a reluctant and unwilling wife is equivalent to necrophilia, coition with a corpse (p. 107). When one reads Angela Carter, one has to accept the bad with the good, and even the explosions of deliberate 'bad taste' which she exploits in an act of aggression against the propriety of the Establishment and of males who do not understand the female perspective she advocates (I mean 'female', not 'feminist': i.e. from a woman's point of view).

Radio 'is, *par excellence*, the medium for the depiction of madness[22]; and Angela Carter has attempted to demonstrate her axiom in the most ambitious of her radio plays, *Come Unto These Yellow Sands*, about the mad Victorian painter and parricide (how many father-murderers there are in the works of this writer!), Richard Dadd: 'A piece of cultural criticism in the form of a documentary-based fiction in which the listener is invited inside some of Dadd's paintings, inside the "Come Unto These Yellow Sands"[23] of the title and into the eerie masterpiece, "The Fairy Feller's Master Stroke"'[24], comments Angela Carter in her *Preface* (p. 12). Paintings described on the wireless? Carter wanted to pursue this vein further, and was planning a radio play based on the life and work of that other madman, Jackson Pollock. Indeed, her descriptions of some paintings are brilliant (for instance, the evocation by Titania herself of the painting *Titania Sleeping*[25] in this radio play is perhaps the

most original page Angela Carter has ever written on
figurative arts). Yet I doubt whether a listener, without
previous knowledge of Dadd's paintings and of his
unhappy life, would make head or tail of these uncanny
sounds: the 'real' sounds of Dadd's Middle Eastern experience; the lugubrious sounds of the God Osiris, of whom the
madman was a devotee, and of the world of fairies, gnomes
and hobgoblins which obsessed and tortured him in his
terrifying miniatures marked by a kind of 'surrealist hyper-
realism' (the other radio plays are easier to understand).

Besides, *Come Unto These Yellow Sands* is heavily con-
ditioned by the ideology of the sixties, so influential on the
writer. I was particularly struck by the facile sociological
conclusions offered by Carter in her analysis of complex
phenomena such as the cult of exoticism, the nature of the
'pastoral exotic', repression and Victorianism: 'The European middle class drank deep of the savage splendours of
the East, the pious grandeur of the Holy Land . . . a
compensatory ideology of innocence.[26] This reminds me a
bit too closely of certain lectures of a sociological nature
which I had the misfortune to hear thirty years ago, plus
the distant echo of a perfunctory reading of Edward W.
Said's *Orientalism*. The 'pastoral exotic' would have been 'a
wilful evasion of the real conditions of life in the insensate
industrial towns such as the Manchester of Engels (an
author Angela Carter's generation read passionately in the
recent past) during the era of imperialist expansion . . .'
(p. 25) Come off it, Ms Carter: what about *Le Roman de la
Rose*? 'Wasn't [Dadd] the product of the most repressed
society in the history of the world?' (p. 53). I wish it were
true, because this would mean that this horrible repression
belonged to the past, and that the Freudian revolution has
freed us from it. Of the whole ideology of the 1960s, to
which we are indebted for the welcome irruption of irres-

pectability, the polemics against the Establishment, the immense freedom of subject matter and the healthy scepticism which has been so useful to us in the last decades, the sociological jargon is, on the contrary, the most obnoxious and pernicious heritage.

Where do radio voices come from? The listener can imagine a source, but he is never sure. Does he hear a real historical character, or a fictional reconstruction of that character, or a radio announcer imitating him, or a god or semi-god impersonating him, or a false animal satirising him with a human voice? Or does the voice come out of nothing? The impersonality of the radio voice makes everything possible. In his brilliant radio plays, Beckett dehumanises human people and dematerialises the physical world. He gets rid of solid reality, personal identity, nouns and pronouns (*Not I*), which freeze the individuals and limit them to their personal responsibility. For Beckett, radio represents the supreme unrealistic attempt. Angela Carter does the opposite, accepting and increasing and expanding the real world through the radio so as to include the private universe of the madman, werewolves and their followers, the traditions and horrors of vampirism, the romps of animals in fables. For her, radio is the supreme example of sur-realism. It is not a simple miscegenation of reality and dreams, which has been present in the theatre since its origins, but an overloading of the frequencies of real life. This is her trademark.

Cinema Magic and the Old Monsters:
Angela Carter's Cinema

••

LAURA MULVEY

Cinema magic was born one day during 1896. Georges Méliès was filming in the Place de l'Opéra when his camera jammed. He put it right and continued to film. When he screened the footage, he saw that the accidental stop motion had transformed an omnibus into a hearse. From then on, of course, he used the stop-motion effect to carry out magic tricks with his camera which he had previously performed on stage as a conjuror. The lady vanished. The India rubber head inflated and burst. Martians disappeared into little puffs of smoke. Bluebeard's wife looked into the bloody chamber. Jack climbed the beanstalk. And the cinema condensed non-narrative conjuring with the long tradition of folk tales which used magic and enchantment as the essential material of their entertainment. According to Marina Warner, Méliès also made three Cinderellas, a Little Red Riding Hood and a Donkey Skin.[1]

Transformations and metamorphoses recur so frequently in Angela Carter's writing that her books seem to be pervaded by this magic cinematic attribute even when the cinema itself is not present on the page. Uncle Perry in *Wise Children* is like a walking special effect, a conjuror who also appears and disappears himself at salient moments. His last great passion, the butterfly, is itself emblematic of metamorphosis. It is when the two Hazard sisters, the story's Ugly

Sisters, fail to be thrilled at the caterpillars he has named after them that Uncle Perry disappears and the Hazard family finally falls to pieces. They are, of course, all reunited in the end, when the Chance twins finally get to go to the ball. Uncle Perry returns in a cloud of butterflies and further confounds the mystery of paternity that runs through the story by presenting the girls with twin babies conjured out of his pockets. Although the Chance twins visit Hollywood, Angela Carter's last novel works as a tribute to cinema more through these near-magical transformations than as an evocation of the home of the movies. However, the studio tycoon's casting couch is itself an innocent-seeming office chair, suddenly changed at the touch of a secret button.

The Passion of New Eve opens with a celebration of cinema in the form of Tristessa de St Ange, 'the most beautiful woman in the world', whose image is preserved on celluloid even though 'the film stock was old and scratched, as if the desolating passage of time were made visible in the rain on the screen, audible in the stuttering of the sound track'. In Tristessa's presence on the screen, Angela Carter manages to capture that other aspect of the cinema, the other side of the coin from its magic effects. This is the cinema as Veronica, preserving the images the camera conveys to the film just as the saint's veil preserved the image of Christ's face. The star is captured like an insect in amber: 'for you were just as beautiful as you had been twenty years before, would always be so beautiful as long as celluloid remained in complicity with the persistence of vision'. Tristessa is an icon of the great movie stars' sublime beauty, but in this short reflection Angela Carter manages to put into a few words something about the cinema that critics and theorists can spread over chapters. Tristessa conflates with the cinema itself, its material properties and its own fragility in the face of time: 'that triumph would die of duration in the end, and the surfaces that preserved your appearance were already wearing away'.[2]

Although Angela Carter wrote about the cinema from the perspective of its decline, she was a child of the cinema and loved it from the time she and her father used to go to the movies in South London: 'It seemed to me, when I first started going to the cinema intensively in the late Fifties, that Hollywood had colonised the imagination of the entire world and was turning us all into Americans. I resented it, it fascinated me.'[3] So the cinema, for her, was the cinema of illusion and glamour: Hollywood. And it was this cinema which, *par excellence*, fetishised the appearance of erotic femininity into the star's image. The star's face, moulded by make-up and lights that seem almost superimposed on the machine, to conceal the mechanisms that create the illusion of beauty. 'Enigma. Illusion. Woman?' 'And all you signified was false! Your existence was only notional; you were a piece of pure mystification, Tristessa.'[4] It is not, of course, *women* who have this privileged relationship with the world's greatest illusion, but an image of feminine beauty, highly stylised by cinema's conventions, and styling them in turn – for instance, in the prevalence of huge close-ups celebrating the merging of the cinema screen and feminine masquerade. And the illusion was conjured up through reality, the star herself and the materials of cinema, but then substance was transformed into the insubstantial and reality subordinated to fantasy: 'She had been the dream itself made flesh though the flesh I knew in her was not flesh itself but only a moving picture of flesh, real but not substantial.'[5] It is hard to think of any more succinct summing-up of the paradox of cinema and its projection of fantasy and illusion on to the female body than the opening of *The Passion of New Eve*.

But Tristessa turns out to be an illusion even in her

corporeal reality: a man disguised as a woman and the mirror-image of Eve, a man remade into a woman. These images of the hybrid recur throughout Angela Carter's writing, bearing witness to her preoccupation with dualisms, not as binary oppositions but as either the merging of two differences into one, as in the androgyne Tiresias, or the separation of sameness into two, as in the mirror-image. (These two hybridities meet in the the story 'Reflections', in which the androgyne inhabits a mirror world.) When the fantastic pushes at the boundaries of credibility, an uncertainty flourishes of the kind that Freud associated with the sensation of uncanniness. In his essay 'The Uncanny', Freud cites stories of the double that convey the strangeness, caught between belief and disbelief, which he was attempting to analyse. But he also discusses the 'living doll' phenomenon, most particularly Olympia, the beautiful automaton made by Dr Coppelius in E. T. A. Hoffman's story 'The Sandman'. Although the Angela Carter story 'The Loves of Lady Purple' deals explicitly with this fantasy, it is in *The Magic Toyshop*, first published in 1967 and then turned into a film by Stephen Morrison in 1988, that she explores the uncanniness of puppets.

The film also gave her the chance to take her fascination with the cinema into the real world, as she scripted and was closely involved with the project. Once again, a metaphor for the cinema itself is animated alongside the puppets. The beautiful automaton, the inanimate object that seems to come to life and entrances its audience, has sometimes been cited as an analogy for the cinema. The cinema, too, is inanimate, consisting of still frames which the projector's movement brings to life. In Villiers de L'Isle Adam's 'The Eve of the Future', Edison designs an automaton to satisfy his friend's desire for a perfect female love-object. In her discussion of the story, Annette Michelson takes the automaton as representing a desire for the cinema at the moment of its own 'eve', that is, at the moment before the birth of cinema; and also as analagous to the oscillation between belief and disbelief that characterises so many kinds of cinema. And she points out that this hesitation, suspension of disbelief, while at the same time acknowledging deception, lies behind fetishism.[6]

In the film *The Magic Toyshop*, Angela Carter implicitly distinguishes between the wonder aroused, on the one hand, by mechanical toys and the miniaturised replicas of familiar things and, on the other, Uncle Philip's fetishistic obsession with his marionettes. Unlike the book, the film opens with a short sequence in the puppet theatre in the basement of the toyshop. We, the audience, are taken into the story through the opening of a stage curtain and the beginning of a performance as Uncle Philip rehearses the marionettes. But the sequence then allows the film to shift, with a beautiful cut-on action, from the marionettes' wooden dance to Melanie, in her own fifteen-year-old flesh and blood, as she dances for herself in front of her mirror. As Melanie admires her image, the film cuts to images of woman by Degas, Renoir and Botticelli, all fixed in poses of feminine allure and frozen in time.

Melanie's narcissistic over-involvement with her image is her fault and her downfall. It is her fascination with her mirror-image that seduces her into wearing her mother's wedding dress. At the moment when she aspires to her mother's sexual rite of passage, attempting to appropriate it prematurely, she stains the dress with blood. This incident is immediately followed by the news of her parents' death in an air crash, in a coincidence that is uncanny and also punitive, in the manner of folk stories. Then Melanie and her younger brother and sister are forced to leave their world of bourgeois security, and their kind nurse and comfortable house in the country are exchanged for the poverty and hard work of their uncle's house in London. Their uncle is introduced into the film by a sinister close-up. A black-gloved hand and a dark shadow fall across the music played by his Irish wife, Margaret, and her two brothers. Uncle Philip's rigid authority and his world of toy manufacture are counterposed to the Irish family's world of music and affection.

Melanie finds herself banished to a house without mirrors, where she narrowly escapes being transformed into a marionette by her Uncle Philip. The crisis is precipitated by Uncle Philip's first show after the three children arrive in London, in which he is assisted by Finn, Aunt Margaret's youngest brother. Finn paints the toys, and Uncle Philip is training him to work the marionettes. It is his resistance to his role as puppet master that provokes the crisis. The marionettes enact the story of Galatea; the sculpture who comes to life under the artist's hands. While the artist is portrayed only by the marionette, the film uses an actress to perform the uncanny moment of Galatea's animation. The film is edited so that the actress appears for only a few seconds. Then, as the artist advances on Galatea and Uncle Philip intones 'Each man kills the thing he loves', her wooden limbs disintegrate in slow motion under Finn's clumsy handling. Uncle Philip, having pushed him down to crash on to the stage, announcing that he is not worthy to pull the strings, decides that Melanie will play the marionette's part in his next production.

Angela Carter reverses the Freudian uncanniness of the beautiful inanimate woman with whom men fall disastrously in love. With an ironic and feminist twist, she draws attention to the fate in store for the young girl who is to be turned into a fetishised object as spectacle, part of a performance in which she is reduced to the status of a wooden marionette. The performance is to be Leda's rape by the Swan. Finn once again rebels against his role as Uncle Philip's surrogate. He refuses ('even though I might want to') to seduce Melanie, although he trains her, as ordered, for the part of Leda. Finn understands not only the sexual implications of Uncle Philip's obsession but also that Melanie is to be turned into an object under his rigid control, playing out, as it were, the Galatea story in reverse. Melanie performs Leda with wooden movements, taking up poses that caricature, with their frozen gestures, her own rehearsals in front of her mirror. And the Swan, Uncle Philip's *pièce de résistance*, swoops down and enacts the rape accompanied by his lurid commentary. That night, Finn destroys the Swan and liberates his family, and Melanie's, as though breaking the ogre's magic power in a fairy story, and all the different characters can then achieve their own heart's desire. The film finishes with an appropriate vengeance. The puppets turn on their master and transform him into one of them, and Uncle Philip ends up as the Guy on the top of the November the 5th bonfire.

The film tells the story of the oppressed characters' liberation from a rigid, rule-governed, totalitarianism that is manifested through a perverse valuation of inanimate puppets and toys over living people. The former are 'brought to life'; the latter are in danger of being transformed into a robotic, silent labour force. From one point of view, the cinema seems to be compromised and placed on the side of Uncle Philip and his fetishism, but from another the cinema has a different role to play in the film. It sweeps into the cold house that lives in fear as dream and escape. Jonathan, Melanie's younger brother, dreams of the sea. He makes boats obsessively. At one point, a doubled sailing ship appears superimposed on the lenses of his spectacles, and his attic room sways like a crow's nest when he first sees it.

But he immediately comes under Uncle Philip's power and loses touch with the people around him, living only for the elaborate boats he makes for the toyshop. He seems destined to carry out his uncle's fantasies until Melanie and the cinema rescue him. The sea sweeps on to the puppet stage and Jonathan rows away, out of the story, in a little boat. This kind of special effect occurs several times. As Finn rehearses Melanie for her role as Leda, the cinema transforms his room into a wave-swept beach, where he can tell her his feelings and his determination to rebel. In Melanie's dream, the rose-covered wallpaper of her room is turned into a rose garden, and the sad antlers nailed to the wall turn Finn into a faun. Towards the end of the story, the film itself becomes freer in its use of cinema, with camera pans and tracks. It is as though the cinema's power to dream participates in the characters' assertion of their own desires and, at the same time, materialises them magically on the screen.

In *The Cinema and the World of Enchantment*, Marina Warner comments: 'Monsters aren't by any means always internal psychotic phantasies. Beasts aren't only within, they can also be without.'[7] Although *The Magic Toyshop* touches on the fantastic, and the story's structure has much in common with a fairy story, and although Uncle Philip's size, cruelty and subjection of Aunt Margaret and her brothers are reminiscent of an ogre, there is a social dimension to the characters' struggle for freedom. The power of the father and the oppression of the poor are real factors in human life. In Angela Carter's retelling of the Little Red Riding Hood story, *The Company of Wolves*, she is reflecting, rather, on the internal fantasies of a young girl at the moment of her adolescence and in the face of her first intimations of sexuality. In 1984 *The Company of Wolves* was made into a film directed by Neil Jordan and co-scripted by him and

Angela Carter. The film version of the story adds a prologue which is in some ways reminiscent of *The Magic Toyshop*, and also deviates from it. Both films share an adolescent girl heroine. In both films she is established within the security of a bourgeois home, and in both films she is thrown into the insecurity of a radically reversed story space. This is the space of adventure and transformation that is familiar from many traditional narrative structures, and bears some resemblance to the liminal space associated with the rite of passage from immaturity to maturity, from childhood to marriageability. However, the narrative space in *The Company of Wolves* emanates unquestionably from the heroine's imagination. Having locked herself in her bedroom, rejecting her sister's demand that she should behave, she dreams herself into the story of Little Red Riding Hood.

As a transition the film uses a nightmare sequence in which the familiar toys in Rosaleen's bedroom have become monstrously enlarged and pursue her through a misty, desolate landscape. She gradually loses her class identity as she moves back in time to a village of the kind in which folk tales were the living oral culture of the people. The village is besieged by the threat of wolves, one of which has killed her sister. These wolves may be a source of terror, but as Angela Carter says in the original story: 'It is winter and cold weather. In this region of mountain and forest, there is now nothing for the wolves to eat . . . wolves grow lean and famished.'[8] This fear is rational. The supernatural creeps into the story through Rosaleen's grandmother, whom she visits in the forest and who tells her stories of werewolves. And then the grandmother's stories pervade Rosaleen's imagination until she re-enacts her version of the Little Red Riding Hood tale. The grandmother is overtaken by the story of her own warnings.

Through its series of transitions, back in time and through

different realms of the imagination, the film reproduces the story of the folk tale itself. As Angela Carter points out in the introduction to her collection *The Virago Book of Fairy Tales*, these tales are known to us in their literary or written form, as they were gathered by the great nineteenth-century collectors such as the Brothers Grimm. Jack Zipes, in *The Trials and Tribulations of Little Red Riding Hood*, shows how Charles Perrault's version of the story (1697) was intended as a warning to the young girls of the bourgeoisie not to stray off the road or speak to strangers. But behind this moralising tale lies another culture and a people whose story-telling power has been subtly inflected and stream-lined for upper-class consumption. In Angela Carter's words: 'So fairy tales, folk tales, stories from the oral tradition, are all of them the most vital connections we have with the imaginations of ordinary men and women whose labour created our world.'[9] She goes on to remind us that the teller of these tales may, more often than not, have been 'an old woman sitting by the fireside spinning – literally spinning a yarn'. And behind her tale, lie ancient animistic beliefs in the presence of the supernatural as an active force in the world which the Church and Protestantism attempted to eradicate through the persecution of witches and were-wolves during the sixteenth and seventeenth centuries. In *The Company of Wolves*, these different layers of story-telling and belief are excavated through the power of the cinema, moving through a young girl's contemporary appropriation of the story for her own interior psychic needs to the social setting of oral culture, and then to the exteriorisation of the irrational in the ancient belief in monsters. In the cinema, worlds can open up and shift from one to another without verbal explanation. The cinema creates links and cross-references that share the imprecision manifested by the workings of the mind or the tangled displacements of collective fantasy.

Angela Carter, with her characteristic love of the hybrid, restored to the Little Red Riding Hood story the werewolf that had been written out of it long ago. The werewolf contributes a more explicitly sexual theme that is only implicitly present in the moralising versions of the tale. In this sense, the modern young girl's interior confusion of desire and anxiety links back directly to the grandmother's stories of werewolves. Zipes claims:

> The witch and the werewolf crazes were aimed at regulating the sexual practices and sex roles for the male-dominated social orders, which were demanding more and more rationalisation in the production and reproduction spheres.[10]

This argument associates social repression with sexual regulation and thus, with sexual repression. In *The Company of Wolves*, Rosaleen comes to terms with the wolf inside the charming hunter, in such a way as to suggest that she is accepting not so much the bestiality of *men* as the presence of her now recognised, but unrepressed, sexuality. The unknown terrors of the outside are now known, and while they might still haunt the interior of the mind, fantasy is more on the side of subversive desire than irrational fear.

Towards the end of the introduction to *The Virago Book of Fairy Tales*, Angela Carter points out: 'Now we have machines to do our dreaming for us. But within that "video gadgetry" might lie the source of a continuation, even a transformation of story-telling and story performance.'[11] And Marina Warner says: 'I would argue that film is essentially an oral medium and shares many characteristics of traditional storytelling.'[12] It may be possible to push this

elective affinity between the cinema and traditional story-
telling one speculative – perhaps fanciful – step further. Did
the cinema, and the illusions that prefigured it, provide a
safe haven for irrational suspension of disbelief, as the old
monsters and their oral culture were being exorcised by the
modern world? The Enlightenment pursued yet another
onslaught on the human mind's stubborn credulity, in the
name of reason rather than the alternative spirits of Christian belief, and hoped to banish 'all of the teeming perils of
the night and the forest, ghosts, hobgoblins, ogres, babies
on gridirons, witches that fatten their captives in cages for
cannibal tables [of which] the wolf is the worst for he cannot
listen to reason'.[13] This spirit world could thus be understood as symptomatic, emanating from the human mind.
And the Beast could be psychologised. But collective invest-
ment in the fantastic retrenched into new technologies of
illusion.

The aftermath of the Enlightenment saw the birth of the
Gothic and a proliferation of phantasmagoric technologies.
For instance, ghosts were summoned up in special perform-
ances in Paris after the Revolution; and magic lanterns and
ghost photography fascinated the nineteenth century. Just
as the materialisations of irrational fears were swept away
from the external world and came to haunt the interiority of
the human psyche, they were re-created through screen
images. During the 1890s Freud was completing the process
of rationalisation, arguing that the unconscious itself could
be interpreted and its workings revealed to logical understanding. But as Freud worked on *The Interpretation of
Dreams*, Méliès was simultaneously discovering the magic
of the cinema, and founding a tradition that would reappro-
priate Freud himself for the 'surreal'. Angela Carter fell
in love with the movies during the fifties, their last decade
of supremacy in the Western world. Hers was the last

generation to experience the moving image in the cinema rather than on television. She despised the small screen. ('Television has extraordinary limitations as a medium for the presentation of imaginative drama of any kind. It has an inbuilt ability to cut people down to size, to reduce them to gesticulating heads or, in long shot, to friezes of capering dwarfs.'[14]) Her work, in books and in the cinema, is a fitting memorial to the power of cinema magic.

Angela Carter:
Bottle Blonde, Double Drag

MARINA WARNER

I

Fairy tales explore the mysteries of love; their earliest forebears are the Greek romances, which were described as *erōtika pathēmata*, or stories of love-in-suffering, and followed heroes and heroines through terrible, protracted ordeals until the last moment of recognition, reconciliation and union.[1] Angela Carter's quest for eros, her perseverance in the attempt to ensnare its nature in her imagery, her language, her stories, drew her to fairy tales as a form, and she wrote some of the most original reworkings in contemporary literature in her collection *The Bloody Chamber* (1979), as well as in some of the contributions to *Fireworks* (1974) and the posthumous *American Ghosts*, which contains a Cinderella story, told with the succinct lyrical poignancy of Carter at her most tender.

In the longer fiction, *The Magic Toyshop* (1967), *Nights at the Circus* (1984) and *Wise Children* (1992), she uses numerous fairy-tale motifs: changelings and winged beings, mute heroines, beastly metamorphoses, arduous journeys and improbable encounters, magical rediscoveries and happy endings. Her recuperation of the form has had a widespread influence, palpable not only in the writings of contemporaries like Salman Rushdie, Robert Coover and Margaret Atwood, but directly on film-making, through *The Company of Wolves*, as well as indirectly on the visual arts as well, for numerous young artists have been inspired by Carter's peculiar blend of romance and cynicism. In his obituary tribute on television, Rushdie called her a Faerie Queene, and in her vintage of comic romance writings she was indeed Titania, the enchantress who discovers eros only to find that her beloved is an ass.

But between the early works (among which I would place the great tales of beauty and the beast in *The Bloody Chamber*) and the later writing – from *Nights at the Circus* onwards – something occurs in Angela Carter's sensibility, and it is bound up with her change of attitude to fairy tales. In the first edition of *Fireworks* she added an Afterword in which she aligned herself with the Gothic tale-tellers, like Poe, like Hoffman of 'The Sandman' and other terrifying *Wundermärchen*:

> cruel tales, tales of wonder, tales of terror, fabulous
> narratives that deal directly with the imagery of the
> unconscious – mirrors; the externalized self, forsaken castles,
> haunted forests; forbidden sexual objects. Formally, the tale
> differs from the short story in that it makes few pretences at
> the imitation of life. The tale does not log everyday experience
> through a system of imagery derived from subterranean
> areas behind everyday experience, and therefore the tale
> cannot betray its readers into a false knowledge of everyday
> experience. . . . Characters and events are exaggerated
> beyond reality, to become symbols, ideas, passions. Its style
> will tend to be ornate, unnatural – and thus operate against
> the perennial human desire to believe the word as fact. Its
> only humour is black humour. It retains a singular moral
> function – that of provoking unease.[2]

Interestingly, this note was removed in subsequent editions of *Fireworks*, and when it is compared to the Introduction to the *Virago Book of Fairy Tales*, written sixteen years later, the reasons become clear. Angela Carter changed her mind about what tales were up to in relation to reality; she became very interested in the way they conveyed the materiality of their tellers' and inventors' lives. Fairy tales came to represent the literature of the illiterate: the divine Marquis yielded pride of place to the anonymous peasant. In that Introduction, she writes: 'So fairy tales, folk tales, stories from the oral tradition, are all of them the most vital connection we have with the imaginations of the ordinary men and women whose labour created our world.'[3] This new understanding of the origin represents a new placing of the interesting, significant margin: the productive transgressions of fantasy no longer arise from self-elected maverick geniuses but among the unacknowledged and nameless crowd, and its anarchic energy does not *ipso facto* constitute revolt against the status quo for reasons of personal realisation, but arises from more pragmatic questions of everyday survival.

This change of perception does not entirely cancel the earlier insights into tales' extravagant fantasising, symbolic landscape, or 'black humour'; indeed, she recognises that all these characteristics of fairy tales relate to the social function of romancing.

Many factors and many writings may have influenced her altered approach: Walter Benjamin's essay on 'The Storyteller', with its emphasis on story-telling as an artisan activity, repairing damage through imagination, and Robert Darnton's historical and provocative essay 'Peasants Tell Tales', about the economic and family conditions which are refracted through the stories.[4] In an interview for the BBC in 1985, Angela once said: 'A fairy tale is the kind of story in which one king goes to another king to borrow a cup of sugar.'[5] Above all, the work of Jack Zipes, a leading scholar

of the Grimm Brothers and an indefatigable champion of
the fairy tale, who has produced volumes of essays, as well
as translations from the Grimms, the Arabian Nights and
the French writers of the seventeenth and eighteenth centuries, exercised a tremendous influence on Angela Carter.[6]
They made friends through corresponding about their
mutual interest in fairy tales, and eventually met, around
1989. Zipes acknowledges that Angela Carter opened his
eyes to the possibilities of fairy tales, and his own theoretical
criticism changed direction under the influence of her
writing – from attacking the materialism and coercive con-
formism he had found inherent in the genre to stressing its
utopian possibilities. He has since dedicated his definitive
study of Red Riding Hood to her memory.

Zipes has argued with hot-headed eloquence, from a
huge range of scholarship, against the narrow psycho-
analytic (largely Jungian) view that fairy tales are deep pools
in which eternal wisdom lies like some wonderful fish that
will bring about everything one desires. They are, in his
view, volatile, adaptive, responsive and instrumental vehicles in which the concerns of both teller and audience are
conveyed – hence the misogynist and puritan morality of
Disney's *Snow White*, for example, and the corresponding
volte-face made by the same company in response to
changing ideas in their recent emancipated *Beauty and the
Beast*.

So how did this changed approach to fairy tale affect
Angela Carter's fiction, and in particular, what bearing does
it have on her undeterred quest for the erotic?

The transformation can be seen, I think, reflected most
clearly in the pronounced shift in her style of dark humour
– from a gorgeous, phantasmagoric eloquence of excess and
voluptuousness, rooted in the work of the Symbolists, in
Baudelaire and in Poe, Baudelaire's great inspiration, to a

more particularly British savoury brand of bawdy, out of
the Wife of Bath and Falstaff to pantomime, music hall, and
Spitting Image. Her Gothic decadence turns into comic
defiance; no longer unfurling the banner of de Sade, she
takes Benjamin's motto, 'cunning and high spirits' for her
own, and her most glamorous and bravura evocations of
sexual allure, like the opening scene in the dressing-room
of Fevvers, the winged aerialiste heroine of *Nights at the
Circus*, are constantly punctured by her almost as soon as
she has cast the spell. Fevvers herself, an icon of dazzling
specular pleasure, keeps moving in and out of focus, by
turns angelically radiant or determinedly farting, winged
and glorious, with huge and grimy underpants tumbled
among the aromatic stew of powder and other remains in
her vicinity. Angela Carter needs to profane her own
fabricated marvels, to blow the raspberries of sin in the
artificial paradises of her own skilled invention.

This characteristic in itself discomfits the reader: like the
gorgeous apparition Fevvers letting rip with a fart, Carter's
own prose keeps dirtying its own hands. Like Fevvers,
she's a bottle blonde herself, and she wants you to see her
roots. The dazzlement, when it happens (in so many *tour de
force* moments of illusion), becomes all the more powerful;
and the disillusion all the more bitter. In *Nights* the hero,
Jack Walser, becomes a clown to run away with the circus
and stay near Fevvers; he too, in this comic disguise,
'experienced the freedom that lies behind the mask, within
dissimulation, the freedom to juggle with being, and,
indeed, with the language which is vital to our being, that
lies at the heart of burlesque'.[7]

Transvestism and female impersonation are staple disguises
of burlesque, and they recur throughout Angela Carter's

oeuvre. But she is not content with simple disguise: her female impersonators are often in double drag – that is, as in Shakespeare's comedies, the boy playing a girl is dressed as a boy, and vice versa. Carter plays with this hall of mirrors to dazzling effect in *The Passion of New Eve*, and again in *Wise Children*, in a specifically Shakespearian context. In *Nights at the Circus*, too, Walser the journalist speculates at the very start that Fevvers, a giantess, might be a male in disguise. But Carter's crucial insight is that women like Fevvers produce themselves as 'women', and this is often the result of *force majeure*, of using what you've got to get by. The fairy-tale transformations of Cinders into princess represent what a girl has to do to stay alive. Carter's treatment of travesty moves from pleasure, in its dissembling wickedness and disruptiveness of convention, to exploring its function as a means of survival – and a specifically proletarian strategy of advancing, through the construction of self in image and language. In this, many of Angela's heroines – both in her writing and in life, like Fevvers, like the Chance sisters, like Lulu/Louise Brooks – resemble the literary text of the kind Angela herself was writing: ornate, bejewelled, artificial, highly wrought prose playing hide-and-seek in *Nights* and *Wise Children*, with the chatty, downmarket, vulgar unadorned personae of the characters underneath the greasepaint and the costume.

So there is a dual development: a new acceptance that the tale (the fantastic or fairy tale) connects to real-life experience, and a change of tone from gaudy near-parodies of nineteenth-century pornography to virtuoso reworkings of Chaucerian and Shakespearian comedy; and this acceptance is enmeshed in – and articulated by – a change in her understanding of self-fabrication. This includes cross-dressing, a 'perversion' Carter was tremendously taken by, and her use of it widens her view of the erotic: power and pleasure are coupled in the early work, but in the later, especially *Wise Children*, their symbiosis is modified.[8] Hedonism has its high costs, for Lulu as well as for Dora and Nora; glamour is a girl's brave stratagem, and Angela Carter's admiration for it has no bounds. But she does recognise that its magic has limits. With that recognition, her glittering humour grows at the same time broader, darker and softer.

Because it was not always so, this broadening of her comedy helps the reader to decipher the risks and the difficulties she suffered as a writer. The transformation itself forms part of the larger shift that has taken place in recent times, which has made humour the weapon of the dispossessed, the marginal – the response of the victim who feels Punch's stick, not the joyous cries of Mr Punch himself. The iconoclast in Carter goes on breaking up the gorgeous images, but finds that they keep reassembling themselves under her blows like squashy cartoon animals

II

There is a group of fairy tales about a silent princess – sometimes a silent prince – whom nothing can move, until someone comes along who does something so funny, or says something so outrageous, that at last the curse is lifted, and the heroine – or hero – is released from the captivity of muteness. The silent princess embodies the audience of fairy tale as well as taking part in the story itself, because the tale can be said to exist in itself to excite responses, to bring life, to assert vulgar rude health against pale misery and defeat, to stir laughter or wonder or tears or hope.

In one seventeenth-century Italian version, by the Neapolitan Gianbattista Basile, the silent princess's first laugh is provoked when an old woman slips on a puddle of oil, falls over and shows her bottom: bawdy and scatology reassert the life principle, literally from below.[9]

The revolutionary Russian philosopher Alexander Herzen commented: 'In church, in the palace, on parade, facing the department head, the police officer, the German administrator, nobody laughs. The serfs are deprived of the right to smile in the presence of the landowners.' (Wipe that smile off your face, says the bullying teacher.) Herzen concludes: 'Only equals may laugh.'[10] So the laughter of the clown, the mockery of the fool, can be the expression of freedom, the gesture that abolishes hierarchy, cancels authority and faces down fear. Its release can lie in the way it abolishes hierarchy and authority. Eighteenth-century riddle books, produced for children's amusement and filled with concealed meanings, knew this function of laughter:

> Of Merry books this is the chief,
> 'Tis as a Purging Pill;
> To carry off all heavy Grief,
> And make you laugh your Fill.[11]

The British pantomime tradition has prolonged the life of the medieval diablerie, and a pantomime character like Mother Goose, irreverently guying her betters, has crossed over from the nursery and the riddle book to flourish on the boards. Significantly, Mother Goose is a drag role; like Widow Twankey or the Wicked Stepmother, she was played by a pantomime dame in the Christmas dramas and music-hall revues. Sex reversals pointed up the magic as well as the absurdity: the name of Pulcinella, Mister Punch's clownish ancestor from Italian masked comedy, ends in the feminine 'a' which retains the memory of his travesty. Mother Goose doubles the inversion: she is played by a man to look like a cross-dressed woman (Pulcinella/ Punch).[12]

In one of her very last pieces, Angela Carter celebrated the British pantomime tradition, its transvestite roles, its use of heavy innuendo and bawdy banter about sexual oppositions:

> The Dame bends over, whips up her crinolines; she has three pairs of knee-length bloomers. . . . One pair is made out of the Union Jack. . . . The second pair is quartered red and black, in memory of Utopia. The third and vastest pair of bloomers is scarlet, with a target on the seat, centred on the arsehole. . . .[13]

The Fool in Dutch painting deals in comic obscenity in this manner; fools can enter where angels fear to tread, and thumb their noses (show their bottoms) at convention and authority: tomfoolery includes iconoclasm, disrespect, subversion.

The Dame became one of Angela Carter's adopted voices (a woman speaking through a man disguised as a woman); this double drag scatters certainty about sexual identity, of course; it puts fixity to the question. But at the same time, it also connects to one form of Carter's utopianism: her dream of synthesis. For the figure of the female impersonator mirrors the hermaphrodite, and this figure of alchemy, wisdom and magic also holds a very potent place in Angela Carter's imagination (the changeling boy over whom Titania and Oberon quarrel in *A Midsummer Night's Dream* becomes a boy-girl in one of her stories[14]). The yearning to achieve synthesis does surface intermittently in her journey to discover, or at least to represent, to write the erotic. In 'Reflections', for example, a metaphysical piece from *Fireworks*, the male questor/narrator passes through the mirror

and actually destroys a god/goddess who perfectly synthesises male and female. She has been ravelling up cosmic
order and harmony by knitting away at a long scarf. Every
dropped stitch is a broken or missing piece in the world on
the other side of the mirror. Though the story is one of
Carter's cloudier tales, the iconoclasm of the protagonist
when he desecrates and destroys the hermaphroditic idol
does not win the author's wholehearted applause. Even
though his act rejects the deity's wholeness as a kind of
tyranny, and stands for the energy of sexual difference (I
think) and for the shaping of identity achieved by resistance, there is irony and sorrow in the last paragraph, too:

> Down she tumbled, the bald old crone, upon a pile of wisps
> of unravelled grey wool as the ormolu furniture split apart
> and the paper unfurled from the wall. But I was arrogant; I
> was undefeated. Had I not killed her? Proud as a man, I
> once again advanced to meet my image in the mirror. Full
> of self-confidence, I held out my hands to embrace my self,
> my anti-self, my self not-self, my assassin, my death, the
> world's death.[15]

Many of Angela Carter's characters have another self in
wonderland, through the mirror, a not-self which defines
them and gives them vitality, but also serves to mark the
absence of the true self and, with that absence, the impossibility of that existence.

But where does that leave coupling, and its double source
– narcissism, which is precisely self-love, and altruism, the
love of another? The difficulty in providing a happy ending
in answer to this question pushed Angela Carter towards
laughter. 'Reflections', written in the seventies, remains
gothically in earnest; *Nights at the Circus*, written a decade

or more later, erupts in laughter, closing with the end of Fevvers's long, sustained joke, her heavenly disguise:

> The spiralling tornado of Fevvers's laughter began to twist and shudder across the entire globe, as if a spontaneous response to the giant comedy that endlessly unfolded beneath it, until everything that lived and breathed everywhere, was laughing. . . .[16]

In *Rabelais and His World*, Mikhail Bakhtin traces the survival of the *risus paschalis*, 'Easter laughter', medieval laughter, blasphemous but permitted, through to its rejection in the seventeenth and eighteenth centuries:

> laughter . . . made its unofficial but almost legal nest under the shelter of almost every feast. Therefore, every feast in addition to its official, ecclesiastical part had yet another folk carnival part whose organizing principles were laughter and the material bodily lower stratum. . . . The origin of the various elements of this theme are varied. Doubtless, the Roman Saturnalia continued to live during the entire Middle Ages. The tradition of antique mime also remained alive. But the main source was local folklore . . . the medieval culture of folk humour actually belonged to all the people. The truth of laughter embraced and carried away everyone; nobody could resist it.[17]

The irony is that Angela Carter clowned more and more over the length of her prolific career because she saw, with her sharp-eyed mordancy, that in her struggle for change she was losing ground – that through Thatcher's eighties and in the world they were creating, all too many were able to resist – by turning a deaf ear to 'the truth of laughter' and much besides. She knew that humour was a last-ditch stratagem, even an admission of defeat: this is the nub of the irony. She understood the limits of merrymaking, burlesque and masquerade, and she spoke clearly in a 1992 interview with Lorna Sage – the editor of this volume, and a close friend – about the power of the carnivalesque to contain rather than to release:

> 'It's interesting that Bakhtin became very fashionable in the 1980s during the demise of the particular kind of theory which would have put all kinds of question marks about the vogue for the carnivalesque. I'm thinking about Marcuse and repressive desublimation, which tells you exactly what carnivals are for. The carnival has to stop. The whole point about the Feast of Fools is that things went on as they did before, after it stopped.'

So Angela Carter's comic disguise, her performance as a bottle blonde with her slip showing, staged a kind of retreat, a retreat brought about by the climate of the Thatcher hegemony. *Wise Children* sustains a tone of dashing, irrepressible vitality, even in the worst adversity, from the lips of her narrator, who is herself not quite a pantomime dame but a chorus girl, a music-hall artiste, a sometime stripper, to whom life gives a raw deal – or nothing at all – but who keeps up her spirits in spite of it. The very last line of the book is, 'What a joy it is to dance and sing!'

The presence of joy in the work of Angela Carter signals her hold on 'heroic optimism', the mood she singled out as characteristic of fairy tales, the principle which sustained the idea of a happy ending, whatever the odds. Angela Carter developed Freud's polymorphous perversity with panache, and played with humour in a wide variety of keys, ranging from flamboyantly upfront ribaldry to the quietest, driest droll asides. She opened the first of her anthologies of fairy tales with the vision of Sermerssuaq, a character of contemporary Eskimo folklore:

> [She was] so powerful that she could lift a kayak on the tips of three fingers. She could kill a seal merely by drumming on its head with her fists. . . . Sometimes this Sermerssuaq would show off her clitoris. It was so big that the skin of a fox would not fully cover it. Aja, and she was the mother of nine children, too![18]

Angela Carter was invited to moderate this passage, as its inclusion, especially in the heraldic position at the beginning of the book, would prevent teachers using the collection in schools. But she stood firm; she practised through her writing a constant stretching of the permitted, of the permissible. Taboo was her terrain, and comedy was one of her ways of entering it. (Not for her the humour of control, of convention, of censure.) She clowned, she fooled, because – as her much-loved (and much-teased) Bard says – 'This fellow's wise enough to play the fool,/And to do that well deserves a kind of wit . . .' Sermerssuaq also, incidentally, symbolised the return of synthesis – the being who manages the ultimate disguise of being both male and female – in a jovial mood.

Angela Carter would have been astonished by the praise in her obituaries; she would certainly have had some caustic phrase for the general enthusiasm. For in England, where she was born and lived, she and her work were viewed askance while she was alive by some of the same media Establishment that gathered in force to praise her in death. Her work sowed discomfort among the British public, which in some ways was all to the good, as she did not seek to be cosy. Her profanity was of the unsettling variety that made it necessary to examine one's own received ideas. It was so very impolite, with its particular feminism, its blend of the irreverent and the Gothic, its dazzling linguistic intricacy and relish for imagery. But it is the humour, its dark and even snaky stabs, that above all, I think, produced the discomfiture people felt at her work, which is of course what she – what Sermerssuaq, what the Panto Dame – intended.

Woolf by the Lake, Woolf at the Circus: Carter and Tradition

ISOBEL ARMSTRONG

Ten years ago, in 1984, two antithetical traditions met in the competition for the Booker Prize: Anita Brookner's *Hotel du Lac* and Angela Carter's *Nights at the Circus*. Brookner's novel is a neo-realist, meticulously circumscribed narrative of middle-class women who experience the punning lack of its title. It is a high-bourgeois elegy, conservative in its impulse to confirm the permanence of those structures – marital, financial – which keep women impotently sad, even if it mourns for them. For Carter, on the other hand, lyricised feminine mourning and melancholy is precisely the trap, the fix, which women have to get out of at all costs. The ballerina in perpetual mourning who figures in Brookner's later novel, *A Closed Eye*, is the object of radical burlesque, aggressive resistance, and resilient postmodern comedy, as the fantasies of masochism are undone in the narrative stunts with the traditional feminine images of oppression – the Sleeping Beauty, Mignon – performed in *Nights at the Circus*.

Prizes polarise. The political and aesthetic differences between the two novelists can be sharpened into an oppositional alignment. One holds to the core of self, and attempts to stabilise the world of middle-class codes and practices with the particularities of documentary detail – rooms, furniture, food, nuances of weather – which give them solidity and illusory permanence. The other sports with displaced subjectivities performing themselves in the cultural debris of a multiplicity of histories and spaces, high-kicking with the conventions of class, gender, genre. With the neo-realist novel, things are meant to be as convincingly solid and opaque as brick even when they are not. With the postmodern novel, things are meant to be as transparent and lightweight as bricolage even when they are not.

But before one goes further with this antithesis, it must be recognised that the two traditions represented by Brookner and Carter have a common precursor: Virginia Woolf. The incompatible siblings of the Booker Prize spring from tensions in Woolf's own work, and from the way feminist theory of the post-Second World War period has read Woolf. Carter's work comes out of the possibilities for bravura fantasy in *Orlando* (1928) and the surreal critique of *Between the Acts* (1941). Brookner's work comes out of the lyric novels, *Mrs Dalloway* (1925) and *To the Lighthouse* (1927) in particular. It is not surprising to find that Carter had worked on a sketch for a libretto of *Orlando*. The point of bringing Carter and Brookner together, and of considering their shared intertextual relation with Virginia Woolf, is not to set up a competition between the conventional and the scandalous successors of the novelist so much as to deepen a reading of both. It also suggests that the pull between different possibilities in Woolf's work comes, perhaps, from deep, conflicted rifts in her thought and social awareness which have been handed on in British fiction.

While Brookner elaborates the strain of elegy in Woolf's fiction, associating the near-fatal misprisions and inhibitions of her protected and self-protected upper-middle-class women with a poetics of loss, it would be a one-sided reading that did not find implicit political analysis in her novels. Woolf wrote that she wanted to criticise the social system in *Mrs Dalloway*, and there is immanent critique of the same kind in Brookner's work. Correspondingly, a one-sided reading of Carter as the novelist who developed her fiction as a fierce cabaret of political correctness, such as that made by John Bayley (and challenged by Hermione Lee), ignores the profundity of Carter's refusal to mourn, and her celebration of the *jouissance* of the *Orlando* tradition. I think these traditions are ultimately incompatible. The need for a centred self and a willingness to accept a constructed self make for real differences of form and ideology. Carter belongs to dissident feminist counterculture; Brookner does not. Despite their differences, however, both, in different ways – helped by Virginia Woolf – are interested in the possibilities of lyrical language and the way it can break into new kinds of experience – and by this I mean not simply expressive experience but new categories and concepts. I shall reflect briefly on what lyrical language can do when I have considered what each novelist developed from Virginia Woolf's work.

Virginia Woolf's work did not immediately become a model for subsequent women writers. Elizabeth Taylor, Elizabeth Bowen, Rosamond Lehmann and Rose Macaulay, for instance – to name a few of the novelists writing between the wars who would certainly have been able to read Virginia Woolf's texts – appear to be almost impervious to the experimental aspects of her work. And certainly, whatever the reasons, it is later feminist theorists rather than women writers who have taken her work up. *A Room of One's Own* (1929) and *Three Guineas* (1938) have become central to the feminist debate, whereas certainly in the immediate postwar period, and well beyond it, she disappeared as a potent precursor for women novelists. Iris Murdoch, with the existential philosophical concerns she derived from France, and Doris Lessing, with her deep and polemical political interest in communism and in the roots of racism, displaced Virginia Woolf. Powerful, robust novelists, reconfiguring modernist techniques with elements of realism, they made her seem a fragile figure, a phenomenon of self-regarding and self-enclosed upper-middle-class aestheticism and sensibility. Avant-garde experiment came from another direction: from the *nouvelle vague*, from Alain Robbe-Grillet and Natalie Sarraute. And until very recently, the critical concerns of high theory, sharpened by both Marxist ideas and deconstruction to an intense awareness of questions of gender, class, and post-colonial culture, passed her by. Curiously enough, she was seen as the exponent of an earlier phase of modernism which was as obsolete in its way, in relation to both Marxist and post-structuralist concerns, as the stodgy Victorians had seemed to the Bloomsbury Group.[1]

We were encouraged to see Virginia Woolf as the *old-fashioned* avant-garde novelist, engaging in purely formal experiment with narrative and time, by such deeply epistemological studies as Eric Auerbach's classic essay 'The Brown Stocking'.[2] Unintentionally, and for some readers, this brilliant study can give the impression that politics and epistemology are mutually exclusive in her work, though this is far from the case. Demonstrating that narrative time is vastly expanded in relation to 'lived' time by analysing the complexities of the flow of consciousness while Mrs Ramsay performs the simple act of measuring her son's leg, Auerbach convinces us of Virginia Woolf's subtlety while enabling us to forget what other work that subtlety performs. For even in the high-modernist preoccupations of her writing – perhaps, in some ways, most of all in these preoccupations – Virginia Woolf's texts are aware of the social meaning implied by formal experiment.[3]

A determinedly high-modernist reading can filter out these meanings, but the narrative experiment does make them possible. In fact, when we put into her texts what, until very recently, was consistently left out of them, the categories of politics and sexual politics, it is also possible to see how novelists writing in the 1980s, in particular, have produced texts which resonate with hers. By a delayed reaction, women's fiction of the last decade, catching up with her sometimes through the renewed examination of her work prompted by feminist readings of the essays on gender which I have mentioned – *A Room of One's Own* and *Three Guineas* – began to respond to the extraordinary challenge of her work.

Carter and Brookner respond to the same dialectic of desire in Woolf's work, the source of both experiment and a sense of loss. How complex the circumstances of Woolf's work often were can be seen from *Orlando*, a text motivated both by extraordinary experiment with a multiple, bisexual subject and by the embarrassing snobbery, as Suzanne Raitt has shown, which was a component of Woolf's adoration of Vita Sackville-West.[4] But Woolf, Maggie Gee reminds us, was capable of writing a preface to a collection of writing by working-class women, as well as being drawn to the 'glamour' of the British aristocracy.[5] Rather than being drawn into a fruitless debate on Woolf's politics (she was and she was not reactionary), it is as well to be reminded that there is a social reading of experience which goes beyond social comment, and this is what Woolf does with her contradictory dialectic of desire.

The pressure of desire in Woolf's work arises because hers is a narrative where everything is *vanishing* or about to vanish. Self and world, a network of interacting drives in which the physiological and the psychological cannot be differentiated, an integument of volatile mental and organic relations, are in perpetual process, always grasped in retrospect, always preparing to be the past. The 'actual event practically does not exist,' Virginia Woolf wrote.[6] Time leaches away, or can be caught only in hypersubtle moments, going on behind one's back. The gaps which arbitrarily mark us off from one another and the world, like gaps in the irradiated signal of the lighthouse at night, are experienced almost as violently as some primal separation, and motivate a longing and for ever incomplete enquiry into the nature of subject and object. The intensity of this felt evanescence, seen through the philosophical tradition of Hume and Pater, is nevertheless greater than any intelectual explanation can satisfy.

Such a ceaselessly relational and yet *disappearing* world simultaneously affirms and abolishes social meanings. Gillian Beer appropriately reads To the Lighthouse as an act of mourning, both a celebration and an exorcism of Woolf's father, Leslie Stephen.[7] Mourning and the separation of death return one through repetition to earlier and paradoxical separations, when consciousness becomes aware of itself as a lonely and separate entity, and, by that very fact, simultaneously as a social being. It is not surprising that in the same novel Lily Briscoe is painting a mother and child, the primal scene both of union and of separation. If the 'event' or experience is actually constructed through the concurrent narratives and multiple relationships of a number of consciousnesses – such as the relation of mother and child, or the double narrative at the end of To the Lighthouse, when Lily works on her painting and the Ramsays approach the lighthouse at last – then the networks of memory, desire and projection which create the event affirm the possibility of collective meaning. On the other hand, 'We perish all alone', as Mr Ramsay is reminded through Cowper. The illusion of narcissistic unity may be all that is gained, as is suggested by Mrs Ramsay's work of art, the dinner party in the first section of the novel. The shock of 'Time Passes', that great fissure in the narrative, disavows such self-absorbed narcissism by conceiving of a universe in which the perceiving subject is not the ordering principle but – displaced, fractured – is disempowered. The individual is no longer mirrored in the external world in a relationship of unity and beauty, which is seen instead as self-regarding and anthropomorphic, an unthinking assertion of power and possession. 'Time Passes' is the other side of the inward-looking unity of the bourgeois dinner party, flickeringly reflected back to itself in the glass of the window, reminded of flux only by the narrator. It constitutes the chasm of the First World War, and, trying to do without the subject and to see what the world would be like without a subject at its centre, it is a fictional and ideological leap. There is nothing quite like it. It is meant to suggest that neither life nor fiction can ever be the same after it. And Virginia Woolf writing her novel about art after upheaval, was aware of another era of change; she saw tanks, manned by soldiers with guns, pass through the street during the General Strike of 1926.

Carter and Brookner take up this crucial narrative break in different ways. While Brookner, one might say, remains, however self-consciously, in mourning for Mrs Ramsay, Carter follows Lily. The split mirrors the conflicting desires of Woolf's narrative itself. After the chasm of 'Time Passes', Mrs Ramsay is no longer there to knit up the fabric of her brown stocking. The very fabric of the house decays. A world has disappeared before Lily returns to her painting. Guns have sounded: the sea has been stained purple – not with paint, but with blood. Lily evolves a non-exploitative

relation to objects, and recognises the dispersal and vulner-
ability of the subject, and the consequential intimation of
bisexuality in this new world. The two novelists fall on
opposite sides of the line with which Lily completes her
picture. In one sense the line signifies finality: 'I have had
my vision'. It means death. Or if it signifies life, it intimates
the harshness of phallic loss and the intransigent fixity of
all relations, including sexual difference, the slash in s/he.
But another way of seeing the line is not as a *terminal* mark
but as a completion which opens up the picture to new
relationships: within itself, with the external world, and
with future time. To say 'I *have* had my vision' is to allow
that it will recur. The line itself becomes that mark of
difference and separation which enables relations to continue and to change – between men and women, parents
and children, the powerful and the powerless, the dead and
the living, war and peace, life and art. Virginia Woolf, in
mourning for her culture while at the same time she saw its
impossibility, oscillated between Mrs Ramsay and Lily,
between one side of the signifying line and the other: I have
had my vision (Brookner): I *have* had my vision (Carter).

Brookner takes up that aspect of elegy, that profound sense
of separation experienced particularly by women in Woolf's
novels, making for a troubled sense of both sexuality and
class. On the other hand, Carter takes up that liberated
sense of a multiple subject which begins to be discovered at
the end of *To the Lighthouse* and leads to an element of
fantasy, openness and play. The rhythm of the death wish
moves as a tragic necessity and limiting of possibility in
Brookner's fiction, while the pleasure principle, playing
with dream-work and transgression, asserts its freedom in
Carter's texts. Both elegy and fantasy are inflections of

desire, and perhaps Virginia Woolf is the first novelist to put desire at the centre of her novels and give it sustained exploration; but the desire of lack and the desire of demand work in different ways as narrative strategies.

The modern fiction of elegy seems to be bound up with the attempt to protect the self from, to ward off, the knowledge of sexuality. Recognising sexual betrayal in advance of its occurrence, Anita Brookner's women are prepared to postpone their sexuality even though that very postponement creates the sense of loss. Recognising desire – but not, except intermittently, its sexual meaning – they are caught in the loneliness desire itself creates. Often single women, or women on their own, or even married women who are spiritually virginal, they are unable to choose, from temperament and circumstance, other than to occlude the sexual in its full complexity until it is too late – or almost too late.

Such studies inherit Virginia Woolf's analyses of women who subtly displace sexuality to the margins of experience. Mrs Ramsay protects both her children and herself from the terrors of the night: she throws her shawl over the great horned boar's head which prevents them from sleeping, warding off and excluding its insistent image of sexual violence. Protection, the prerogative of the mother, extends to an exclusion, almost an amnesia, of the sexual. Richer emotionally and more powerful than her predecessor, Mrs Dalloway, who knows, without quite knowing, in her virginal upper room, that she has 'failed' her husband, Mrs Ramsay nevertheless reduces the sexual to silence. In an unspoken exchange with the 'roused' Mr Ramsay at the end of the day, she withdraws from him: 'Will you not tell me just for once that you love me? . . . But she could not do it: she could not say it.' In 'Time Passes', the excluded element has its revenge; simultaneous with the springing loose of the landing floorboard, the shawl swings loose 'with a roar'.

It is sound, repeated sound, which insists on sexual meaning in *Hotel du Lac*. Edith hears, or thinks she hears, the sound of a softly closing door early in the morning of her first day in the padded protection of the high bourgeois hotel. The sound of the closing door – subliminally present in the narrative, an almost repressed detail – recurs. The door closes on taboo experience, but simultaneously draws attention to the possibility of entering upon it. Edith hears the sound, but – honourably incurious, fatally ignorant – does not attach meaning to it even when the woman who turns out to be her rival almost tells her what it means. Almost too late, she discovers that the man courting her for her class and taste is behind the recurrently sounding door with someone else.

Anita Brookner's world is more directly cruel and drily ironic than Virginia Woolf's, but she also inherits from her, in overdetermined, delicate sensuous detail, the scent, touch, feel and texture of the bourgeois woman's feminine appurtenances, with their multiple functions of suppressing, displacing, masking, substituting for, something that is not there. Food (Mrs Ramsay's *boeuf en daube*), flowers, furniture; clothes, possessions, purchases – these are not expressions of delight and exuberant representations of the feminine so much as a more literal aggregation of things intended to repair and assuage. But the less their symbolic meaning, the more necessary it is to accumulate more things. Both novelists are sharply aware – and perhaps Virginia Woolf saw this for the first time in the novel – that women are encouraged in the addiction of buying things. Anita Brookner has an immediate response to the object of consumption – the scent of evening baths in the hotel, for instance – but is only too aware that her women are reduced to consuming; that their experience, paradoxically, is actually attenuated by the act of consumption. The dinner party, Mrs Ramsay's artwork, is thinned down to shared hotel meals. When her characters are not frantically buying clothes, they are reduced to the humiliation of simply eating, to woman as eating subject: 'They ate in silence, feeling exposed and guilty, graceless, as women eating alone without enjoyment do feel. The sweetness burst in Edith's mouth, cloying quickly.'[8]

Like *To the Lighthouse*, *Hotel du Lac* begins from the vantage point of a window; and, with a kind of grey lyricism, a threnody on the greyness of the lake transmutes the colours of water in Virginia Woolf's novel to a monochrome uniformity. Anita Brookner's women are always experiencing the poetics of lack. They are always at the edge of another world: Edith, as the mistress of a married man, is at the edge of the private world of marriage; the words 'Your car or mine?', exchanged between wife and husband, epitomise for her the exclusive intimacy made by the shared bonds of property and habit. On the other hand, because such women can never enter the domain of public action from their women's world, men are always at the margins of their experience: it is a double alienation from both public and private. These are women who never seem quite to exist, either for themselves or for anyone else.

The meek do not inherit the earth. In this greedy upper-middle-class environment, those with a strong sense of self win out, occasionally extending lacerating pity: '"I said, she has such sad eyes"', Edith is told, when asked by the Puseys to join them. But the meek can be destructive. Edith, though honourably, has run away from the brink of marriage to an honourable man. In *A Closed Eye* (1991), the novel following *Hotel du Lac* (which might just as well have been called *A Closed Door*), unacted desires blight. Harriet, married to a man old enough to be her father, masks sexuality with a willed and wilful innocence on one side of her life, and is passionately and silently in love with her best friend's husband on the other. She refuses her husband warmth, collusively spoils her own daughter, and neglects the emotional needs of her best friend's daughter, even while she clings possessively to her for the sake of her father. Understanding her loneliness, like Mrs Dalloway, she misrecognises its cause: 'I might be tempted to go in search of that empty room, with the single shaft of sunlight across the undisturbed bed.'[9] Her defacing birthmark, sign of the victim and outsider at one level, is also the Cain's mark of the middle-class woman's repression.

Desire bleeds perpetually into elegy. 'The Woman does not exist', Lacan's notorious epigram about the place of the feminine, forced to be the other of the masculine subject, is both apposite and not apposite to Brookner's novels. It is the negation of the feminine subject, the emptying out of meaning from the self, not the existence of the feminine as representation, which preoccupies Anita Brookner. Or at least, the lived experience of negation converges with a culturally made image, and the result is a perpetual outflow of energy and vitality into grief and depression.

The dissipating outflow of the poetics of lack and suffering would become inchoate but for the tight formal control exerted on the novels. Unlike Hélène Cixous, Anita Brookner is not a celebrant of the flow of desire and feeling, feeling indistinguishably of the body's physiological rhythms and of the mind. Indeed, the body is left out of her characters' calculations as something that cannot be easily dealt with. The botched abortion of Harriet's daughter is witness to the body's independent existence, which can be mutilated at will, and moves against rather than with the mind. And just as elegy threatens to take over as elegy, so form threatens to take over as *form*. *Hotel du Lac* circles back periodically from Edith's present desolation to the reasons for her virtually enforced holiday, and explanation of the past and discovery of the present meet at the end of the novel when she decides to choose – not present betrayal within a comfortable new marriage, but a past betrayal out of it. The formal control does not seem to have the same epistemological and political purpose as it does in the novels of Virginia Woolf, however. In *A Closed Eye* there is a persistent symmetry: two friends, two husbands, two daughters, the two swans, black and white, of *Swan Lake*, that ballet of a soft and a hard woman, which the little girls see almost at the novel's midpoint. Like the ballet, whose union of body and pattern is described as a rebuke to the inchoateness of life, such meticulous formalism is there simply to show what life lacks – form, order. The daughter of Harriet's friend worries with anxious distrust about the fate of the white swan, asking the questions which the ballet's form fails to ask. In Anita Brookner's work, middle-class protectiveness longs for the closure of form commensurate with its sense of order – but rarely gets it.

The poetics of lack begins and ends with the experience of the individual consciousness. Angela Carter, on the other hand, does not write from subjectivities and their centre of self. Hers is not the expressive mode, the inwardness of the feeling self. Instead she writes in a stylised, objectifying, external manner, as if all experience, whether observed or suffered, is self-consciously conceived of as *display*, a kind of rigorous, analytical, public self-projection which, by its nature, excludes private expression. The critique through fantasy which is the prerogative of what has come to be called magical realism demands such impersonality. The kind of fixed and passive suffering explored by Anita Brookner belongs, in Angela Carter's *Nights at the Circus*, to the terrible museum of death where the woman as victim is on display to gratify the sick sadomasochistic fantasy of visitors – the sleeping beauty who scarcely ever wakes up, the miniature woman who never grows up. Big Ben chimes throughout the first part of Fevvers's narrative and at the end of it, as if in parody of the reference to the leaden circles of sound which punctuate *Mrs Dalloway*. For now time is completely elastic, an *a priori* category, only because we can do what we like with it.

In *To the Lighthouse*, Virginia Woolf had begun to think of consciousness as a multiplicity of discontinuous subjects. This, and her increasingly questioning interest in exploring the limits of family and the possibility of other kinds of love outside it – between Lily and Mrs Ramsay, for instance – is what makes her a precursor of Angela Carter's work. But it is the surreal *sprezzatura* of *Orlando* (1928) which is the real antecedent of a novel such as *Nights at the Circus*: the 'biography' of a man who lives from the Elizabethan period to the present (1928), becoming a woman before the nineteenth century begins.

Place and time dissolve in *Orlando*. Orlando is first seen practising swordplay on the dessicated head of a Moor, a macabre reminder of the violence of Elizabethan society and its territorial aggression. The novel actually mocks the idea of the self-contained nation and its culture by transgressing local boundaries: Orlando courts a Russian and serves in Constantinople. The huge flood which marks the breaking up of the Great Frost in Jacobean England – breaking up as well a phase of Orlando's life – also marks the unfreezing of historical time into the fantastic, and the dissolution of established categories. The undermining of accepted categories goes hand in hand with the unorthodoxy of the narrative discourse. Orlando, skipping to Constantinople, avoids the English revolution, and returns as a woman to the reign of Queen Anne. True to the class to which he/she belongs, it is the gaiety and brio of the pleasure principle which conditions his/her experience. A hidden politics of narrative flouts historical 'events' to play with the forms of life made possible by the class position s/he holds, and its determined nature. Throughout, s/he finds that his/her social identity is defined in carnival, fiesta, masque, parties and social gatherings – even the visit to the department store in the twenties is an orgiastic experience.

There are huge differences between the privileged Orlando and the disenfranchised Fevvers, but in just the same way, space, place and temporality are at the service of Fevvers and her party and their *pleasure* in *Nights at the Circus*.[10] From London to Siberia, from Circus Manager to Grand Duke to Shaman, transported by a toy train which disappears when its function is over, Fevvers lives (literally, by making a living from it) through entertainment, masquerade, travesty, saturnalia, spectacle. The novel becomes a kind of rebus in which meaning is made in and through display and *spectacle*. It is through spectacle that gender identity is made, and women come into economic existence in this novel, if they are lucky, only by *being* spectacles. Fevvers, the central character, a woman who has grown wings, comes into being through a dream-work pun on 'bird', for that is one of the words for woman. The novel asks: if a woman *was* a bird, what would she be? Other women in the novel are locked into display and the necessity to *pose* as a *representation* of someone else's ideas about women's role or function ('Woman does not exist'). Fevvers poses as the Winged Victory in the brothel where she grows up (significantly, the Winged Victory is decapitated, mutilated) but can fly away. On the other hand, the Sleeping

Beauty and the midget pose in the museum of horrors: Mignon, the Ape-Man's woman, poses as the long-lost daughter in the gimcrack deceptions of a medium to whom she is a virtual slave. To be the representation of a fantasy which is itself a representation is to be enslaved indeed, a violence confused by a further violence, as animals – pigs, monkeys – represent women, too, and are treated as women. Yet, the novel, aware of violence and at the same time exuberant, uses fantasy to unmask fantasy, and thus liberates Fevvers into her *own* world of fantasy and play.

To see how this is possible, we can go back for a moment to Orlando's change of sex: 'He [not she] was a woman.' Both before and after this transformation Orlando experiences moments of androgyny and bisexuality which intrigue and fascinate her/him. Her/his name, suggesting the alternation of difference (either/'Or'), begins and ends with two noughts which indicate that the *content* of this either/or of sexual difference is variable and relative. The nature of identity and sexual identity is entwined, for instance, with economic structures. Orlando's intense 'Elizabethan' sexuality is bound up with a violently acquisitive need for valuable objects in which worth inheres intrinsically in things as an unmediated relationship. Her/his 'modern' consciousness, on the other hand, obeys the taxonomy of consumption organised in the department store. Just as it splits goods into classes and parts – sheets and bathsalts – so there is a parallel splitting of the feminine subject, who is a plurality, a multiplicity of selves: 'How many different people are . . . having lodgement at one time or another in the human spirit? Some say two thousand and fifty two.'[11] History divides us vertically, the present horizontally, but sexuality seems to be distributed under and across these divisions. Orlando's masculine sexuality can 'communicate' with her feminine self, but they remain apart, ununified, and they are not *fixed*. The 'movable' nature of sexual meaning is testified by the comic motif of Orlando's leg. His/her body is exactly the same, we are told: yet at one time his masculine calf thrills Nell Gwyn, while at another a sailor nearly falls into the sea at the sight of her ankle.

What really ensures the fixing of sexuality is the masque of purity (which is at the same time a masquerade) overseeing Orlando's change of sexual identity. Modesty, Chastity and Purity, allegorical figures, cast the *veil* of representation and repression over sexuality, which is constructed by the law: it is ideology; 'virgins and city men; lawyers and doctors; those who prohibit, those who deny; those who reverence without knowing why'.

Nights at the Circus liberates Fevvers into making the meaning of her own sexuality because, in exactly the same way as *Orlando*, the novel refuses to regard sexual difference in terms of fixed categories. It permits a dance of possibility. Fevvers's wings create an eroticised hermeneutic enquiry: what *is* she? Is she a bird or a woman? Or could she, given her size and strength, be a man? Is she a hoax? All these possibilities are expressed by Walser, the cipher of Fevvers's narrative and eventually her lover. Much of the comedy is created by the intense, hyperbolic, libidinal curiosity gathering round Fevvers's wings, which begins to parody the taboos and suppressions associated with the unspoken and the scandalous in sexual experience – biological sexual characteristics and their functions. Fevvers's discovery of wings is treated as if it were something like the onset of menstruation: the hump they make, like a second breast, has to be concealed; or the hump may be phallic, ambiguously bisexual; above all, a shockingly outrageous immodesty is imputed to the action: 'I spread'. By transferring taboo from one area of the body to another, Angela Carter parodies the language of sexual *pudeur* and shows that what *is* a hoax is the attaching of permanent, literal sexual meaning to particular parts of the body. In a self-conscious frolic of Freudian, carnivalesque and Lacanian reference – a frolic which sports with the authority of these writers as well as invoking them – she explores what experience would be like if, as Freud believed, libidinal feeling lives by substitution, and is displaced from one object of desire to another, one part of the body to another.·

In the end, though, despite – or perhaps because of – such mobility, you have to have the 'confidence', as Fevvers says in her robust final words, to fix things where you want. Love is possible when that is possible. Doctrinaire positions limit. That is partly why Fevvers is so often irritated by Lizzie, her loving mother figure, and her farcical eagerness to take a Marxist feminist line on everything. Until they release themselves from spectacle and the fixity of its fantasy, the women in the novel cannot do what the clowns, their male but sexually ambiguous opposites in the circus, can do – make up their identities. Sad, lyrical and clumsy, the clowns offer a paean of delight and laughter for the gift they are allowed – make-up. With greasepaint they can make up their personae and be in control of the representation which is and is not the self. One might compare the way Brookner's women use clothes and make-up as reparation, to staunch their loss of identity and give themselves a stable sexual being.

To make up, of course, outside the circus, is the woman's prerogative, and it is typical of the novel's crisscrossing of gender that this should often be taken to be a sign of oppression in another context. And make-up, the temporary invented self hypostasised, can indeed push one into madness. Walser, posing as a human chicken in the free-floating world of the circus, is almost chopped to death during the leading clown's sudden but irrevocable fit of insanity, and is temporarily almost as traumatised as his attacker. But such a weird fatality is yet another example of the exchange and remaking of roles in the novel. Walser's near-fatality parallels the near-violation and ritual murder of Fevvers earlier, when she is sold by the owner of the museum to one of the upper-class maniacs who haunt it. When Walser has not only imagined but *experienced* life from Fevvers's position, he is capable of loving her. It is salutary to remember that in this novel the hidden sword is a weapon possessed by men and women alike. Phallic violence is not the characteristic of masculinity alone. Mr Ramsay's 'beak' of destructive aggression, which so often hurts his family and himself, is held in common.

The fiction of elegy and what we might call the fiction of sport and play are, arguably, positive and negative poles of desire, the desire of the death wish and of the pleasure principle, manifesting themselves in the new cultural conditions following Woolf's modernism. While Anita Brookner, as the punning title of her novel suggests, is concerned with exploring the desire issuing from lack, in a dessicated middle-class world, Angela Carter is buoyantly concerned with the assertive desire issuing from the need to make demands on life, with redefining desire itself with the farce, cunning and high spirits of Benjamin's story-teller. If Anita Brookner's women are caught in the world of 'those who prohibit, those who deny', cramped by a class and sexual status which never recognises their worth, Angela Carter's characters are outcasts from it, the international tramps and refugees whose suffering creates a kind of macabre entertainment industry, and whose very existence is a critique of the prohibitions and denials which have resulted in such brutality and violence.

Realist narrative from the edges of the bourgeois world, magic narrative commensurate with its underside – these are both powerful modes. What really divides them is the narrative written from the centred self, and the narrative written through the fractured consciousness of multiple selves. This is likely to be the ground of debate about women's writing, for some feminist theory affirms that the realism which conveys the specific and immediate details of women's lives constitutes a politics of concrete detail, and this implies a centred narrative.[12] It is remarkable that Virginia Woolf's writing was sufficiently capacious to provide the possibilities for both modes of writing – lyrical neo-realism and discontinuous postmodern narrative pluralism – going far beyond the brief of modernism and the narrow class beliefs and aesthetics of the Bloomsbury Group as we have come to understand them. True, the poetics of lack, always prompted towards mourning, with an uneasiness about class and sex – particularly in the case of the lone woman without family – and transgressive fantasy, were never resolved in her work. And yet fantasy, stringently aware of feminist theories she herself made possible, dissident, moving with the energies of the pleasure principle and its delights and terrors, celebrates the multiplicity of possibilities which *Orlando* first explores. Though admittedly, Orlando wonders, with reservations not to be found in her/his followers, whether s/he can reconcile Burkean continuity with modern fracture.

Perhaps neo-realism and magical realism might be combined in a new grand narrative? That ambition – for the grand narrative – was certainly part of Virginia Woolf's project, and there seem to be no good reasons why it should be given up by women (we do not have to produce master narratives at the same time as grand narratives) at this historical moment, whatever is argued about the anachronism of attempting such texts. But brickwork and bricolage, like Barthes's work and text, seem a contradiction in terms. I have said, however, that both novelists explore the possibilities of lyrical language. This unique poetic register, deriving from Virginia Woolf, remains the least-explored element of her work and that of her followers. People are embarrassed by what they think of as 'poetic prose', but it is not that. 'Poetic prose', the fetishistic expressive language of self-absorbed sensibility and private soliloquy, is not what any of these writers produce. Rather, lyrical language opens up new categories and concepts and, as such, is the precondition of knowledge – not feminist knowledge alone, but any knowledge. It does this – to go back to the dividing line with which Lily ends her picture – by finding a language which is capable of troubling that signifying slash (Lily's line could well be the division between signified and signifier) which makes us aware of difference and likeness. In other words, it troubles the founding distinctions by which categories are constructed, and thus opens the way for the reconstruction of categories. It suspends meaning for a moment, troubling the line between signifier and signified, conscious and unconscious, subjectivity and culture. Its strength is that it refuses to fix the line between the private and the cultural, but makes it mobile. In her libretto for *Orlando*, Carter recognised the intensity of longing even while she so stringently burlesqued it by asking at one point, as Hermione Lee points out in her essay, for a music expressing 'the absolute quintessence of romantic melancholy'. And it may be that the rhetoric of desire, recognised so potently and in such different ways by the three novelists discussed here, is what loosens the hold of that distinction between inner and outer worlds, and prepares us for those shifts of meaning which question the world.

It is a mode which searches into the unconscious, floating

semiotic material into the realm of conscious experience and making it ask questions of the very basis of that experience, its nature, its history, the culture to which it belongs. It is to be found in the strange indeterminacy of what is half intensely private reverie and half cultural memory in Mrs Dalloway's recall of Shakespeare's 'Fear no more the heat of the sun'; it is to be found in Mrs Ramsay's incorporation of the pulse of the lighthouse, that public beacon, into her own being; it is to be found in Edith's grey evocation of Dantesque feeling standing above the hotel lake; it is to be found in the Byron poem sung by the battered and starving Mignon in her bath: 'We'll go no more a-roving'. Mignon, who has just stuffed herself with luxury chocolates encased in frilled tutus of paper, suddenly becomes a tragic rather than a pathetic figure to her listeners. She knows the words of the song, but not their meaning, and this understanding, of which she herself cannot be aware, brings tears to their eyes and gives new meaning to the song. The suspension, or indeterminacy, of meaning 'means' that consciousness and culture meet on new terms. The poetic register, created here by both Mignon and her listeners, reconfigures everyone's experience. The poetic register prepares to make new relationships with reality, but remakes what is reality in the process. It is profoundly social utterance, and deeply private. This is a germinal mode which is still waiting to be fully explored.

Seriously Funny:
Wise Children

∙∙∙

KATE WEBB

1   Introduction: Crisscross

I'm sure Angela Carter would have been pleased to hear that the hottest thing in pop music these days[1] are two young mixed-race American rappers who wear their trousers back to front and call themselves 'CrissCross'. Carter's last work of fiction, *Wise Children* – in the spirit of the novel one could call it, perhaps, an old bird's-eye/I view of the social, cultural, imperial and sartorial history of the century now ending – is itself patterned with intersecting tracks and grooves that are made by her characters 'crossing, crisscrossing'[2] the globe; by the zigzagging lines of familial and artistic descent that reach across and into their lives; and by the writing itself, which passes through – often parodying – many genres and styles, yet remains something completely authentic and her own.

2   Family and Culture: Twin Peaks

Wise Children is the story of 'the imperial Hazard dynasty that bestrode the British theatre like a colossus for a century and a half', and its bastard progeny, Dora and Nora Chance, identical twin girls who are illegitimate twice over: by birth, because their father, Melchior Hazard, denies his paternity of them time after time; and by profession, where, as a novelty act, they dance the boards in music hall, appear briefly as extras in an ill-fated Hollywood musical, and finally undress (though never beyond the G-string) in seedy postwar strip shows like 'Nudes Ahoy!' and 'Nudes of the World!'.

The story is told by one of these lovely bastards, Dora, the wisecracking, left-handed, southside twin sister who rakes over more than a century of family romance and history. As in all the best modern fiction, the action of the novel takes place in just one day. A special day, however: it is the anniversary of Shakespeare's birthday, which happens also to be Dora's and Nora's own – this year their seventy-fifth. It's the birthday and centenary, too, of another set of twins, Melchior and Peregrine Hazard, father and uncle (but which is which?) of these performing sisters, 'The Lucky Chances'. The double-faced Hazard/Chance family is served up to the reader as a model for Britain and Britishness, obsessively dividing itself into upper and working class, high and low culture. And just as Dora proves these strict lines of demarcation to be false within her own family, so, too, her story shows the reader how badly they fit the complexity and hybridity of British society and culture.[3]

If it is relatively easy (and Carter has a lot of fun doing this) to show how we foster and exploit binary oppositions in culture in order to justify the domination and exclusion of others, and to sustain elite privilege in society, it is a much more complicated thing to respond to the fictions, the romances – family and otherwise – which we have built upon the idea of legitimacy and illegitimacy. Master of this dialectic is William Shakespeare, whose 'huge overarching intellectual glory'[4] dominates the English literary canon and whose work, like Carter's own, is brimful with ideas of doubleness, artificiality and parody. In *Wise Children*, Carter not only weaves Shakespeare's stories in and out of her own, she also reminds us of the extent to which his words and ideas impregnate English culture and life: his face is on the £20 note that Dora doles out to the fallen comic, Gorgeous George; and contemporary television programmes that poach their names from him, like *The Darling Buds of May*, *May to September* and *To the Manor Born*, all make pointed, if somewhat disguised, appearances in the novel.

Part of what attracts Carter to Shakespeare is his playing out of the magnetic relationship of attraction and repulsion that exists between the legitimate and the illegitimate, between energy and order. This occurs most famously, perhaps, in the sliding friendship of Prince Hal and Falstaff. Near the close of her story, Dora tries to reimagine one of Shakespeare's cruellest moments: what if Hal, on becoming king, had not rejected Falstaff, but dug him in the ribs and offered him a job instead? What if order was permanently rejected, and we lived life as a perpetual carnival? These questions are not answered directly (and I will return to her implied answers later), but this challenge to order, to the legitimate world, is made throughout the novel.

Dora, illegitimate as she is, may sympathise with some of Falstaff's bastard qualities, but her story is not one of martyrdom or victimhood. She knows that as outsiders she and her sister Nora are given freedoms for which their legitimate twin sisters, Imogen and Saskia, could never hope. When Dora describes Nora's first sexual experience, she warns her reader not to:

> run away with the idea that it was a squalid, furtive
> miserable thing, to make love for the first time on a cold
> night in a back alley with a married man with strong drink

on his breath. He was the one she wanted, warts and all,
she *would* have him, by hook or by crook. She had a passion
to know about Life, all its dirty corners, and this is how she
started. . . . (p. 81)

Wise Children, then, not only challenges legitimacy, it is also
a celebration of the vitality of otherness. Paradoxically,
though, because the legitimate and illegitimate world rely
upon one another's mirror-image of difference through
which to define themselves, such a celebration of illegitimacy necessarily implies a valorisation of the system which
produces outcasts. Knowing this, one of the questions
Carter asks us in the novel is: What, then, should a wise
child do? Revel in wrong-sidedness and, therefore, the
system that produces it, or jettison the culture of dualism
altogether? In answer, Carter's wise – though by now
somewhat wizened – child, Dora, pulls of the sort of
conjuring trick that her Falstaffian Uncle Perry is famous
for: she manages both to have her cake and eat it, to revel
in her wrong-sidedness, to sustain her opposition to authority, and yet to show that the culture and society she inhabits
is not one of rigid demarcation, but has always been mixed
up and hybrid: Shakespeare may have become the very
symbol of legitimate culture, but his work is characterised
by bastardy, multiplicity and incest; the Hazard dynasty
may represent propriety and tradition, but they, too, are an
endlessly orphaned, errant, and promiscuous bunch.

3   Culture and Imperialism

(i)   'High' Culture: William's Word

The Hazard family is a patriarchal institution, but its father
figures (Ranulph and later his son, Melchior) find their

authority deriving not from God, but from a Shakespeare who has come to seem omnipotent in the hegemony of British culture, to embody not only artistic feeling but religious and national spirit too: for Ranulph, 'Shakespeare was a kind of God. . . . It was as good as idolatry. He thought the whole of human life was there.' By becoming, each in his generation, the 'greatest living Shakespearian', Ranulph and then Melchior assume a kingly status themselves. Having so often rehearsed the role of Shakespearian prince or king, these actors take on the mantle of royalty itself: 'the Hazards belonged to everyone. They were a national treasure.'

At a late stage in the family's history, mirroring the collapse both of empire and of royalty, the imbrications of 'The Royal Family of the theatre' make them appear as vulgar and commercialised as our latter-day House of Windsor. Like them, the Hazard dynasty become national sport, soap opera masquerading as news. But in earlier times this regal troupe of players are not only commodities for the country ('national treasure'), they are agents of Britain's colonial ambition. Before the fall of the House of Hazard, Ranulph's evangelical zeal for spreading the Word of Shakespeare is so great that he 'crosses, crisscrosses' the globe, travelling 'to the ends of the empire' in his efforts to sell the religion of Shakespeare and the English values he represents:

> Ranulph. He was half mad and thought he had a Call. Now he saw the entire world as his mission field . . . [in] the family tradition of proselytizing zeal . . . the old man was seized with the most imperative desire, to go on spreading the Word overseas. (p. 17)

In Tasmania, Shanghai, Hong Kong, Singapore, Montreal, Toronto, Alberta and even Gun Barrel, North Dakota,

Ranulph Hazard's travelling theatre troupe meet in their audience a passion for self-fashioning as great as Shakespeare's own. As a consequence, they leave in their wake around the globe a string of towns called Hazard.

Throughout *Wise Children* Carter celebrates the vital and carnivalesque in life. 'What a joy it is to dance and sing!' is Dora's refrain, but she is aware of the effect that the enthusiasm and self-absorption of carnival can have upon others: aware, too, of the ways in which this power can be harnessed by a dominant group and brought to bear upon a weaker one. So she celebrates the craziness, 'a kind of madness', that drives old Ranulph to travel the world taking Englishness to foreigners, yet deftly shows how intimately connected are Shakespeare's cultural domination and British imperialism.

Carter's connecting of art and religion reinforces this idea: Ranulph sees it as his 'mission' in life to perform Shakespeare throughout the world in order to persuade other people of the greatness of the Bard's words, just as missionaries took the Bible and tried to persuade 'natives' of the truth of God's Word. Ranulph Hazard's theatre troupe literally follow in the steps of religious evangelicalism – his 'patched and ravaged tent went up in the spaces vacated by the travelling evangelicals'. They perform in 'wild, strange and various places', and their costumes are 'begged or improvised or patched and darned.' Cultural hegemony may have been an important part of the imperial vision, but acting, Carter reminds us, has always been an illegitimate profession: peripatetic, thrown-together, made-up and sexually ambivalent (in Central Park, Estella plays Hamlet in drag). Theatre, and particularly the theatre of Shakespeare, has played its role in colonising the minds of other countries, but it is also a potentially destabilising and subversive force.

(ii) 'Low' Culture: Gorgeous George

'Tragedy, eternally more class than comedy,' sighs Dora, meaning both that it has a classier pedigree than comedy and that it is associated with the classes rather than the masses. Carter's qualification, however, points to her conviction that, like everything else in life, art form (choosing to write comedy rather than tragedy) is a question of politics.[5] 'Comedy is tragedy that happens to other people,' she says (taking in the process, perhaps, a swipe at Martin Amis,[6] whose comedies often are).

Dora first encounters the comic Gorgeous George when she is thirteen, entertaining the masses on Brighton pier. Uncle Perry arrives unexpectedly in Brixton with a carload of good things to eat and drink, and packs the ersatz Chance family (Dora and Nora, Grandma and one of Perry's many foundlings, 'our Cyn') off to Brighton for the day. There they find George; a combination of Frankie Howerd ('*Filthy* minds, some of you have') and Larry Grayson ('Say no more'), he comes in the tradition of the holiday *camp* entertainer and his jokes are endlessly insinuating, every phrase or object carrying with it some double, sexual meaning. Sex is everywhere and with it, therefore, the possibility of incest. Reflecting England's fallen status, George's jokes mock ideas of strength and purity, and fuel paternal anxiety about redundancy and impotency. His comedy is parodic and slippery and perfectly timed, and his punchline, when it's finally delivered, is a withering attack on a foolishly deluded old patriarch who thinks himself the greatest stud around: the son, taken in by his father's boasts of promiscuity, becomes worried about committing incest with some unknown bastard offspring, but his mother tells him not to worry because, after all: '*E*'s not your father.' *B-bum!*

George's final *coup de grâce*, after singing 'Rose of England', 'Land of Hope and Glory', 'God Save the King' *and* 'Rule Britannia', is to strip off before his dazzled audience and reveal a torso tattooed with a map of the world: 'George was not a comic at all but an enormous statement.' But even a statement as blatant as the pink- (for British colonies) dominated world (Dora smartly picks out Ireland, South Africa and the Falkland Islands) emblazoned across the body of this latter-day St George is fraught with ambiguity. Unlike St George of old, Gorgeous George no longer wins battles and rules the waves; he merely represents the idea of conquest. He is a walking metaphor, an effete mirror-image. George shows us an empire falling: having once dominated the world, this Englishman can now be master of only one space: his own body.

George's decline, like the British Empire's, continues apace. Dora encounters him once more as an anachronistic Bottom (his kind of peculiarly English comedy doesn't travel) in the Hollywood production of *A Midsummer Night's Dream*, a débâcle over which Melchior presides, and in which she and Nora have bit parts (they play Mustardseed and Peaseblossom). Finally, back in London, George ends up hitting rock bottom: Dora, catching a glimpse of his pink tattoo, recognises him in the pathetic street beggar who approaches her for the price of a cup of tea.

(iii)   Fallen

If Shakespeare provides English literary culture with a model for plurality, it is in Milton, particularly in *Paradise Lost*, that we find a model for dualism in the world, a dualism resulting from the patriarchal and monistic vision of Christianity. One of Dora's refrains (she has a few up her sleeve) is the Miltonic phrase 'Lo, how the mighty are fallen', which is both a silly semantic joke and a serious intimation of the world she inhabits. Many of the descriptions of fallenness in *Wise Children* are specifically Miltonic or Christian: for instance, both Melchior and Peregrine are figured as Godlike *and* Satanic. Peregrine lands into the lives of the naked, innocent, unselfconscious and therefore Eve-like Nora and Dora as Adam arrived on earth: out of nowhere. And it is of Adam that Dora thinks when she sees him, because this is to be her First Man, the man who, like the fallen angel Lucifer, will first seduce her. In the same way, Melchior, 'our father' who 'did not live in heaven' but who, God-like, is worshipped by the girls from afar, is also given a Satanic side: he appears 'tall, dark and handsome' with 'knicker shifting' eyes, dressed in 'a black evening cape with a scarlet lining'. Later he is Count Dracula (a late-nineteenth-century Satanic pretender), ordering Dora and Nora to carry dirt over from Stratford – as Dracula had carried it from Transylvania – to scatter on the Hollywood set of his film of *A Midsummer Night's Dream*.

In Hollywood, the English colony represents a parody version of the once great Empire, playing Disraeli, Queen Victoria and Florence Nightingale. Just as in Ranulph's generation English theatre was shown to embody the nation's imperial strength, so now the film industry in Hollywood symbolises America's new role as a world power. Melchior's attempt to produce a film version of *A Midsummer Night's Dream* is his way of trying to conquer Hollywood, 'his chance to take North America back for England, Shakespeare and St George.' But the trip to Hollywood is presaged by the burning down of Melchior's manor house, and with the English theatre symbolically erased in the fire, 'the final degeneration of the House of Hazard' ensues. Ultimately we find Melchior's son, Tristram, the 'weak but charming, game-show presenter and television personality, last gasp of the imperial Hazard dynasty', presiding over an S/M game.

(iv) The End

> The sense of limitless freedom that I, as a woman,
> sometimes feel *is* that of a new kind of being. Because I
> simply could not have existed, as I am, in any other
> preceding time or place. I am the pure product of an
> advanced industrialized, post-imperialist country in
> decline.[7]

It is typical of Carter that unlike many modernist writers she sees in the decline of empire – to adapt Brecht – not the death of bad old things but the birth of good new ones – her own liberation, for instance. Symbolising the newness that the death of the old might now bring into being, *Wise Children* is secreted with what Salman Rushdie, in a short story, called 'the eggs of love'[8]: Dora's and Nora's bottoms jiggle like hard-boiled eggs; there are dried eggs during the war and smuggled black-market ones; Scotch eggs that landladies put out for supper; and in the snow, Dora sees egg-shaped depressions.

This is a cuspy, millennial novel, and 'millennia', Carter believes, 'always get strange towards the end'.[9] Part of *Wise Children*'s strangeness is due, perhaps, to the disconcerting sense of beginnings and possibility at the moment of ending, of death. The story's final has a riotous celebration for the now-centenarian Melchior and Peregrine, after which Dora (who, at seventy-five, has herself been thinking about calling it a day), finds that she and Nora have suddenly had motherhood thrust upon them. They toddle home – these unmarried, non-biological and overage mothers – 'Drunk in charge of a baby carriage'.

Death has a strong presence in this book – not just the end of empire or the death of the patriarch, which Dora is happy to let go, but a sense of the presence of death in the midst of life. Dora is someone who wrestles with this, a spirited fighter who refuses to grieve for long, or give in to defeat. 'Let other pens dwell on guilt and misery', our autodidact narrator recites from Jane Austen. Dora's optimism derives from both a moral and a political sense of duty learned at her grandma's knee, whose often-recited maxim 'Hope for the best, expect the worst' lies on the map somewhere between Gramsci's 'Pessimism of the intellect, optimism of the will' and St Augustine's 'Don't presume, don't despair'. Neither she nor Nora sheds a tear at the news of their beloved Tiffany's death, though both are heartbroken by it. 'Life must go on,' says Nora, refusing to be engulfed by despair.

One of *Wise Children*'s characteristic inversions of the supposed order of life is that no one dies of old age, all are 'untimely' deaths – the only 'true tragedy', Dora says wisely: Grandma, hit by a flying bomb on her way to the off-licence; Cyn's husband, killed in North Africa in the war, and Cyn herself succumbing to the Asian flu of '49 (the cat to the cat flu of '51); Dora's lover, Irish, makes his last exit in Hollywood, caused by too much booze and a 'dicky-ticker'; finally, there is the apparent suicide of their godchild, the young, mixed-race Tiff, who, Ophelia-like, seems to have made her suicide a watery one, into the bosom of Old Father Thames. But this is just one of the instances in which – to use Edward Said's[10] phrase – Carter 'writes back'. Her Ophelia does not give in to patriarchal abuse (by committing suicide in Father Thames): like Carter she, too, imagines herself as 'a new kind of being', and in the end it is she (the illegitimate outsider) who lays down the new rules of play for the Hazard dynasty.

4   A Looking-Glass World

(i)   Pluralism and Difference

In *Wise Children*, Carter is able to suggest a jumbled, impure multiculture, while showing clearly that class, racial and sexual elites which seek to exclude otherness are still a powerful and conditioning force. A reader of Foucault, Carter fully understood the way in which the dualistic structures that belong to the dying past – to Christianity, patriarchy and empire – are still extant in the present.[11] By showing Shakespeare at the heart of English culture, as the 'author of our being', father to both the Hazards and the Chances (legitimate and illegitimate share his birthday), Carter is arguing that plurality and hybridity are not simply conditions of modernity, products of its wreckage, but have always existed and are characteristic of life itself. From this it follows that she does not see in plurality, as many postmodernists do, a nihilistic loss of value; rather, an existential acceptance of the facts of life and death in which contradictions are a sign of hope, and difference has to be negotiated rather than fought over as if there were only one place of rightness, one correct way of living that must be identically reproduced the whole world over. This is something that Dora's grandma knows innately – feels it, as Dora does, 'in her ancient water'. When, in wartime, she waves her stick in the air at the bombers overhead, she recognises that war is a result of patriarchal insistence upon monism: men fight to wipe out women and children (whom 'she knew they hated . . . worst of all' – because they are most other); but forever locked in some recidivist oedipal struggle, they fight, as well, to stop younger men stealing their thunder, to stop them taking away their distinguished mantles of poet or god.

(ii)   Glasshouse Fun

But while men continue to fight wars, to battle for absolute control of land or language, Carter tells us we live now in a world of endless refraction. The days when a looking-glass reflected just one wicked witch, one absolute image of otherness, are gone. Now we have cinema, television, radio and video splintering the world 'in a gallery of mirrors',[12] a glasshouse of perpetual reproduction. Our relationship to these multiple, often contradictory reflections, especially for women, is as important and as determining as our relationship to other people. It is this awareness, critics like Lorna Sage[13] have argued, that defines much of Carter's work, and makes it unique.

In *Wise Children*, however, the glasshouse is not the house of horror, the bloody chamber we have peered into with Carter so often in the past. These characters are not the glassy, fragile forms of some of her reworked fairy stories, eternally caged by images not of their own making. Dora's narrative is a much freer, bouncier one, with a resilience that comes from a new kind of resourcefulness. Perhaps we have now lived long enough with our shadow selves, Carter seems to be suggesting, that we are at last learning how to gain some control over them. Dora is a toughie, a survivor and a canny self-observer, and is not imprisoned by her female sexuality or the multitude of images of femininity that surround her. Rather, she seems like one of Shakespeare's bastards, Edmund, determined not to let the Dionysian wheel of fate[14] settle her life, but to find in the *chance* of her wrong-sidedness neither shame nor restraint, but opportunity. Because of this Dora is able to enjoy her own body, and the bodies of other women too. Maybe one of the meanings of the twins is a rather Laingian[15] one: the idea that one need not be afraid of one's image, but should embrace it, love it instead. Like the autoerotic Dora and Nora, one can 'feast' on oneself. (However, this enlightening idea finds its dark equation on the Hazard side, where the family seal is of an animal devouring itself – a pelican pecking at its own breast. This is because in a value system that is monistic, self-love – as I suggested above in the case of Ranulph and Melchior – inevitably implies incest or its correlative, cannibalism.)

5   Family Romance and Family Secrets

'Dread and delight coursed through my veins. I thought what have I done . . .' Perhaps part of the reason for Dora's dread and delight, when she momentarily wonders whether, as a young girl, she had fucked her Uncle Perry, has to do with the idea of gaining power not with a man's weapon – his strength; but with a woman's – her sex. One way for Dora, the outsider, to gain access to the power and legitimacy of 'the House of Hazard' is to fuck her way inside, or at least to bring it to its knees by transgressing its laws of order and hierarchy: uncles are not supposed to have sex with their nieces, particularly not when they are only thirteen – Dora's age, it finally transpires, when Peregrine first seduced her.

Wise Children is like the proverbial Freudian nightmare – aided and abetted (as Freud was himself) by Shakespearian example. Dora's family story is crammed with incestuous love and oedipal hatred: there are sexual relationships between parent and child (where this is not technically so, actor-parents marry their theatrical offspring – in two generations of Hazards, Lears marry Cordelias); and between sister and brother (Melchior's children Saskia and Tristram). And there is oedipal hatred between child and parent

(Saskia twice tries to poison her father, and she and her twin sister Imogen are guilty either of pushing their mother down a flight of stairs or at least of leaving her there, an invalid, once she has fallen); and between parent and child ('All the same, he [Ranulph] loved his boys. He cast them as princes in the tower as soon as they could toddle.'[16])

Nor is Dora's name accidental. In another example of 'writing back', Carter's Dora, unlike her Freudian namesake, suffers very little psychic damage from lusting after her father (she 'fell in love the first time she saw him') or her uncle, or a string of father substitutes (men old enough to be) with whom she has affairs. The fact that it is the female (sisterly) body which seems most erotic to her (the nape of Saskia's neck, Nora's jiggling bottom) is for this Dora a cause for celebration, rather than self-hatred. Her half-sisters, Saskia and Imogen, fare less well in this game of family romance. On hearing that her father, Melchior, is about to marry her best friend (another form of incest), 'Saskia's wails approached hysteria, whereupon Melchior smartly smacked her cheek . . . She shut up at once.' It is because of this betrayal, and her father's silencing of her anger, that Saskia takes revenge by seducing the couple's son and her half-brother, Tristram.

Ironically, then, it is the legitimate daughters, Saskia and Imogen, who end up emotionally crippled by their family relationships (though this, perhaps, is a reflection of how rotten the family has become). These weird and troubled sisters might have received greater attention in Carter of an earlier vintage, but here Dora asserts: 'I refuse point-blank to play in tragedy.' Perhaps because in dealing with illegitimacy in the past, particularly female illegitimacy, Carter, in her highly wrought and self-conscious work, had sometimes aestheticised pain, even death, now, facing her own, she wanted to face it more squarely or not at all:[17] 'We knew nothing was a matter of life and death except life and death.'

Dora's story-telling is a spilling of all the family secrets, bringing the skeletons out of the closet and exposing them to bright lights. This is a comment in itself: no more family secrets, no more lies, no more illegitimacies, Dora seems to assert, yet there is a powerful and unresolved tension in *Wise Children* between the idea of family secrets and family romance. As the Hazard/Chance family has been shown in the novel to symbolise the broader culture, so too, there is a tension between a desire for openness and equality – a world without secrets or bastards – and the seductive pull of romances from unofficial places, stories from the wrong side of the blanket, from 'the wrong side of the tracks'.

6   How She Writes

Mikhail Bakhtin argued that language is inherently dialogic because it implies a listener who must also be another speaker.[18] It's a proposition that Carter, the iconoclast, agreed with and tried to illuminate in her writing: 'A piece of fiction is never static. I purposely try to make what I write open-ended, "user-friendly".'[19] She demonstrates this in *Wise Children* by employing a first-person narrator (a form, she said, that men were afraid to use, because it was too revealing). Carter's mouthpiece, 'I, Dora Chance', speaks to her reader as if she expected him or her to reply: 'There I go again! Can't keep a story going in a straight line, can I?' At the beginning of the book Dora tells us that she is writing her autobiography on a word-processor on the morning of her seventy-fifth birthday, but the vernacular force of her speech is so great that later she magically appears to transcend the written word, becoming, instead, the old bird who's collared you in the local boozer:

> Well, you might have known what you were about to let yourself in for when you let Dora Chance in her ratty old fur and poster paint, her orange (Persian Melon) toenails sticking out of her snakeskin peep-toes, reeking of liquor, accost you in the Coach and Horses[20] and let her tell you a tale. (p. 227)

Dora's a reader-teaser, endlessly drawing attention to herself by postponing the moment of revelation ('but I don't propose to tell *you*, not now . . .') or prodding her reader into paying attention because 'Something unscripted is about to happen'. She's also a demythologiser, keen to let her reader in on the tricks of the trade: a chronicler not just of the Hazard and Chance families but of fashion through the ages – talking about brand names, she says: 'If you get little details like that right, people will believe anything'. As with this last sentence, her gist is always more than surface level, and a huge part of the fun of reading *Wise Children* lies in seeing how far you can unpack the layers of meaning. How far, too, you can unpick the words of others that have been woven into Carter's/Dora's own. There is Shakespeare everywhere, but other writers also: Milton, Sterne, Wordsworth ('If the child is father of the man . . . then who is the mother of the woman?'), Dickens, Lewis Carroll making an appearance as a purveyor of 'kiddiporn', Samuel Butler, Shaw, Dostoevsky ('My crime is my punishment'), Henry James and Tennessee Williams ('They lived on room service and the kindness of strangers') are just a random selection.

Like any postmodern novel worth its salt, *Wise Children* not only steals freely from other literary texts but also takes from the texts of other people's lives and uses these too. In

Hollywood, Carter has a field day. Armed, I'd say, with the dirt-dishing Kenneth Anger,[21] she has a roster of stars making guest appearances – sometimes as themselves, sometimes in various kinds of drag: featured players are Charlie Chaplin 'hung like a horse', Judy Garland (Ranulph's wife is known as Estella 'A Star Danced' Hazard, and was 'born in a trunk'), Busby Berkeley, Fred Astaire and his wife Adele, Astaire and Ginger Rogers, Ruby Keeler, Jessie Matthews, Josephine Baker, Jack Warner, W. C. Fields, Gloria Swanson, Paul Robeson, Orson Welles ('old buffers in . . . vintage port and miniature cigar commercials'), Clark Gable, Howard Hughes, Ivor Novello and Noël Coward (Dora's and Nora's first dancing teacher is called Mrs Worthington). Daisy Duck with her missing back molars (it enhances the cheekbones) is a mixture of Lana Turner and Jean Harlow, ending up like Joan Crawford in TV soaps giving 'good décolleté'. Daisy's 'peel me a prawn' line is Mae West's 'Beulah, peel me a grape' from *I'm No Angel*, and her Puck, with a 'face like an old child', is Mickey Rooney, who starred as Robin Goodfellow in the original Hollywood version of *A Midsummer Night's Dream*. Erich von Stroheim is the model for Genghis Khan, the whipcracking, jodhpured director with a penchant for cruelty and steak-eating orchids, and Dora's alcoholic, scriptwriting boyfriend Irish is an amalgam of many writers – Scott Fitzgerald, Nathaniel West and William Faulkner – finally succumbing to the abundant alcohol and indifference doled out in equal measures by the studio system. There's a veiled portrait, too, of Brecht in Hollywood, whom Dora employs to teach her German and likes because he's one of the few people she meets out there who aren't terminally optimistic: 'What I say is, fuck the bourgeoisie.'

Wise Children has songs, too: music-hall and patriotic war songs, jazz and pop. And good and bad jokes: as well as

Carter's own ('Why are they called Pierrots?' . . . 'Because
they do their stuff on piers'), she pastiches older camp
comedians like Frankie Howerd and Larry Grayson, and
picks up on the more recent Thatcherite humour of Harry
Enfield's 'Loads a'money', turning it into Tristram's ghastly
catchphrase 'Lashings of Lolly'.

If her sources of material are eclectic, so too is her method
of writing – Carter trips lightly through many styles and
genres: she is an expressionist who paints 'a female city,
red-eyed, dressed in black . . .'; a magical realist, a student
of Hawthorne, Nabokov and Borges, wreathing Perry in
magic butterflies; a graffitist scratching 'Melchior slept here'
across her page; and a montage Surrealist: 'She was our air-
raid shelter; she was our entertainment; she was our breast.'
Carter is a conjuror baiting her audience – 'All in good time
I shall reveal to you how . . .'; a romance novelist who
knows where the big bucks are to be found – 'Romantic
illegitimacy, always a seller'; a teller of tall tales – 'If you'll
believe that . . .', and wise old wives' tales. She's a reteller
of fairy stories – 'Once upon a time . . .'/'It had come to
pass . . .'; an autobiographer and 'inadvertent chronicler',
farceur and tragedian, fabulist and 'rival realist' – Sage's[22]
phrase for Carter's through-the-looking-glass world.

But just as this is a wise book, knowing about culture,
history and politics, it is also a childlike one. The house at
49 Bard Road that Dora and Nora live in all their lives is
reminiscent of the kind found in English children's stories.
Its large musty rooms and odd-striking grandfather clock,
(mysteriously) absent father and mother, and presiding
grandmother left to eke out the rent by taking in strange
boarders, are all staples of the genre. Orphaned children
are free children – free of the sexually proscribing authority
of their mum and dad, at least, so perhaps the (Wildean)
habit of rather forgetfully losing your parents in these

stories (as it patently is in *Wise Children*), is strategic: a way of allowing characters a little more space in which to fashion themselves.

Finally, as well as employing all these styles in her own writing, Carter shows us how a familiarity with many ways of seeing is a part of the modern condition: Dora is not only a passive observer of different genres, she also employs them to shape her own world. She does this to heighten experience, but also self-consciously, even paradoxically, to gain a sense of the constructedness of life by turning people into actors. For instance, when Estella leaves for America she imagines herself in a scene from a movie, and when Melchior, at the age of twelve, absconds from the home of his 'dour as hell' puritan aunt, he does so as a character from a children's story, as Dick Whittington.

7   The Anxiety of Paternity

(i)   Literal Fathers

The question of paternity arises everywhere in *Wise Children*. Just 'what does a father do?' and 'what is he for?', Dora asks. And well she might, given the example of the Hazard men, all of whom disown their children in one way or another. Ranulph leaves his twin sons Tristram and Gareth, fatherless, abandoning them when he shoots their mother and himself in a lovers' quarrel; Melchior and Peregrine, learning from their father's example, are equally forgetful about their fatherly responsibilities. Melchior forgets to love his children, and when he remembers, it's the chilly, arm's-length affection that the wealthy inadequately bestow on their young. He denies paternity of Dora and Nora altogether, of course – the bastard girls he sired with his landlady one night in Brixton. (Perhaps the reason

Grandma creates a romance out of her origins and out of Dora's and Nora's is to protect them from their repudiating father, to allow them the freedom of making themselves up rather than being determined by Melchior's dismissal.) His brother Peregrine, a lavisher of all kinds of love, while watching wistfully after Saskia (and this is ambivalent – are his feelings for her sexual or fatherly?), denies his paternity of both her and her twin sister Imogen.

At the end of this line, Tristram stands no chance as a parent. Not, that is, until his lover, Tiffany, fights back, makes demands upon him, setting down preconditions for his fatherhood. What Carter hints at here is that it is the absence of practising fathers that causes so much grief and confusion: meaning that fathers, having never properly experienced fatherly feelings, often confuse them with sexual ones – hence the tradition of marrying your daughter, of Lears loving Cordelias, in the Hazard family. In the same way, absent fathers are mysterious fathers, which is why these enigmatic creatures become, for their children, the object of such longing and romance.

However, it is the errant behaviour of fathers that creates, among the Hazards and the Chances, so much opportunity for the breakdown of order, for transgression. It seems that in some way fatherly absence is what creates the carnival. That men are such recalcitrant parents stems from their carnival instincts, a sense of narcissism (Peregrine is far too self-involved to be able to give himself permanently as a parent); selfishness (Melchior is more interested in his work than in his children); and a desire not to be controlled or determined within a family order which limits the patriarch just as it confines women.

The only father who escapes this pattern of paternal abuse is Gareth, Tristram's twin brother, who carries on the evangelical tradition of the Hazard family in the Church rather than the theatre. A disciple of 'liberation theology', Gareth is the only 'non-combatant' father, not engaged in the 'titanic' warfare between parent and child. But he achieves this new stance in the same old Hazard way: by abandoning his children, leaving them with Perry, who passes them on at the birthday finale as a very special gift to Nora, who had always wanted to be a mother.

(ii)   Literary Fathers

Such fatherly ambivalence, Carter suggests in *Wise Children*, might be rooted not only in carnival selfishness but in the anxiety of paternity: the eternal 'gigantic question mark over the question of their paternity'. It is this forever unresolved uncertainty about their role in biological creativity that has led men to create a mystique around artistic, and especially literary, creativity: as critics like Gilbert and Gubar have shown, the anxiety of paternity is translated into the anxiety of authorship. Here, however, Carter seems to be arguing that women, whose role in biological creativity is not in doubt ('"Father" is a hypothesis but "mother" is a fact'), should now begin to shrug off the male anxiety that they, as writers, have been made to assume, and stop asking questions such as 'Is the pen a phallus?'[23] Dora does not romanticise or transform sex into something other than it is (which is what men do in their mystifying of the creative process, to cover their feelings of inadequacy); she enjoys it for what it is. A straight-thinking woman, Dora would never mistake a pen for a penis.

8   Carnival Girls and Carnival Boys

As I suggested above, the Bakhtinian idea of carnival is
central to *Wise Children*. In particular, Carter plays out ideas
about sexuality's relationship to the carnivalesque
transgression of order – a transgression that is, according to
Bakhtin, at once both sanctioned and illegitimate. Jane
Miller has argued in a collection of essays[24] that because of
the breakdown of all barriers, particularly linguistic and
bodily ones, that carnival entails, women do not appear in
Bakhtin's work as distinct from men: carnival's amassing
experience, which collapses laughter with fear, pleasure
with nausea, where the world becomes 'infinitely reversible
and remakeable',[25] ends up denying female difference. The
reason Miller tenders for 'the inability of even these writers
[Bakhtin, Volosinov and other Formalists who are interested
in power] to make gender difference and sexual relations
central to their work' is that they are limited by their
'particular history and their own place in it'. What Carter
seems to suggest in *Wise Children*, however, is a prior
problem. It is not just a question of Bakhtin denying
difference, denying 'those pains and leakages that are not
common to both sexes',[26] but that women and carnival
might, ultimately, be inimical because female biology and
the fact of motherhood make women an essentially connecting force, while carnival is essentially the celebration of
transgression and breakdown.

Without entering into the debate about whether transgression can be revolutionary if it is sanctioned by authority,[27] perhaps it is in this seeming paradox in Bakhtin's
argument – that carnival's transgressions are both allowed
and disallowed – that we can see how well suited a model
carnival is to masculinity, and how ill suited it is to femininity.

Although some women in *Wise Children* possess characteristics that might be thought of as carnivalesque, it is a
man, Peregrine, who embodies it: he is 'not so much a man,
more of a travelling carnival'. Peregrine is red and rude, a
big man and, in the classic Rabelaisian manner, a boundary-
buster, growing bigger all the time. To Dora and Nora he is
the proverbial rich American uncle, a sugar daddy whose
fortunes dramatically rise and fall but who, when he is in
the money, spreads his bounty around with extravagance
and enjoyment. He is a big bad wolf of an uncle, too, a
randy old devil who seduces the pubescent Dora when she
is just thirteen. He is a multiple man, and his multiplicity
makes him as elusive as the butterflies he ends up pursuing
as a lepidopterist in the Brazilian jungle: to Dora and Nora
'He gave . . . all his histories, we could choose which ones
we wanted – but they kept on changing, so. That was the
trouble.' He is a contradictory presence, a very 'material
ghost', in whom Dora sees all her lovers pass by as she and
he make love at Melchior's tumultuous birthday party.

If Peregrine's history is unknowable because it is so
multiple, Grandma's origins are unknown because she
refuses to reveal them: 'our maternal side founders in a
wilderness of unknowability'. Grandma arrived in Bard
Road at the beginning of the century with no past but
enough money to set her going for a year. She is a mystery
woman, dateless, nameless, 'She'd invented herself, she
was a one-off', just as later she invents her family. And like
Perry, she is a woman of contradictions, a naturist who
happily reveals her naked body to the world, yet speaks
with an elocuted voice, a disguise that sometimes slips as
she forgets herself and 'talks up a blue streak'. She and
Perry get along famously – they are kindred spirits who
joke about the idea of their being married.

Estella, Dora and Nora's 'real' grandmother, also comes

close to one of the few descriptions of womanhood in Bakhtin's work ('she represents . . . the undoing of pretentiousness, of all that is finished, completed, exhausted'): Estella's 'hair was always coming undone . . . tumbling down her back, spraying out hairpins in all directions, her stockings at half-mast, her petticoat would come adrift in the middle of the street, her drawers start drooping. She was a marvel, and she was a mess.' And through her affair with a younger man, Estella is the undoing of Ranulph's old order. But unlike Perry, who is able to skip away from all his sexual transgressions, Estella is destroyed in the Othelloesque orgy of jealousy and retribution that ensues from her affair.

In the same way, Saskia is a force who wreaks havoc, but like Estella she, too, pays a price. If Saskia's disruptiveness is carnivalesque, there is little of the carnival's laughter in her. Saskia's anger, as it commonly is in women, is directed to the domestic sphere of food and cooking. As a child she'd played a witch in a production of her father's Macbeth, 'but she'd shown more interest in the contents of her cauldron than her name in lights'. In later life she continues to be an 'unnatural' witchy woman who, rather than nurturing, seems intent upon poisoning people. From the age of five, when she's seen under a bush devouring the bloody carcass of a swan, to her twenty-first birthday party, when she serves up a duck 'swimming in blood', her conspicuous consumption of meat is perhaps some sort of profane attempt to make herself feel legitimate, to be flesh of her father's flesh. But finally, Melchior's marriage to her best friend forces Saskia to recognise herself as a terminal outsider and, unable to gain the love she needs from her father, she sets about poisoning him instead. (Conversely, the motherly Grandma, who repudiates men, is an avid vegetarian: 'she'd a passion for salads, it went with all that naturism. During her strictest periods, she'd make us a meal of a cabbage, raw in summer, boiled in winter.')

The Lady Atalante Lynde, Melchior's first wife, after falling downstairs (or was she pushed by Saskia and Imogen?), comes to live in Dora and Nora's basement, and is rechristened Wheelchair in honour of her new invalid status. Once at Bard Road she seems to undergo some sort of a transformation: losing her upper-class tightness, she becomes another bawdy, bardy woman: she asks a grocer 'Have you got anything the shape of a cucumber, my good fellow?' But her transformation isn't only psychological. Rather like Flann O'Brien's bicyclists, or one of Bruno Schulz's fabulous creatures, Lynde passes through a 'migration of forms'[28] – the woman becomes her wheelchair, or at least, they become a part of one another. Welded together they now, like twins, contain something of the other's personality. After a breakfast of bacon, Dora describes Wheelchair as 'nicely greased'.

All these women, and Dora too, have elements of carnival in them, but none of them personifies it as Peregrine does. Perhaps this has something to do with carnival's relationship to order. Carter has argued that in the 'real' world, 'to be a woman is to be in drag'.[29] If in the carnival world, by putting on masks and being other than what we are, we transgress the order of the 'real' world, then what does this play-acting mean for women who, in the 'real' world, *already* exist in a duplicitous state of affectation? The idea of carnival seems to presuppose a monistic world: the experience of femininity contradicts this, implying that the 'real' world is itself a place of diversity, of masks and deception.

We can understand better the idea of carnival being both licensed and illicit if we see how masculinity operates within it. In *Wise Children* the anarchic solipsism of carnival allows a forty-year-old man (Peregrine) to seduce/rape a thirteen-year-old girl (Dora). It could be argued that patriarchy relies upon such masculine transgression of order as a reminder and a symbol of the very force which shores it up. This is what Carter seems to be saying in *Wise Children* about the function of war in society: that patriarchy legitimates the violent disorders of war in order to sustain itself. Attractive as carnival's disorder can be to women who have been trapped by patriarchy, when women become the object of this disorder – as they are in war, or in rape, or in 'kiddiporn' – then the idea of carnival becomes much more problematic for them, and their relation to it becomes an inevitably ambivalent one: as with Estella and Saskia, carnival is as likely to defeat women as it is to bring down order.

9   Bringing the House Down

> Nora and I were well content. We'd finally wormed our
> way into the heart of the family we'd always wanted to be
> part of. They'd asked us on the stage and let us join in,
> legit. at last. There was a house we all had in common and
> it was called the past, even though we'd lived in different
> rooms. (p. 226)

At the end of *Wise Children*, when Dora and Perry are having sex for the last time ('you remember the last time just like you remember the first'), Dora fantasises about what it would be like to bring the house down, to fuck it away in some glorious carnival orgy of destruction. She toys with the idea, sensing the excitement of exerting such eradicating (warlike) power. In the end, though, Dora decides that this is not something she wants to do, because although her historical house has sometimes been a painful place to live in, a place from which people have tried to eject her, it is also where her history, her story, lies. Bastard that Dora is, this is a house that she has built, too. (That the house is a metaphor for the literary canon is quite clear. Should those left outside trash the house of fiction, or try to renovate it?)

For all Dora's carnivalesque enthusiasm, and despite her part in conjuring the fantasy world of illusion, of having lived amidst the 'bruising dew-drops', she's always able to tell the difference between what is real and fake, between what is tragedy (untimely death) and what isn't (a broken heart). In an interview in 1984,[30] Angela Carter said that she was essentially 'an old-fashioned feminist'; her preoccupations were with the material condition of women: 'abortion law, access to further education, equal rights and the position of black women'. On pornography she said: 'I don't think it's nearly as damaging as the effects of the capitalist system.' Dora, too, is of this materialist persuasion:

> wars are facts we cannot fuck away, Perry; nor laugh away either.
> Do you hear me, Perry?
> No. (p. 221)

Perry cannot hear Dora because at some level the irrational, possibilising, illusion-making carnivaler cannot entertain the ordered, hard 'real world'. But just as Dora would not throw away the historical house of order, she would not banish the chaos of the carnival either. Because it seems to her 'as if fucking itself were the origin of illusion', and in this carnival world of illusion – in fucking, laughter and art – there is the possibility to *conceive* of the world differently, to break down the old. There are 'limits to the power of laughter' – the carnival can't rewrite history, undo the effects of war or alter what is happening on the 'news'. And there is no transcendence possible in life, Carter tells us, from the materiality of the moment, from the facts of oppression and war. But carnival does offer us the tantalising promise of how things might be in a future moment, if we altered the conditions which tie us down. It is only the carnival which can give us such imagined possibilities, which is why the creative things that make it up in life are so precious: laughter, sex and art.

Dora's art reports from both sides of the tracks, chronicling a history of exclusion and opposition, but also of wrong-sided exuberance. She ends her story, and her day, with Gareth's new babies, pocketed deep inside the folds of Perry's greatcoat (carnival bringing newness into the world). As ever in the dialectical Hazard/Chance family, they turn out to be twins, but this time the old sexual divisions are broken, for this latest double-act signals a change of direction – these wise children are 'boy and girl, a new thing in our family'. And who knows where such a strange combination might lead? With this challenge, Angela Carter signed off. Leaving the reader, in the best Bakhtinian fashion, holding the babies. But if we attend, we can hear her out there riding Dora's wind: 'What a wind! Whooping and banging all along the street . . . The kind of wind that gets into the blood and drives you wild. Wild.' Listen, wise children, can't you hear her shouting to us: 'What a joy it is to dance and sing!'

'A Room of One's Own, or a Bloody Chamber?': Angela Carter and Political Correctness

HERMIONE LEE

Nine weeks after Angela Carter's death on 16 February 1992, an overview of her work by John Bayley appeared in *The New York Review of Books* for 23 April.[1] It was a striking exercise in insidious disparagement. The essay, which needs to be quoted at some length for its strategy to be apparent, began with a description of postmodernism, in fiction, as writing in which 'everything goes': a self-consciously permissive fusion of 'fantasy and realism, satire and social comment'. Angela Carter qualified as a postmodernist because of the element of 'communality' in her work: postmodernism claims to be a 'single ongoing subcultural event', and doesn't distinguish between what is private and what belongs to everyone, just as it doesn't distinguish between 'high art and pop art'. Like other 'very capable modern authors', Carter was postmodernist in being 'good at having it both ways'.

Though Bayley repeatedly alluded to Carter's 'brio' and professionalism, her originality and her 'literary charm and drive' – especially in the novel he paid most attention to, *Love*, her 'vaudeville version of the Sixties' – it became apparent that in defining her as a postmodernist *con brio* he came to bury Angela Carter, not to praise her. For, like all postmodernists, she 'sticks . . . to the party line':

Indeed if there is a common factor in the elusive category of
the postmodernist novel it is political correctness: whatever
spirited arabesques and feats of descriptive imagination
Carter may perform she always comes to rest in the right
ideological position.

The 'position' (a slightly giggling innuendo here?) was
repeatedly illustrated. A comic passage in *Love* on the man's
fear of the woman's 'perilous interior' 'sticks' (we are told)
'even here to the party line: instructing us that female
bodies must not be treated as objects'. In *The Bloody Chamber*,
the wolf who ends up in a blissful embrace with Little Red
Riding Hood is 'a politically correct animal at heart'. The
wolf-girl is 'inducted via menstruation into a correct and
liberated social and sexual awareness' which reminded
Bayley of Peter Redgrove and Penelope Shuttle's 1978
panegyric for the menses, *The Wise Wound*. The 'rollicking
vaudeville plots' of *Nights at the Circus* and *Wise Children* act
out postmodernism's hostility to elitism. The literary models
that lurk behind *Wise Children* – not only Shakespeare but
Dickens and J. B. Priestley's *The Good Companions* – are given
(again) 'the proper party line'. The 'Carter girl' of the novels
– mellow, warmhearted, sensible, earthy – has provided 'a
new kind of persona for real women to copy': not a good
thing, says Bayley, for 'girls' who are 'not like that by
nature'.

So the novels were made to look like vehicles (albeit
original, charming and vivacious ones) for a hardline feminist ideology which equates menstruation with 'all the
female virtues opposing male violence and aggressiveness'
and provides a pressurising prototype for female behaviour.
Bayley followed this with a cunning coda which asked
whether her fiction would stand rereading. Probably, he
suggested, she had been too hyped by her 'enthusiasts and

publicists': 'A process of inflation seems unavoidable.' A slight sleight-of-hand led us on to the thought that 'few novels today seem aware of the old canonical notion of "good writing": they can even seem programmed for auto-destruction'. Carter's ideological messages, in her novels and her retelling of fairy stories, are 'committed to the preoccupations and to the fashions of our moment.' The implication was clear: they are built to auto-destruct, not to be reread. Carter, for Bayley, represented the politicising of good writing. Her female subversiveness, praised by Margaret Atwood, made 'imagination itself into the obedient handmaid of ideology'. 'That would not worry many in the latest generation of critics, who read literature past and present by the light of political correctness.'

Rarely can a recently dead writer have been so travestied by an ostensibly enthusiastic appraisal. For a writer who spent much of her life out of fashion, who failed or declined to fit into any orthodoxies of feminism, whose novels notoriously did not win big literary prizes and whose name has become generally well known only since her death, this was indeed an ironic postmortem.

Not that there is anything misleading about John Bayley's identification of Carter with a feminism which employs anti-patriarchal satire, Gothic fantasy, and the subversive rewriting of familiar myths and stories, to embody alternative, utopian recommendations for human behaviour. Her obituaries paid tribute to a person whose character *was* her politics. Other postmodernist fiction writers who were also her close friends – Robert Coover, J. G. Ballard, Salman Rushdie – praised her magical wizardry and her wonderful inventiveness. Rushdie called her a 'high sorceress', a 'benevolent witch-queen'. Women friends – Marina Warner, Lorna Sage, Margaret Atwood – described her as a Fairy Godmother or Faerie Queene (without the feyness), whose

friendship was as nourishing and as imaginatively challenging as her writing. They noted her conversational wickedness, her unpredictability, her down-to-earthness, and her
valuing of democracy, folklore and pleasure. Marina Warner
made an eloquent case for Carter as a vital figure in the
British feminist movement, through her identification with
Carmen Callil and Virago, in helping to establish 'a
woman's voice in literature as special . . . as a crucial
instrument in the forging of an identity for post-imperial,
hypocritical, fossilised Britain'.[2] Warner and Ballard, Carter's
best elegists, avoided the tendency to sentimentalise their
lost friend as an infallible White Witch of feminism by
keeping in focus her edgy refusal to please. By contrast, the
Times's anonymous obituarist[3] expressed his (or her) bias by
omitting any mention of Carter's last and most-praised
novels, *Nights at the Circus* and *Wise Children*, and by
drawing attention instead to her intermittent 'vulgarity', the
dangers of cult status, her preoccupation with sexual violence, and her late signs of 'succumbing to polemicism'.

'Succumbing to polemicism' is one thing – Carter does let
rip all over the place when she wants to – but identifying
her with 'political correctness' is quite another. It's no
accident that the book Bayley concentrated on in *his* 'obituary' was her satire on the 1960s, *Love*. He enjoyed her
sardonic treatment of what he calls 'young people seduced
by the heady climate of the revolution . . . and licensing in
the communal setting whatever private violence was haunting them'. But by favouring this book over her others, he
insisted on an association with the 1960s which, for the
American readership of *The New York Review of Books*, would
have put the seal on the link he was making between
postmodernism and political correctness. For it is one of the
standard features of the attacks on 'PC' (especially in the
States) that it is identified as a tyranny born out of sixties

radicalism. Out of the old libertarian movements for individualism, sexual freedom and recognition for oppressed minorities, for bold avant-gardism in the arts and for deconstruction in literary criticism, has arisen a neo-McCarthyism of political repression and censorship.

This 'politics of identity' has led over the last few years to intransigent confrontations between group cultures struggling for power. So, an extreme conservative denunciator like Hilton Kramer, editor of *The New Criterion*, fulminates against 'the new barbarians', the 'self-proclaimed victim groups', who claim that the sole function of the arts is to redress 'every social, political, sexual, [and] ethical grievance that one or another "minority" may wish to bring as an indictment against our society'.[4] Intellectuals more in sympathy with minorities, such as Edward Said, but who find in 'PC' a censorious zealotry, refuse to accept that in the effort to 'deconsecrate Eurocentrism' it is enough to 'surround ourselves with the sanctimonious piety of historical or cultural victimhood as a way of making our intellectual presence felt'.[5] And those arguing on the side of 'PC' claim that their opponents are right-wing fundamentalists, defenders of the status quo of the white hegemony against cultural pluralism, in the name of 'choice' and intellectual freedom.

Since 'PC' is all about language, the now-stale American jokes about usage (fit, mobile people should now be referred to as 'temporarily able'; very short people will soon be known as 'vertically challenged'; and so on) reflect the unease and confusion of those on the edges of the battleground. If you constantly clean up your language to keep pace with the claims of every interest group, are you being timidly fashionable, or genuinely right-thinking and unprejudiced? Horror stories of campus intimidation (students in creative writing classes being forbidden, in their fiction, to impersonate characters of a race or a gender not their own; teachers being refused tenure or dismissed because they want to teach dead white males, or have made unacceptable sexist or racist remarks; students forced to retract and apologise for bad attitudes) give ammunition to those who speak intemperately of the takeover of the 'new barbarians'. Audiences for David Mamet's punishing satire on feminist correctness, *Oleanna*, have tended to leave the theatre irreconcilably divided.

These arguments would seem to have nothing to do with Angela Carter. It is hard to imagine her referring to her winged heroine Fevvers as 'differently abled', or refusing to write on de Sade or Freud because they were sexist. But by reviewing her life's work in this way in America, where she is not yet well known, John Bayley posthumously maligned her, and perhaps cleared the way for future attacks on her work. If you now want to dismiss a feminist author, you can make her sound rigid and intolerant by giving her the 'PC' label.

Carter is traduced by that association. For speakers of 'PC', certain issues – anti-harassment codes, for example – are sacrosanct, and certain kinds of speech must be silenced, or 'chilled'. This may be for good ends, but it makes for a pious and humourless language. Carter's obituaries repeatedly referred to her dislike of the 'sanctimonious' (the word Said uses in his critique of 'PC'). She was 'a defiler of sacred cows', said Rushdie, with feeling. 'She demolished the temples and the commissariats of the righteous.' The title of her excellent 1982 collection of cultural commentary, reviews and autobiographical pieces was *Nothing Sacred*. In *Nights at the Circus* there is great distrust of the Shaman who exercises authority through his 'power of looking preternaturally solemn' and his 'own utter confidence in his own integrity'. And the hero of that novel is collecting a series called 'Great Humbugs of the World'.[6]

In *Expletives Deleted* (1992), Carter's last, posthumously published collection of essays and reviews – understandably not her best book, but full of characteristic and characterful ingredients – she certainly did not 'come to rest' in a politically correct position. Carter's *Englishness* prevents that, for a start. The mix of Yorkshire-inherited bluntness and a caustic, chirpy South London cynicism (vividly parodied and perhaps too-endearingly celebrated in the voice of Dora Chance, narrator of *Wise Children*) stops her from sounding righteous or dogmatic. The tone is laconic, unpretentious and robust. 'Filthy work, but somebody's got to do it', as she liked to say, and says here of a fiction-writing that disrupts traditions. ('Kingsley Amis isn't going to try.'[7]) In the bits of autobiography which slip out enjoyably here and there, she comes on as a local girl:

> My London consists of all the stations on the Northern
> Line, but don't think I scare easily: I have known the free-
> and-easy slap-and-tickle of Soho since toddlerhood, and
> shouldered aside throngs of harlots in order to buy my
> trousseau casseroles from Mme Cadec's long-defunct
> emporium, undeterred by rumoured crucifixions in nearby
> garages. Nothing between Morden and Camden Town
> holds terror for me.[8]

A serious politics does make itself felt by way of this slap-happy manner. It is not polemical, but it is consistent and direct: passionate sympathy for the 1984–5 miners' strike; convinced opposition to Clause 28 ('Nobody who has seen the inside of a closet would wish to condemn anyone to return to it'); an understanding of Irish Anglophobia; support for Rushdie (to whom she sends a moving last message of comfort and encouragement in her introduction); detestation of Thatcherism. She did not include some of the more straightforwardly feminist pieces of recent years – her preface to the *Virago Book of Fairy Tales*, or her introduction to the Virago anthology of stories, invitingly titled *Wayward Girls & Wicked Women*, where she described the heroines of her selection, as if describing herself, as 'sharing a certain cussedness, a bloodymindedness', evading 'the victim's role by the judicious use of their wits'.[9] It's typical of the tone of *Expletives Deleted* that its most pugnacious piece of feminist criticism takes the form of a splendid joke-review of Paul Theroux's exercise in libidinous hubris *My Secret History* (1989), the story of 'Parent', who wants to 'fuck the world': 'I suggest a vasectomy. As it stands, Parent's career usefully demonstrates the interconnectedness of sexism and racism: I hope this was Theroux's point.'[10]

Her democratic literary politics makes her prefer folklore and oral 'illiterate' narratives to, say, Henry James, and she reserves her most uncritical language for John Berger's documentary elegies for peasant life. Here she does allow for something sacred: 'a sense of the sacred quality of everyday things that recalls the interiors of Vermeer'.[11] She takes pleasure in fiction as game-playing, like Pavic's *Dictionary of the Khazars*, playfully built out of deconstructable, reassemblable blocks in imitation of traditional fairy tales. Her heart goes out to writers of 'outlawry' or illicitness, who make us uncomfortable, or don't fit in: Moorcock, Burroughs, Christina Stead, Hanif Kureishi, J. G. Ballard, whose peculiar obsessiveness she captures very well. (Her reviews are usually benign, and often seem to be about friends: or perhaps they became friends after she reviewed them.)

The two outsanding pieces in the collection are quirky,

illuminating readings of English novels. One is a fine essay on *Jane Eyre*,[12] very good on the novel's sexuality, which speaks eloquently of Brontë's 'fierceness' and 'profligate imagination' – and hopes that St John Rivers is the type of missionary who will end up in the pot. The other is an interesting introduction to a now little-known novel by Walter de la Mare called *Memoirs of a Midget*.[13] De la Mare's curious and troubling picaresque story of a vertically challenged Victorian lady who goes mad and tries to kill herself lets Carter loose on her best subjects: alienation and loneliness. She describes the alarming taboos and repression lying beneath the novel's 'gentle charm and elegant prose'. De la Mare made a tragic, misanthropic story out of estrangement and peculiarity; Carter's fictional gift was to turn 'polymorphous perversity' – sadism, deformity, illegitimacy, freakishness – to pleasurable ends, to let it run free and enjoy itself. But the clear influence of *Memoirs of a Midget* on *Nights at the Circus*, revealed by this essay, also suggests how much disturbing, solitary feeling underlay her own celebratory stoicism.

Carter periodically lived abroad (in Japan, from 1969 to 1972, teaching in the States in the 1980s), which helped with her edge-on view of British life. And because she was always in revolt against the 'tyranny of good taste', she had a passion for America – its discordancy, its weirdness, its inexhaustibility. She loved those American supermarket headlines ('73-year-old mother's 16-month pregnancy'); she loves the grandiose, Gothic bizarrerie of Hollywood (see *Wise Children*) which 'colonised her imagination' in the 1960s. But she is also full of fear and alarm at the tragic drama of 'Amerika"s 'gigantic fuck-ups'.

But the most interesting details in these posthumous pieces are perceptions of Englishness. She makes good blunt jokes about British habits of mind, like the suspicion of Euro-bestsellers such as Eco's *The Name of the Rose*, which seemed 'to some British critics to spring from an EEC conspiracy to thwart exports of genuine, wholesome, straightforward British fiction the same way French farmers block the entry of English lamb'.[14] She is merciless about British snobbery, particularly foodism: 'Oh, that coconut kirsch roulade in the first issue!' (of a magazine called *À la Carte*). 'Even if the *true* foodie knows there is something not quite . . . about a coconut kirsch roulade as a concept. It is just a bit . . . just a bit *Streatham*. Its vowels are subtly wrong. It is probably related to a Black Forest gâteau.'[15] Elizabeth David's anecdote of Virginia Woolf's bread-baking has her spitting and cackling:

> Virginia Woolf? Yes. Although otherwise an indifferent cook, Virginia could certainly knock you up a lovely cottage loaf. You bet. This strikes me as just the sort of pretentiously frivolous and dilettantish thing a Bloomsbury *would* be good at – knowing how to do one, just one, fatuously complicated kitchen thing and doing that one thing well enough to put the cook's nose out of joint. 'I will come into the kitchen, Louie', she said to this young employee of hers, 'and show you how to do it.'[16]

Carter's ambivalent relationship to Virginia Woolf shows how inappropriate it is to mark her down as a militantly correct feminist. Her evasiveness and playfulness with feminism, her resistance to any predictable orthodoxy, her inventiveness and love of fantasy, are all very like Woolf's. But as the passage about bread-making shows, she partly dislikes her. A year before her death, she appeared on a Channel Four *J'Accuse* programme attacking Virginia Woolf, and made a memorably satirical remark about *Orlando*'s 'brown-nosing' of the aristocracy.[17] But among the fragments she left was the draft of a libretto for an opera based on *Orlando*, to be scored by Michael Berkeley.[18]

Carter's theatricality and her passion for spectacle, vaudeville and pageant became increasingly apparent in her work – not just in *Nights at the Circus* and *Wise Children*, but in her 1985 radio drama based on the painter Richard Dadd, or in her imaginative influence on the sinister spectacles in Neil Jordan's film *The Company of Wolves*. (She also left an unperformed stage version of *Lulu*.) Like Virginia Woolf, she loved to weave masquerades and plays and echoes of Shakespeare into her fiction. In her tantalisingly unfinished notes for *Orlando: An English Country House Opera* (a few scenes written, a structure sketched in) Carter leaps at all the possibilities the novel offers of pagentary and farce. The high camp of the Elizabethan scenes with the old Queen are made the most of (just as they are in Sally Potter's film, which I imagine Carter would have enjoyed). The masque of the three goddesses Purity, Chastity and Modesty, who survey Orlando's sex-change, is closely modelled on the novel. And Carter adds, entirely in the spirit of Woolf, a splendid spoof on *Ivan the Terrible* for the scenes with Orlando's Russian princess, Sasha, and a fine idea for a pageant set in the 'Age of Scandal' and denoting the passage of time. Orlando dances with Casanova, Kit Smart prays with Dr Johnson, and, to increasingly ominous music, Nelson and Lady Hamilton appear, the sound of the 'Marseillaise' is heard, and the men all go off to fight Boney. Where Carter alters Woolf's emphasis is in her foregrounding of Orlando's servants, who occupy central and crucial roles in the libretto as chorus, observers, and figures of stability and wisdom. As one might have expected from her remarks on *J'Accuse*, Carter's *Orlando* is more emphatically egalitarian and democratic than its model.

John Bayley was at his most acute about Carter when he

noted the affinity between her and 'the Virginia Woolf of *Orlando* and *The Waves*'. But his argument necessitated that he should mark the difference between them as being Carter's intransigent politics. 'A room of one's own, or a bloody chamber?' he asks. The choice is between 'privacy' and polemic. Carter's political correctness, according to Bayley, takes her out of the room of one's own – what he calls 'the privacy and individuality, the more secret style of independence' of Virginia Woolf (and Jane Austen) – and into the bloody chamber of 'politicized' writing, 'the literary wing of militant orthodoxy'.

According to this argument, one would expect Carter's *Orlando* to have concentrated on the novel's considerable overlaps with *A Room of One's Own* (a more 'politicized' and less 'secret' book than Bayley would allow), to have introduced Orlando's difficulties as a woman writer and the novel's questioning of gender identity. But – at least in the unfinished draft – Orlando is not even a writer, and it is the private, 'secret' side of his (or her) character which has attracted Carter. Instead of mulling over her manuscript, this Orlando contemplates her loneliness. The main plot becomes a search for love. What Carter catches beautifully is the tenderness and poignancy of the novel, under its flashy surface. One of her humorous directions for the music asks that 'the absolute quintessence of romantic melancholy' should be reached.

Carter parts company from Virginia Woolf in her admiration for James Joyce, who is quite as important a model for her. Joyce, too, has been used as ammunition in the argument on political correctness. Stanley Fish, writing in 1992 on the necessity for regulating 'hate speech' – on the hateful choice between offensiveness and censorship, of 'either allowing

or policing the flow of discourse' – comes down on the side
of censorship. In order not to 'permit speech that does
obvious harm', we must 'shut off speech in ways that might
deny us the benefit of Joyce's *Ulysses* or Lawrence's *Lady
Chatterley's Lover* or Titian's paintings'.[19]

Carter's words on Joyce in *Expletives Deleted* take the
opposite position, and are about freedom, not policing. She
reads *Ulysses* as the great linguistic liberator, the book which
'decolonialised English', whose 'magisterial project of bug-
gering the English language, the ultimate revenge of the
colonialised', set Carter, in her turn, free to 'treat the Word
not as if it were holy but in the knowledge that it is always
profane'. (She likes Joyce too because, unlike Virginia
Woolf, he was the 'poet of the upper-working and lower-
middle classes'. 'He never succumbed to the delusion that
people who do not say complicated things do not have
complicated thoughts.') Give offence, give pleasure: that is
what fiction can do. Joyce was the writer 'who showed how
one could tell the story of whatever it is that is going to
happen next'.[20] Angela Carter, whose heroines always make
the most of the 'hazard of events', learnt to be such a writer
from Joyce, as well as from Woolf. 'Whatever it is that is
going to happen next' is much less interesting without her.

An earlier version of this essay was published as 'Angela
Carter's Profane Pleasures', *Times Literary Supplement*, 19
June 1992, pp. 5–6.

Notes

■■■

Introduction   *Lorna Sage*

1.   'Gabriel García Márquez', in *Writers at Work: Paris Review Interviews*,
Sixth Series, ed. G. Plimpton, with an Introduction by Frank Kermode,
Harmondsworth: Penguin, 1985, pp. 313–39 (p. 324).

2.   *The Virago Book of Fairy Tales*, London: Virago, 1990, pp. ix–x.

3.   *Six Memos for the Next Millennium*, trans. P. Creagh, Cambridge,
MA: Harvard University Press, 1988, pp. 116–17.

4.   'The Savage Sideshow', *New Review* 39/40 (1977), pp. 51–7 (p. 56).

5.   *Shadow Dance* (1966), reprinted as *Honeybuzzard*, London: Pan, 1968,
p. 25. Subsequent references are to this edition.

6.   *Heroes and Villains* (1969), Harmondsworth: Penguin, 1981, p. 86.
Subsequent references are to this edition.

7.   'Angela Carter interviewed by Lorna Sage', in *New Writing*. ed. M.
Bradbury and J. Cooke, London: Minerva Press, 1992, pp. 185–93 (p. 190).

8.   *American Ghosts and Old World Wonders*, London: Vintage, 1994,
pp. 110–20 (p. 115). Subsequent references are to this edition.

9.   ibid., pp. 121–39 (p. 127).

10.   *Nothing Sacred: Selected Writings*, London: Virago, 1982, p. 28.

11.   'Flesh and the Mirror', in *Fireworks* (1974), London: Virago, 1987,
pp. 61–70 (p. 63). Subsequent references to *Fireworks* are to this edition.

12.   *Nothing Sacred*, p. 28.

13.   'Notes From the Front Line', in *On Gender and Writing*, ed. M.
Wandor, London: Pandora, 1983, pp. 69–77 (p. 70).

14.   'Truly, It Felt Like Year One', in *Very Heaven: Looking Back at the
1960s*, ed. S. Maitland, London: Virago, 1988, pp. 209–16 (p. 215).

15.   *The Sadeian Woman*, London: Virago, 1979, pp. 56–7. Subsequent
references are to this edition.

16.   *The History of Sexuality. Volume One: An Introduction*, trans. Robert
Hurley, Harmondsworth: Penguin, 1981, pp. 105–6. Subsequent
references are to this edition.

17.   *Come Unto These Yellow Sands: Four Radio Plays*, Newcastle Upon
Tyne: Bloodaxe Books, 1985, p. 13.

18.   ibid., p. 7.

'Mutability is Having A Field Day': The Sixties Aura of Angela Carter's Bristol Trilogy: *Marc O'Day*

1.   See, for instance, 'Angela Carter', in John Haffenden, *Novelists in
Interview*, London: Methuen, 1985, p. 76.

2.   The most notable example is John Bayley, 'Fighting for the Crown', *The New York Review of Books*, 23 April 1992, pp. 9–11.

3.   See Haffenden, p. 80; Helen Cagney Watts, 'An Interview with Angela Carter', *Bête Noire*, 8 August 1985, p. 165; and Angela Carter, 'Truly, It Felt Like Year One', in *Very Heaven: Looking Back at the 1960s*, ed. Sara Maitland, London: Virago, 1988. What isn't clear from published statements is whether Carter consciously intended to work over the same local territory three times. She once referred to *The Passion of New Eve* as the second in a 'project of three speculative novels', which suggests that she did sometimes conceive things in threes: see Lorna Sage, 'The Savage Sideshow: A Profile of Angela Carter', *New Review*, 4, 39/40 (1977), p. 56. And it can scarcely be accidental that the Trilogy comprises her first, third and fifth published novels, interspersed with the earliest of the speculative fictions, *The Magic Toyshop* (1967) and *Heroes and Villains* (1969). *Toyshop*, strictly, is the crossover text: its initial 1950s setting allies it with the realism of the Bristol Trilogy, but the period details and the laws of nature obtaining in its fictional world become far less certain once the action moves into the toyshop, marking the advent of the speculative tendency in Carter's fiction. The novel's 'magical realist' potential is fully exploited in the 1986 film version.

4.   Barthes, 'The Reality Effect' (1968), repr. in *The Rustle of Language*, trans. Richard Howard, Oxford: Blackwell, 1986, p. 141.

5.   Margaret McDowell, in *Contemporary Novelists*, ed. James Vinson, 3rd edn, London: Macmillan, 1982, p. 129.

6.   Quoted respectively in Haffenden, p. 80 and Watts, p. 165.

7.   Sage, p. 55.

8.   Carter, *Shadow Dance* (1966), repr. as *Honeybuzzard*, London: Pan, 1968, pp. 168, 83. Subsequent page references to this reprint edition – I haven't been able to get hold of the original – are bracketed in the text.

9.   Carter, quoted in Watts, p. 165. She refers to her early sixties self as 'a wide-eyed provincial beatnik' in Sage, p. 54. For slightly contradictory statements on the drafting and typing up of *Shadow Dance*, see Watts, p. 166; and Ian McEwan, 'Sweet Smell of Excess', *Sunday Times Magazine*, 9 September 1984, p. 43.

10.   Carter, *Nothing Sacred: Selected Writings*, London: Virago, 1982, p. 84.

11.   On the revision of *Love*, see Carter, 'Living in London – X', *London Magazine*, 10 (March 1971), p. 55.

12.   Sage, p. 54.

13.   Carter, 'Notes For a Theory of Sixties Style' (1967), repr. in *Nothing Sacred*, pp. 86–7.

14.   Levin, *The Pendulum Years*, London: Cape, 1970, p. 9.

15.   Quotations in this paragraph are taken from, in order: Marina Warner, 'Introduction', in *The Second Virago Book of Fairy Tales*, ed. Angela

Carter, London: Virago, 1992, p. xiii; *Honeybuzzard*, p. 1; Atwood, 'Magic Token Through the Dark Forest', *Observer*, 23 February 1992, p. 61; and Lorna Sage, 'Death of the Author', *Granta 41· Biography* (Autumn 1992), p. 241.

16.   On hippies as entrepreneurs, see Angela McRobbie, 'Second-Hand Dresses and the Role of the Rag Trade', in *Zoot Suits and Second-Hand Dresses: An Anthology of Fashion and Music*, ed. McRobbie, London: Macmillan, 1989.

17.   Wilson, *Adorned in Dreams: Fashion and Modernity*, London: Virago, 1985, pp. 230–31.

18.   ibid.

19.   Thompson, 'An Anatomy of Rubbish' (1969), repr. in *Arts in Society*, ed. Paul Barker, Glasgow: Fontana/Collins, 1977, p. 40. Subsequent page references are bracketed in the text.

20.   Nuttall, *Bomb Culture* (1968), repr. London: Paladin, 1970, p. 72. Subsequent page references are bracketed in the text.

21.   Fiedler 'The New Mutants' (1965), repr. in *The Collected Essays of Leslie Fiedler*, 2 vols, New York: Stein & Day, 1971, 2.

22.   Carter, *Several Perceptions*, London: Heinemann, 1968, p. 16. Subsequent page references are bracketed in the text.

23.   Carter, 'Truly, It Felt Like Year One', p. 211.

24.   Sage, 'Angela Carter', in *Dictionary of Literary Biography, Vol. 14, British Novelists Since 1960*, ed. Jay L. Halio, 2 vols, Detroit: Bruccoli Clark, 1983, 1, p. 207.

25.   This is comparable to the description given by Carter of her own childhood household, where 'a curious dream-time operated . . . and none of the clocks ever told the right time': 'The Mother Lode' (1976), repr. in *Nothing Sacred*, p. 14.

26.   Old Sunny may well be based on a man called Charlie whom Carter writes about in one of her earliest journalistic pieces for *New Society*: see 'A Busker (Retired)', *New Society*, 30 March 1967, p. 471.

27.   'Black Innocence', *Times Literary Supplement*, 1 August 1968, p. 817.

28.   Carter, *Love* (1987), repr. London: Picador, 1988, p. 114. The original edition was published by Hart-Davis in 1971. Subsequent page references to, first, the 1971 text and, second, the paperback edition of the revised version cited above, are bracketed in the text.

29.   Hewison, *Too Much: Art and Society in the Sixties* (1986), repr. London: Methuen, 1988, p. 179.

30.   Lee's age is changed to twenty-four in the revised version.

31.   Peter Berger and Thomas Luckmann, *The Social Construction of Reality* (1966), repr. Harmondsworth: Penguin, 1971, p. 39.

32.   ibid.

33.   Carter, 'Notes for a Theory of Sixties Style', p. 86.

34.   On the sixties gothic revival, see Bart Moore-Gilbert, 'The Return of the Repressed: Gothic and the 1960s Novel', in *Cultural Revolution? The*

Challenge of the Arts in the 1960s, ed. Moore-Gilbert and John Seed, London: Routledge, 1992.

The Disorder of *Love*: Angela Carter's Surrealist Collage: *Sue Roe*

1.   Angela Carter, 'The Alchemy of the Word', in *Expletives Deleted*, Vintage, 1933, p. 69.

2.   ibid., p. 73.

3.   *Honeybuzzard* (published in Britain as *Shadow Dance* [1966]); *The Magic Toyshop* (1967); *Several Perceptions* (1968); (*Heroes and Villains* (1969).

4.   Carter describes it thus in her Afterword to the new, fully revised edition of *Love* (Chatto, 1987). This latter is the text under discussion throughout. The first edition of *Love* was published by Rupert Hart-Davis in 1971. I have elected to write about the revised edition largely because the first edition is no longer widely available.

5.   Angela Carter, 'Flesh and the Mirror', in *Fireworks* (Chatto, 1987), pp. 61–70, which considers the construction of the other in relation to the need to construct the (female) self (p. 63).

6.   Afterword to *Love* (1987), p. 113.

7.   Ian Turpin, *Ernst*, Phaidon, 1993 (first published 1979), p. 5.

8.   ibid., p. 15.

9.   Quoted by Harry Matthews in 'Some Sexual Positions: Surrealist Discussions of Bodily Pleasures and Psychic Mysteries', *Times Literary Supplement* 4715, 13 August 1993, p. 3, reviewing José Pierre (ed.) *Investigating Sex: Surrealist Discussions, 1928–1932*, trans. Malcolm Irmie, Verso, 1993.

10.   ibid.

11.   Matthews: 'The participation of real women in several of the sessions does little to restore any consequent balance between the sexes. . . . Of course, these men were unaware in varying degrees of the realities of women's experience – how could they not be? They were speaking in a pre-feminist age . . .'. (e.g.:

Paul Eluard:	I'd like a woman to ask a question. Approval.
Nusch [Paul Eluard's wife]:	How do you like to make love?
Albert Valentin:	You mean one sex inserted into another?
Paul Eluard:	As you know very well, to make love means to ejaculate. [ibid.]

12.   Leonora Carrington, 'Cast Down by Sadness', in *The Seventh Horse*, Virago, 1989, p. 51.

13.   Leonora Carrington, 'My Mother is a Cow', in *The Seventh Horse*, pp. 190–91.

14.   A Surrealist game in which a sentence or drawing was made up by several people working in turn, none being allowed to see any of the

previous contributions. Sarane Alexandrine, *Surrealist Art*, Thames & Hudson, 1991 (first published Paris, 1969), pp. 50–52. The *cadavre exquis* will be discussed more fully in section II below.

15.   Angela Carter, 'The Alchemy of the Word', in *Expletives Deleted*, p. 73.

16.   James Brockway, review of *Love* in *Books and Bookmen*, February 1975.

17.   Angela Carter, *The Magic Toyshop*, Virago, 1992 (first published 1967), p. 1.

18.   Anita Van Vactor, review of *Love* in *The Listener*, 20 May 1971.

19.   Turpin, *Ernst*, p. 8.

20.   Roger Shattuck, *The Banquet Years*, Vintage, 1955, p. 348.

21.   Afterword to *Love*, p. 113.

22.   Benjamin Constant, *Adolphe*, Penguin, 1964 (first published 1816).

23.   Roland Barthes, *Camera Lucida*, Farrar, Straus & Giroux, 1981 (first published Editions du Seuil, 1980), p. 85.

24.   'Ernst's experiments with word-image combinations – which were to influence the development of *peinture-poésie*, which the Surrealists opposed to the pure abstraction of the avant-garde – came to a head in a series of Picture-Poems dating from 1923–4 . . . the words not only react with the image, they form part of the very structure of the composition' (Ian Turpin, *Ernst* pp. 8–9). In 'Men Shall Know Nothing of This' (1923), by contrast, the poem is inscribed in full on the back of the canvas (Turpin, p. 54).

25.   Alexandrine, *Surrealist Art*, pp. 49–50.

26.   ibid., pp. 50–52.

27.   ibid., p. 62.

28.   Carl Jung, 'Psychological Aspects of the Mother Archetype' (1938), in *Aspects of the Feminine*, Routledge, ARK paperbacks, 1992, p. 126.

29.   Angela Carter, *The Sadeian Woman*, Virago, 1983 (first published 1979), p. 124. Carter is basing her remarks on her reading of de Sade's *Philosophy in the Boudoir*.

30.   ibid.

31.   Carl Jung, on the ' "Nothing-But" Daughter': 'Finally, it should be remarked that *emptiness* is a great feminine secret. It is something absolutely alien to man; the chasm, the unplumbed depths, the *yin*. The pitifulness of this vacuous nonentity goes to his heart (I speak here as a man). . . .' ('Psychological Aspects of the Mother Archetype', p. 127.

32.   Nadia Choucha, *Surrealism and the Occult*, Oxford: Mandrake, 1991, p. 47. Coucha also draws attention to the Surrealists' Jungian interests: 'Although the surrealists claimed to be Freudians, their interests are closer to the French psychologists Charcot, who had conducted studies on female hysteria, and Janet, who had been a teacher of C. G. Jung' (p. 48).

33.   Marina Warner, Introduction to Leonora Carrington, *The Seventh Horse*, p. ii.

34.   Leonora Carrington, *The House of Fear*, Virago, 1989, discussed in Choucha, *Surrealism and the Occult*, p. 116, in her chapter on Ernst and Carrington (pp. 105–121).

35.   'If plumes make the plumage, it is not glue [*colle*] that makes collage.' Ernst, quoted in Alexandrine, *Surrealist Art*, p. 64.

36.   Angela Carter, talking about her own work at the Cheltenham Festival, 1990 (in a sudden remark about psychoanalysis which sent her into peals of laughter).

37.   The 'decalcomania' technique consisted of sandwiching ink between layers of paper; Ernst applied it to oil paint and canvas, producing some of his most penetrating social commentary out of this technique. (Turpin, *Ernst*, p. 20.)

38.   Alexandrine, *Surrealist Art*, pp. 140–41.

39.   Psychoanalysts say that masquerading corresponds to women's desire. That seems wrong to me. I think the masquerade has to be understood as what women do in order to recuperate some element of desire, to participate in man's desire, but at the price of renouncing their own. . . . What do I mean by masquerade? In particular, what Freud calls 'femininity'. The belief . . . that it is necessary to *become* a woman, . . . whereas a man is a man from the outset. . . . a woman . . . to become a normal woman, . . . has to enter into the *masquerade of femininity*.' (Luce Irigaray, 'Questions', in Margaret Whitford [ed.], *The Irigaray Reader*, Blackwell, 1991, pp. 135–6)

40.   Sigmund Freud, *Totem and Taboo*, Routledge, 1961 (first published 1950), p. 31.

41.   André Breton, *L'Amour fou* (1937), the novel in which he used images resulting from unforeseen associations of forms or themes. He spoke of it as 'the most fabulous source of unfindable images' (Alexandrine, *Surrealist Art*, p. 52).

42.   Breton, *Manifestos of Surrealism*, University of Michigan Press, 1972, quoted in Choucha, *Surrealism and the Occult*, pp. 47–8.

43.   Choucha, *Surrealism and the Occult*, p. 48.

44.   See Matthews, 'Some Sexual Positions: Surrealist Discussions of Bodily Pleasures and Psychic Mysteries', pp. 3–4 (and Note 11 above).

45.   Austin Osman Spare, *The Book of Pleasure (Self-Love): The Psychology of Ecstasy* (1909–13). 'Spare describes art as the "instinctive application (to observations or sensations) of the knowledge latent in the subconscious".' (Choucha, *Surrealism and the Occult*, pp. 49–51.)

46.   Irigaray, 'Questions', pp. 134–5: the 'other' syntax, the one that would make feminine 'self-affection' possible, is lacking, repressed, censured: the feminine is never affected except by and for the masculine. What we would want to put into play, then, is a syntax that would make woman's 'self-affection' possible. A 'self-affection' that would certainly not be reducible to the economy of sameness of the One, and for which the syntax and the meaning remain to be found.'

47.   Anita Van Vactor, review of *Love*. See note 18 above.

48.   For example, the Collinses' school motto, 'the Kantian imperative: DO RIGHT BECAUSE IT IS RIGHT', *Love*, p. 10. Cf. Charles Taylor: 'What is peculiar to the modern West . . . is that its favoured formulation for this principle of respect has come to be in terms of rights' – a bias which calls into the question the issue of what personal moral dignity consists in: this must have gendered connotations, and must hence become a question for feminism. Carter hints at this nexus of problems here in *Love*. (Charles Taylor, *Sources of the Self: The Making of the Modern Identity*, Cambridge University Press, pp. 11–15)

49.   Compare, perhaps, Max Ernst's 'Carnal Delight Complicated by Visual Representations' (1931), one of the paintings which 'moved him towards the materialization of the imaginary' (Alexandrine, *Surrealist Art*, pp. 65–6).

The Fate of the Surrealist Imagination in the Society of the Spectacle: *Susan Rubin Suleiman*

1.   Ado Kyrou, *Surréalisme et Cinéma* (Paris: Arcanes, 1953); *Amour-Erotisme et Cinéma*, Paris: Le Terrain Vague, 1957.

2.   Carter, 'Tokyo Pastoral', in *Nothing Sacred: Selected Writings*, London: Virago, 1982, p. 33.

3.   *Nothing Sacred*, p. 28.

4.   The unidentified quotes attributed to Angela Carter in the preceding pages are from that telephone conversation, London, 16 May 1991. My memory of the conversation remains especially vivid and poignant, for Angela Carter was already undergoing daily treatments for lung cancer; yet her extraordinary sense of humour (including her ability to laugh at the doctors' disagreements about how to treat her illness), as well as her kindness and interest in others, remained as alive as ever. She died less than a year later, on 16 February 1992, aged fifty-one. I dedicate this essay to her memory.

5.   Brian McHale, *Postmodernist Fiction*, New York and London: Methuen, 1987, p. 10.

6.   Angela Carter, *The Infernal Desire Machines of Doctor Hoffman*, London: Penguin, 1982, p. 97. The novel was first published in 1972. Subsequent page references to the Penguin edition will be given in parenthesis in the text.

7.   André Breton, *Point du jour*, Paris: Gallimard, 1970, p. 26. The essay was first published in September 1924. My translation.

8.   Susan Rubin Suleiman, *Subversive Intent: Gender, Politics, and the Avant-Garde*, Cambridge, MA: Harvard University Press, 1990, p. xv.

9.   Linda Hutcheon, *A Poetics of Postmodernism*, New York and London Routledge, 1988, p. 5.

10.   Auberon Waugh, 'The Surreal Thing', *Spectator*, 20 May 1972, p. 772.

11.   David Punter, 'Angela Carter: Supersessions of the Masculine',

Critique XXV:4 (Summer 1984), p. 211. Further page references will be given in parentheses in the text.

12. Ricarda Smith, 'The Journey of the Subject in Angela Carter's Fiction', *Textual Practice* 3:1 (1990), note 5.

13. Herbert Marcuse, *Eros and Civilization*, with a new Preface by the Author, New York: Vintage, 1962, p. 135.

14. Guy Debord, *La Société du spectacle*, Paris: Champ Libre, 1971, p. 9; my translation.

15. Donna Haraway's 'A Manifesto for Cyborgs: Science, Technology, and Socialist Feminism in the 1980s', first published in 1984 (*Socialist Review*, 50), has often been reprinted since, and has acquired an international audience; Lyotard's hopefulness about computers and postmodern society, expressed in *La Condition postmoderne* (Paris: Minuit, 1979; English trans. 1981), has been somewhat tempered since then (see his *Le Postmoderne expliqué aux enfants*, Paris: Galilée, 1986.

16. Gilles Deleuze and Félix Guattari, *L'Anti-Oedipe*, Paris: Editions de Minuit, 1972; the phrases in quotation marks are on p. 34.

17. Carter, *The Passion of New Eve*, London: Gollancz, 1977; *Nights at the Circus*, London: Chatto & Windus, 1984.

18. This essay has benefited greatly from the discussions I have had with various audiences who heard it as a public lecture – in Austin, Texas in 1992, and Amsterdam and Valencia in 1993. My special thanks to Giulia Colaizzi and Thomas Elsaesser, whose questions and challenges concerning postmodernism and technology pushed me to define Carter's position more clearly.

Running with the Tigers *Margaret Atwood*

Angela Carter, *The Sadeian Woman*, London: Virago, 1979.
—— *The Bloody Chamber*, New York: Harper & Row, 1980.
Donald Haase (ed.), *The Reception of Grimm's Fairy Tales: Responses, Reactions, Revisions*, Detroit: Wayne State University Press, 1993.

'Mother is a Figure of Speech . . .' *Nicole Ward Jouve*

Only works actually quoted are included here. Among criticism that has made me think, I wish to mention Elaine Jordan's essay in Linda Anderson (ed.), *Plotting For Change*, Avon, 1991; Lorna Sage's essay in *Women in the House of Fiction*, Macmillan, 1992; and Geraldine Meaney's bits and pieces in *(Un)like Subjects: Women, Theory, Fiction*, Routledge, 1993.

Carter, Angela, *The Passion of New Eve*, London: Virago, 1982 (first published Gollancz, 1977).
—— *The Bloody Chamber*, Harmondsworth: Penguin, 1981 (first published Gollancz, 1979).
—— *The Sadeian Woman*, London: Virago, 1979.

—— *Nothing Sacred*, London: Virago, 1982.

—— 'Notes from the Front Line;, in M. Wandor (ed.), *On Gender and Writing*, London: Pandora, 1983.

—— 'Sugar Daddy', in U. Owen (ed.), *Fathers by Daughters*, London: Virago, 1983.

—— *Nights at the Circus*, London: Picador, 1984. (first published Chatto & Windus).

—— *Wise Children*, London: Vintage, 1992 (first published Chatto & Windus).

Chodorow, Nancy, *The Reproduction of Mothering: Psychoanalysis and the Sociology of Gender*, University of California Press, 1978.

Cixous, Hélène, 'Castration or Decapitation?' *Signs*, No. 7, Fall 1981, pp. 41–55.

Colette, *Journal à rebours*, in *Oeuvres complètes*, Paris: Flammanion, 1948–50, vol. XII, p. 50.

Freud, Sigmund, 'Female Sexuality', 1931, in Pelican Freud Library, vol. 7.

Gallop, Jane, *Feminism and Psychoanalysis: The Daughter's Seduction*, London: Macmillan, 1982.

Gilbert, Susan and Gubar, Sandra, *The Madwoman in the Attic*, New Haven, CT and London: Yale University Press, 1979.

Humbert, Elie J., *C.G. Jung*, Paris: Editions universitaires, 1983, p. 59.

Irigaray, Luce, *This Sex Which Is Not One*, Ithaca, NY: Cornell University Press, 1985.

—— *The Irigaray Reader*, ed. M. Whitford, Oxford: Blackwell, 1991.

Joyce, James, *Ulysses*, Harmondsworth: Penguin, 1971.

Keenan, Sally, *From Myth to Memory: The Revisionary Writing of Angela Carter, Maxine Hong Kingston and Toni Morrison*, University of Essex Ph.D. thesis, 1992.

Kristeva, Julia, *The Kristeva Reader*, ed. T. Moi, Oxford: Blackwell, 1986.

Rich, Adrienne, *Of Woman Born: Motherhood as Experience and Institution*, London: Virago, 1977.

Roberts, Michèle, *The Wild Girl*, London: Methuen, 1984.

Rose, Jacqueline, *Sexuality in the Field of Vision*, London: Verso, 1986.

Sage, Lorna, 'The Death of the Author', *Granta*, 1992, pp. 235–54.

New New World Dreams: Angela Carter and Science Fiction
Roz Kaveney

1.   'The literary men (and women) will now treat Ballard as the sf writer who came in from the cold. Who finally put away childish things, man-powered flight, landscapes of the flesh, the erotic geometry of the car crash, things like that, and wrote the Big Novel they always knew he had in him' (review of *Empire of the Sun* in *Expletives Deleted*).

2.   'Posterity will certainly give him that due place in the English literature of the late Twentieth Century which his more anaemic contemporaries grudge; indeed, he is so prolific it will probably look as

though he has written most of it, anyway' (review of *Mother London* in *Expletives Deleted*).

3.   I have seen a copy of Moorcock's later fantasies inscribed to a friend with the comment 'See, that extra week makes all the difference'. And it did.

4.   Ironically, Sladek's most successful book is probably the pseudonymous spoof *Arachne Rising*, in which he argued, from a feigned true believer's position, that astrologers had got it all wrong and there needed to be a thirteenth sign of the zodiac, Arachne, to fit the lunar cycles more precisely. Sladek learned that this is not the sort of thing you joke about, because the book became very popular in California.

5.   All of whom have, in their time, been guests at SF conventions, usually at Mexicon, one of the smaller conventions and one specifically aimed at the fans of written SF rather than attempting to be a broad church in which players of games, watchers of films, tinkerers with computers and wearers of costumes all have their programmes and demand respect for their sensibilities. Angela Carter, by contrast, was guest of honour at an Easter convention, at which there was no chance that the sections of the SF community which its more sober-sided littérateurs might consider embarrassing could be kept out of the way; she was not someone who was going to be phased by blaster fights in the hallways or green nudes with twenty-foot wingspans.

6.   Towards the end of the novel, Leilah, herself now reborn as Lilith, Adam's first and unacknowledged wife, asked by Eve why 'the sky never grew completely dark, but remained stained with a smoky rose', says: 'Those are the flames of Los Angeles' (p. 175).

7.   Basically, one of the defining features of SF as genre is an inward-looking but often productive process which I have elsewhere called dialectical motonymy, in which a previous handling of a theme or plot twist is deliberately evoked in order to take political or moral issue with it. Joanna Russ's *We who are about to . . .*, with its heroine who slaughters the rest of her party of castaways, is not the gratuitous separatist rant it had been accused of being, but a riposte to a whole sub-genre of castaway stories in which women are expected to become breeding machines for the sake of species survival. One of the reasons why many people who come to genre SF late, without soaking themselves in it in early adolescence, find it impenetrable is because so much work in the genre is so heavily referential, complex skeins of variation on classic ideas.

There is also, in both SF and fantasy, a further but overlapping category which the critic John Clute has christened Twice Told Tales, where the retelling of stories, or elements of stories, is less a polemical revision than a way of meditating on Story itself. The stories in *The Bloody Chamber* tend to be both revisionist fantasies and Twice Told Tales, but the former, on balance, more than the latter; by contrast, the Shakespearian echoes and parallels in *Wise Children* or the transposed Westerns of *American Dreams and Old World Wonders* are Twice Told Tales, which is not to say that they do not score the odd polemical point as they go.

The version of 'Puss-in-Boots' in *Bloody Chamber* is a revisionist fantasy in that it makes sensuous use of the cruelty implicit in the original tale, a Twice Told Tale inasmuch as it is more about the tone of voice in which Puss narrates than it is about transforming the plot.

The Dangerous Edge   *Elaine Jordan*

1.   Editions of Carter's work used:
Heroes and Villains (1969) Penguin, 1981
The Infernal Desire Machines of Doctor Hoffman (1972) Penguin, 1982
The Passion of New Eve (1977) Virago, 1982
The Sadeian Woman Virago, 1979
The Bloody Chamber (1979) Penguin, 1981
Nights at the Circus (1984) Pan, 1985
Wise Children (1991) Vintage, .1992

2.   ICA interview with Lynne Segal and Peter Osborne, October 1993, forthcoming in *Radical Philosophy*, Summer 1994. *Gender Trouble* was published by Routledge in 1990. Butler's *Bodies That Matter* (Routledge, 1993) responds to criticisms – often misapprehensions – of *Gender Trouble*.

3.   John Bayley, 'Fighting for the Crown', *The New York Review of Books*, 23 April 1992, pp. 9–11. He ends by setting up Thatcher and Carter as twin British anti-heroes while hinting, with a proper British modesty, that this is of no great interest 'to Europe and America'. Though she did say of the local situation, in a private letter, 'if I'm so bloody subversive, how come Thatcher got in the third time' (a depressed, mocking, as well as angry, moment), I find that students from across the world are startled and inspired by possibilities which come new to them through reading Carter. Bayley contrasts Carter's kind of writing to the 'privacy and individuality, the more secret style of independence' of Jane Austen and Virginia Woolf; and also to a more 'modest' exercise in the new fashion, Penelope Fitzgerald's *The Gate of Angels*, which he'd recently reviewed. Modesty, privacy and secrecy offer little resistance to traditional models of female 'influence' and 'manipulation'; and it strikes me that his 'Carter girl of the Eighties' is more like Fitzgerald's heroine than any of Carter's, who disapproved of role models and preferred more open and challenging imaginative experiment.

It is surprising to find Bayley having a good word to say for Woolf. Reviewing Vanessa Bell's letters, he typically misses no chance to set one sister up at the expense of the other (*London Review of Books*, Christmas Issue, 15:23, 2 December 1993, p. 20). Maybe he should think less about Virginia's spite and aggression, and more about his own.

4.   When Bayley writes that 'Carter's brand of magic realism is also a democratic magic', it sounds like a borrowing of Lorna Sage's 'a magical democracy', from her obituary for her friend, but it deadeningly turns

round the feel of it – that democracy can be spirited – to something duller, branded as 'ideologically sound' (*The Guardian*, 17 February 1992). This obituary is the finest and most broadly conceived valuation of Angela Carter's work. Recent surveys of post-1945 British fiction – Malcolm Bradbury's (1993) and Randall Stevenson's *The British Novel Since the Thirties* (Batsford, 1986) – fail, in their deliberate insularity, to acknowledge the stature and the European dimensions of Carter's writing, and its more than European concerns. I do not think her writing is very like that of Gabriel García Márquez, nor that it depends on his; and the innovations with which Salman Rushdie is identified postdate Carter's, yet Carter and Rushdie are seen by Bayley and Stevenson as importing an alien 'magical realism'. Each writer shares influences and concerns – which neither, I think, would be inclined to deny – but each inflects them differently. Another writer associated with comparable strategies and concerns, with interplaying the local and the larger, is the South African J. M. Coetzee.

5.   I discuss this in 'Enthralment', in *Plotting Change*, ed. Linda Anderson, Edward Arnold, 1990; and in 'The Dangers of Angela Carter', in *New Feminist Discourses*, ed. Isobel Armstrong, Routledge, 1992 (the latter essay predates the former). In a scrawl to me Carter wrote: 'if I can get up Suzanne Kappeler's nose, to say nothing of the Dworkin proboscis, then my living has not been in vain'. However, she had some respect for Kappeler's *The Pornography of Representation*, as I do (and, in my case, for Andrea Dworkin when I've heard her quietly and convincingly tackle hecklers).

6.   Lorna Sage, *Women in the House of Fiction*, Macmillan, 1992, p. 168. However, Jane Campion's film *The Piano* shows something of this line of thought about nineteenth-century women, and is wonderful in its romantic cine-graphing of strength and passionate will under restraint (I don't identify romance or romanticism with lack of critical intelligence).

7.   Mandy Merck, *Perversions*, Virago, 1993, p. 72. This is dedicated to 'partiality, irony, intimacy and perversity' – rather different from Bayley's preferred secrecy, privacy and modesty, the values which Virginia Woolf mocked in writing the sex-change in *Orlando*. Although she has trumpets heralding 'the Truth', Woolf does, however, mask what needs to happen physically if it's no more than gender in the head – unlike Carter's transsexual operation in *The Passion of New Eve*, when Sophia tucks Evelyn's severed genitals into the pocket of her shorts (p. 71). My impression is that women rather than men find this scene funny. There could be no single judgement as to whether one should or should not roar at it.

8.   *Sex Exposed: Sexuality and the Pornography Debate*, ed. Lynne Segal and Mary McIntosh, Virago, 1992, Introduction and pp. 65–91. This collection of essays criticises feminist overemphasis on issues of sexual

abuse and violence, which necessarily represents the victimage rather than the powers of women.

9.   Merck, *Perversions*, p. 266. Much earlier Cora Kaplan argued against reformed sexual desire as a prerequisite for feminism, in 'Wild Nights', reprinted in *Sea Changes*, Verso, 1986.

10.   Luce Irigaray, *This Sex Which Is Not One*, trans. Catherine Porter, Cornell University Press, 1985. Equivalent to impersonation, mimicry as a political practice is 'to make "visible" by an act of playful repetition, what was supposed to remain invisible', the logic of the ruling discourse (p. 76). Irigaray distinguishes such mimicry from the idea that femininity is always a masquerade, playing a required role without resistance. An array of cross-references is possible here, from Joan Riviere's 'femininity as masquerade' to Roland Barthes's cultural politics, the exposure of naturalised myths as artificial, in *Mythologies* ('Myth Today'). Mimicry in Irigaray's sense is congruent with the general account of irony as 'echoic utterance' that queries the kind of discourse echoed, or its use, which is proposed by Deirdre Wilson and Dan Sperber, 'Rhetoric and Relevance', in *The Ends of Rhetoric*, ed. John Bender and David E. Wellbery, Stanford University Press, 1990. Carter experimented in a twentieth-century way of thought whose emergence we can see more clearly in retrospect, and which it would be stupid to see as mere will to militancy or correctness. If 'femininity' is understood as a masquerade, and 'masculinity' too, we can look for more choice, more enjoyment, more responsibility of an active kind, in what we personate, which can be more subtle than all becoming New Madonnas, or their enemies.

Irigaray's work on women and the law – ambivalent and controversial, like her earlier writing – is reviewed by Peter Goodrich in a special issue on 'Gender, Law and Justice' of *Women: A Cultural Review*, 4:3, Winter 1993, Oxford University Press, pp. 317–27.

11.   *Perversions*, pp. 260–62.

12.   The way of putting things here is indebted to an unpublished paper, 'The Fictions of Radical Democracy', by Mark Devenney, University of the Witwatersrand and South Africa, which reminded me how literary and political theory can well be linked. Devenney's paper draws on the theory of Chantal Mouffe and Ernesto Laclau, and takes its examples from the fiction of Nadine Gordimer and J. M. Coetzee.

13.   Judith Butler (1982), quoted in *Perversions*, pp. 248, 291.

14.   Post-Christian, post-Romantic, post-Marxist, 'postmodern' or anti-foundational resistance to the 'eschatological plot' of origins and ends is widespread, for example in the work on early German Romanticism of Jean-Luc Nancy and Philippe Lacoue-Labarthe, *The Literary Absolute*, trans. P. Barnard and C. Lester, State University of New York Press 1988. An important guide for me has been the optimistic scepticism of Ernesto Laclau, for example the title essay of his *New Reflections on the Revolution of Our Times*, Verso, 1990.

15. Sage, *Women in the House of Fiction*, p. 177.

16. From Andrew Marvell's 'The Unfortunate Lover', one of the epigraphs to *Heroes and Villains*.

17. Carter gave seven explanations for the role of the blind piano tuner in 'The Bloody Chamber', one of which, apart from the happy ending, fits the vindictive element in the loving representation of Jewel: he 'has only the function of the anonymous princess the fairy tale hero marries in the last paragraph and lives happily ever after with because the storyteller gives them no other option' (Correspondence).

18. *Wise Children*, p. 148. 'The Merchant of Shadows' is the title of a story in Carter's *American Ghosts & Old World Wonders* (Chatto & Windus, 1993), originally published in the *London Review of Books*, 26 October 1989. This needs to be read in conjunction with *The Passion of New Eve*. The star and the great director figure, but not quite as expected.

19. The picaresque sequential structure of *The Passion of New Eve*, crossed by arcane imagery of albatrosses and hermaphrodites, uses Eisenstein's working metaphor of cinema montage as an alchemical process, imaginary and technological (*nigredo, albedo, rubedo*: mass breakdown, separation, and the red-gold fire of revolutionary transformation). See Sergei Eisenstein, *Film Form*, ed. Jay Leyda, Harcourt Brace Jovanovich, 1949.

20. Elisabeth Bronfen, *Over Her Dead Body: Death, Femininity and the Aesthetic* (Manchester University Press 1992), pp. 420–24.

21. Reduction of human flesh to meat, as well as the revaluation of purely reproductive sex and the dubious 'nature' of drives to reproduction *and* destruction, are discussed in an essay by Simone de Beauvoir, 'Faut-il brûler Sade?', published in *Les Temps Modernes*, December 1951–January 1952. Carter's bold look at the liberatory possibilities of de Sade's writing, the incitement to enjoy, in *The Sadeian Woman*, is indebted to this essay, which has mostly been ignored by feminists and biographers when it is not dismissed as an aberration. De Beauvoir herself rightly considered it an important part of her thinking about sexuality and sociality (you can find a friend in an enemy, without ceasing to hate what you hate; arguments take on some of the assumptions of those we argue against; see Harriett Gilbert's essay on Andrea Dworkin in *Sex Exposed*, pp. 216–29). Translated by Annette Michelson, de Beauvoir's 'Must We Burn Sade?' was published as *The Marquis de Sade: An Essay*, (London: John Calder, 1962).

Louise J. Kaplan has also revalued de Beauvoir's insights into Sade; for example (ironically): 'She . . . knew he would never . . . sentimentally mistake the human flesh as an object of enchantment', *Female Perversions* (1991; Penguin, 1993), pp. 354–9. Kaplan, who could well be read alongside Merck's final essay, 'The feminist ethics of lesbian s/m', also discusses fear of the mother or of wishes regarded as feminine, and the perverse terror of destroying the body representing this weakness (p. 27), which returns us to the desire to destroy knowledge of sexual difference, to descrate and abject what cannot be assimilated (p. 355).

22.   Gerardine Meaney, in *(Un)Like Subjects* (Routledge, 1993), gives an interesting analysis of this episode in relation to horse-cults and feminine sexuality.

23.   Charles Taylor, *Sources of the Self: The Making of Modern Identity*, Harvard University Press, 1989, pp. 211–33. Taylor quotes Puritans on this supposedly unitary 'modern identity' ('there is a difference between washing of dishes, and preaching of the word of God: but as touching to please God none at all'); this is 'pleasingly' linked to Herbert's Anglican discourse in Jonathan Glover's review of Taylor, 'God loveth adverbs', *London Review of Books*, 22 November 1990.

24.   One of the allusions in the naming of Fevvers, her written flesh animated and loaded with cultural signifiers, is to Socrates' comical and poignant account in Plato's *Phaedrus* of how love makes us sprout feathers and soar. Carter grounds this transcendence in celebration of a spirited body, and makes it a vulgar available miracle.

In the Alchemist's Cave: Radio Plays   *Guido Almansi*

1.   In a personal interview.

2.   Henry Miller, *Tropic of Cancer*, New York: Grove Press, 1980, p. 235.

3.   London: Chatto & Windus, 1993.

4.   She had murdered her father and his family with an axe in a celebrated massacre known as *The Fall Axe Murders*.

5.   On the morning of the bloody murder in the short story 'The Fall River Axe Murders', in *Black Venus*, London: Chatto & Windus, 1985, pp. 101–21, and at the age of four in 'Lizzie and the Tiger'.

6.   'Burnt the fire of thine eyes', William Blake, *The Tyger*.

7.   Job I:7.

8.   In a personal interview, published in an Italian magazine.

9.   *Come Unto These Yellow Sands*, Newcastle upon Tyne: Bloodaxe, 1985.

10.   Carter first wrote a short story with the same title in *The Bloody Chamber*.

11.   *Nights at the Circus*, p. 9.

12.   *Wise Children*, p. 115.

13.   Angela Carter, *The Bloody Chamber* p. 121.

14.   *Come Unto These Yellow Sands* cit., p. 154.

15.   Carter first wrote a short story with the same title, published in *The Bloody Chamber* cit. pp. 110–8. The story was afterwards made into a film by the director Neil Jordan, in 1984, called *The Company of Wolves*.

16.   This was first written as a short story, entitled 'The Lady of the House of Love', published in *The Bloody Chamber* cit., pp. 93–108.

17.   *Come Unto These Yellow Sands* quoted, *Preface*, p. 8.

18.   In the short story of the same title in *The Bloody Chamber* we have

the identical expressions but as part of a description of Red Riding Hood, not uttered by her.

19.   *American Ghosts & Old World Wonders*, cit., p. 13.
20.   *Come Unto These Yellow Sands*, cit., *Preface*, p. 9.
21.   In *The Bloody Chamber*.
22.   *Come Unto These Yellow Sands*, *Preface*, p. 8.
23.   A painting of 1842.
24.   A painting Dadd worked on for nine years, from 1855 to 1864.
25.   A painting of 1841.
26.   *Come Unto These Yellow Sands*, pp. 31–2. But the phrase 'compensatory idology of innocence' also appears on p. 23.

Cinema Magic and the Old Monsters: Angela Carter's Cinema
Laura Mulvey

1.   Marina Warner, 'The Uses of Enchantment', in Duncan Petrie (ed.), *The Cinema and the Uses of Enchantment*, London: British Film Institute, 1993.
2.   *The Passion of New Eve*, p. 1.
3.   *Expletives Deleted*, p. 5.
4.   *The Passion of New Eve*, p. 2.
5.   ibid., pp. 7–8.
6.   Annette Michelson, 'On the Eve of the Future', *October* no. 29.
7.   'The Uses of Enchantment', p. 21.
8.   *The Company of Wolves*, p. 110.
9.   *The Virago Book of Fairy Tales*, London: Virago, 1990, p. ix.
10.   *The Trials and Tribulations of Little Red Riding Hood*, ed. J. Zipes, London: Routledge, 1993, p. 71.
11.   *Virago Book of Fairy Tales*, p. xxi.
12.   'The Uses of Enchantment', p. 24.
13.   *The Company of Wolves*, p. 111.
14.   'Acting it up on the Small Screen', *Nothing Sacred*, p. 124.

Angela Carter: Bottle Blonde; Double Drag   *Marina Warner*

1.   Arthur Heiserman, *The Novel before the Novel*, Chicago and London, 1977, pp. 3–6; see also B. E. Perry, *The Ancient Romances: A Literary-Historical Account of Their Origins*, Berkeley and Los Angeles, 1967; Bryan Reardon, 'The Form of Ancient Greek Romance', in R. Beaton (ed.), *The Greek Novel*, London, 1988, pp. 205–16.
2.   *Fireworks*, London, 1974. I am grateful to Alison Marks for bringing this afterword to my attention.
3.   *The Virago Book of Fairy Tales*, London, 1990, p. ix.
4.   Walter Benjamin, 'The Storyteller: Reflections on the work of Nikolai Leskov', in *Illuminations*, trans. Harry Zohn, New York, 1969, pp. 83–109; Robert Darnton, 'Peasant Tell Tales: The Meaning of Mother

Goose', in *The Great Cat Massacre and Other Episodes in French Cultural History*, London, 1984, pp. 13–34.

5.   *Cinderella*, *Arena*, BBC2, directed by Melissa Llewellyn Davies, script by Marina Warner.

6.   Jack Zipes, *Breaking the Magic Spell*, London, 1979; *Fairy Tales and the Art of Subversion*, New York, 1983; 'The Rise of the French Fairy Tale and the Decline of France', in *Beauties, Beasts and Enchantments: Classic French Fairy Tales*, New York, 1989; 'Introduction' to *Spells of Enchantment; The Wondrous Fairy Tales of Western Culture*, New York, 1991; (ed.), *The Trials and Tribulations of Little Red Riding Hood*, London, 1994, rev. edn.

7.   Angela Carter, *Nights at the Circus*, London, 1984, p. 103.

8.   See Marjorie Garber, *Vested Interests: Cross-Dressing and Cultural Anxiety*, London, 1993, for a very fine study of this theme.

9.   Gianbattista Basile, *Il Pentamerone ossia La Fiaba delle fiabe*, ed. and trans. Benedetto Croce, 2 vols, Bari, 1982, pp. 3–12.

10.   Alexander Herzen, *On Art*, Moscow, 1954, p. 223, quoted in Mikhail Bahktin, *Rabelais and His World*, trans. Helene Iswolsky, Indiana, 1984, p. 92. Iris Gillespie's paper, 'Iconoclasm and the Subcontinent' 1994 (unpublished), about Rushdie was an inspiration to my thinking about Carter's inconoclasm.

11.   *A Whetstone For Dull Wits, or a Poesy of New Ingenious Riddles*, in John Ashta ed., *Chapbooks of the Eighteenth Century*, London, 1988.

12.   See Marina Warner, 'Speaking with Double Tongue: Mother Goose and the Old Wives' Tale', in *Myths of the English*, ed. Roy Porter, Oxford, 1992, pp. 33–67.

13.   'In Pantoland', in *American Ghosts and Old World Wonders*, London, 1993, pp. 98–109.

14.   'Overture and Incidental Music for *A Midsummer Night's Dream*', in *Black Venus*, London, 1985, pp. 63–76.

15.   Angela Carter, 'Reflections', in *Fireworks*, London, 1987, p. 101.

16.   *Nights at the Circus*, p. 295.

17.   Bakhtin, *Rabelais and His World*, p. 82.

18.   *The Virago Book of Fairy Tales*, p. 1.

Woolf by the Lake, Woolf at the Circus: Carter and Tradition
Isobel Armstrong

This essay is a shortened version of 'Virginia Woolf: Founding Feminist or Anxious Influence?', first published in *La Huella De Virginia Woolf*, ed. Mercedes Bengoechea; Universidad De Alcala De Herares, 1992. Reprinted with permission of Mercedes Bengoechea and the University of Alcala de Henares.

1.   Even feminist readers have experienced some difficulty in incorporating Virginia Woolf into their criticism. See, for instance,

Chapter 10 in Elaine Showalter, *A Literature of Their Own: British Women Novelists From Brontë to Lessing*, London, 1978; see also Chapter 1 in Toril Moi, *Sexual/Textual Politics: Feminist Literary Theory*, London, 1985.

2.   Erich Auerbach, 'The Brown Stocking', in *Mimesis: The Representation of Reality in Western Literature* (1946), trans. Willard R. Trask (Princeton; NJ, 1953), pp. 525–3.

3.   The social meaning of form in Virginia Woolf's work has been recognised in different ways by a number of critics, of whom the following are notable: Gayatri Chakravorty Spivak, 'Unmaking and Making in *To the Lighthouse*', in *Women and Language in Literature and Society*, ed. Sally McConnell-Ginet, Ruth Borker and Nelly Furman, New York, 1980; Makiko Minow-Pinkney, *Virginia Woolf and the Problem of the Subject*, Brighton, 1987; Rachel Bowlby, *Virginia Woolf: Feminist Destinations*, Oxford, 1988.

4.   Sazana Raitt, *Vita and Virginia: The Work and Friendship of Victoria Sackville-West and Virginia Woolf*, Oxford, 1993.

5.   'Male and Female in the Woman Who Writes', in *La Huella De Virginia Woolf*, 29–43; 37.

6.   Virginia Woolf, *A Writer's Diary*. ed. Leonard Woolf, London, 1965, p. 102.

7.   Gillian Beer, 'Hume, Stephen and Elegy in *To the Lighthouse*', in *Arguing with the Past: Essays in Narrative from Woolf to Sidney*, London and New York, 1989, pp. 183–202.

8.   Anita Brookner, *Hotel du Lac*, 1984; Triad/Panther, 1985, p. 147.

9.   Anita Brookner, *A Closed Eye*, London, 1991, p. 125.

10.   Angela Carter, *Nights at the Circus*, 1984; London, 1985.

11.   Virginia Woolf, *Orlando: A Biography*, 1928; London, 1977, p. 235.

12.   See Rita Felski, *Towards a Feminist Aesthetic*, London, 1989. When I wrote this essay (1991), I had not read Judith Butler's *Gender Trouble: Feminism and the Subversion of Identity*, London and New York, 1990, but it is clearly a book relevant to my argument.

Seriously Funny: *Wise Children*   Kate Webb

1.   Spring 1993.

2.   Angela Carter, *Wise Children*, Vintage, 1992, p. 19.

3.   If this seems rather too schematising a response, then I call in my defence Carter herself, who often iterated the idea that she intended her fiction to have direct political meaning: 'My characters always have a tendency to be telling you something' (*Omnibus*, BBC1, 16 September 1992); 'in the end my ambition is rather an eighteenth-century "Enlightenment" one – to write fiction that entertains and, in a sense, instructs' (*Contemporary Writers: Angela Carter*, Book Trust for the British Council, 1990); 'I believe that all myths are products of the human mind and reflect only aspects of material human practice. I'm in the

demythologising business' (Angela Carter, 'Notes from the Front Line', in Michelene Wandor [ed.], *On Gender and Writing*, Pandora, 1983).

4.   *Omnibus*.

5.   'All art is political and so is mine. I want readers to understand what it is that I *mean* by my stories . . .' (unpublished interview with Kate Webb, 18 December 1985).

6.   Martin Amis, *Other People*, Penguin, 1981.

7.   Angela Carter, 'Notes from the Front Line'.

8.   Salman Rushdie, 'Eating the Eggs of Love', in *The Jaguar Smile*, Picador, 1987.

9.   Interview with Mary Harron: 'I'm a socialist, damn it! How can you expect me to be interested in fairies?', *Guardian*, September 1984.

10.   Edward Said, *Culture and Imperialism*, Chatto & Windus, 1993.

11.   Foucault makes this argument in many of his works. It is a particularly strong theme of *Discipline and Punish*, Penguin, 1975, and *The History of Sexuality, Volume One*, Penguin, 1976.

12.   *Omnibus*.

13.   *Contemporary Writers*, Book Trust.

14.   Carter gets the wheel of fate into the novel by having Tristram spin a wheel (of fortune) on his s/m game show.

15.   This is an idea which permeates all of R.D. Laing's work, but is the cornerstone of *The Divided Self*, Pelican, 1965.

16.   It would take another full essay to delineate all the Freudian and Shakespearian connections in *Wise Children*. Here, I am just trying to indicate the extent to which they penetrate the novel.

17.   Angela Carter died of cancer on 16 February 1992.

18.   Mikhail Bakhtin's work on carnival is to be found in *Rabelais and His World*, Indiana University Press, 1984; *Problems of Dostoevsky's Poetics*, Manchester University Press, 1984; and *The Dialogic Imagination*, University of Texas Press, 1981.

19.   *Contemporary Writers*, Book Trust.

20.   There is a pub called the Coach and Horses on Clapham Road, equidistant from where Angela Carter lived in Clapham and the road where we might suppose that Dora lives in Brixton. Not Bard Road, of course (this is Carter's invention), but Shakespeare Road, which – with Milton Road, Spenser Road and Chaucer Road – runs off Railton Road and parallel to Coldharbour Lane. Coldharbour Lane was the place known traditionally for providing digs to the theatrical profession: it is there that Marilyn Monroe's showgirl lives in the film *The Prince and the Showgirl*. Railton Road was the heart of the area known as the 'Front Line' before the riots of 1981 and 1983, after which Lambeth Council knocked half of it down. When, later in the novel, Dora says that she prefers the heat of Railton Road at half-past twelve on a Saturday night to the freezing country house of Melchior's first wife, she is both making a political statement – choosing the culture of the colonised over that of the

empire-builders – and talking about the relative culture of these two groups. At Lady Lynde's house, she is offered lousy food and a cold bed. On a Saturday night on Railton Road, Dora would have found blues parties, drugs, booze and many other people who felt 'What a joy it is to dance and sing!'

21.   Kenneth Anger, *Hollywood Babylon*, Straight Arrow Books, 1975.
22.   *Contemporary Writers*, Book Trust.
23.   Sandra M. Gilbert and Susan Gubar, *The Madwoman in the Attic*, Yale University Press, 1979.
24.   Jane Miller, *Seductions: Studies in Reading and Culture*, Virago, 1990.
25.   ibid.
26.   ibid.
27.   I'm thinking here in particular of the New Historicist writing on Shakespeare, and of Linda Hutcheon's *A Theory of Parody*, Methuen, 1985.
28.   Bruno Schulz, *Sanatorium Under the Sign of the Hourglass*, Picador, 1980.
29.   *Omnibus*.
30.   Interview with Mary Harron.

'A Room of One's Own, or a Bloody Chamber?': Angela Carter and Political Correctness   *Hermione Lee*

1.   John Bayley, 'Fighting for the Crown', *The New York Review of Books*, 23 April 1992, pp. 9–11.
2.   Marina Warner, 'Angela Carter', *The Independent*, 18 February 1992, p. 25.
3.   'Angela Carter', *The Times*, 17 February 1992.
4.   Hilton Kramer, 'The Prospect Before Us', *New Criterion*, September 1990, reprinted in *Debating PC*, ed. Paul Berman, Dell Publishing, 1992, pp. 315–21.
5.   Edward Said, 'The Politics of Knowledge', *Raritan*, vol. XI, no. 1, Summer 1991, in Berman, *Debating PC*, pp. 172–89.
6.   *Nights at the Circus*, Chatto & Windus, 1984; Pan, 1985, pp. 263–4.
7.   'Milorad Pavic: *Landscape Painted with Tea*' (1991), in *Expletives Deleted*, Chatto & Windus, 1992, p. 18.
8.   'Iain Sinclair: *Downriver*' (1991), in *ibid.*, pp. 119–20.
9.   *Wayward Girls & Wicked Women*, Virago, 1986, Introduction, pp. ix–xii.
10.   *Expletives Deleted*, p. 145.
11.   ibid., p. 31.
12.   'Charlotte Brontë: *Jane Eyre*' (1990), ibid., pp. 161–72.
13.   'Walter de la Mare: *Memoirs of a Midget*' (1982), ibid., pp. 51–66.
14.   ibid., p. 12.
15.   'An Omelette and a Glass of Wine and other Dishes' (1984), ibid., p. 79.
16.   'Elizabeth David: *English Bread and Yeast Cookery*' (1987), ibid., p. 98.

17.   'J'Accuse: Virginia Woolf', written and presented by Tom Paulin, directed by Jeff Morgan, Channel Four, 29 January 1991.

18.   Forthcoming in Angela Carter, *The Curious Room: Collected Works, Volume I*, Chatto & Windus, 1995. Copyright, Estate of Angela Carter. Michael Berkeley's obituary notice for Carter in *The Independent* in February 1992 described the 'hilarious meetings' between himself, Carter and John Cox, working on *Orlando*, when she 'immediately came up with lines that simply begged and beg yet to be set'.

19.   Stanley Fish, 'There's No Such Thing as Free Speech and it's a Good Thing, Too', in *There's No Such Thing as Free Speech: and it's a Good Thing, Too*, Oxford University Press (NY), 1994.

20.   'Envoi: Bloomsday' (1982), in *Expletives Deleted*, pp. 207–13.

Notes on Contributors

Guido Almansi was formerly Professor of English and Comparative Literature at the University of East Anglia, and is presently theatre critic of the Italian weekly *Panorama*. His *L'estetica dell'osceno*, first published in 1974, is being re-issued this year by Einaudi.

Isobel Armstrong was Professor of English at Southampton from 1979–89 and has been Professor of English at Birbeck College, University of London, for five years. Her latest book is *Victorian Poetry: Poetry, Poetics and Politics* (1993). She is co-editor of *Women: A Cultural Review*. Her (then) teenage daughter introduced her to Angela Carter's work.

Margaret Atwood is the author of more than twenty-five books of poetry, fiction and non-fiction. Her latest novel, *The Robber Bride*, was published by Virago in paperback in autumn 1994. She lives in Toronto, Canada.

Elaine Jordan is Senior Lecturer in Literature at the University of Essex, where she directs the MA in Women Writing and the interdisciplinary Doctoral Programme in Feminist Theory. She has published essays on Angela Carter, Toni Morrison, and Christa Wolf.

Nicole Ward Jouve is a French writer and academic who holds a Chair at the University of York. Her latest book is *White Woman Speaks with Forked Tongue* (1991).

Roz Kaveney is a journalist and publisher's reader living in London. She is active in civil liberties and anti-censorship work and is a contributing editor on the forthcoming *Encyclopaedia of Fantasy*.

Hermione Lee is Professor of English Literature at the University of York. Her books include *Willa Cather: A Life Saved Up*

(Virago, 1989) and she is currently working on a new biography of Virginia Woolf.

Laura Mulvey is a film-maker and film theorist. Her collected essays were published by Macmillan as *Visual and Other Pleasures* in 1989. She contributed the volume on *Citizen Kane* to the British Film Institute's series Film Classics. Her films (co-directed with Peter Wollen) include *Riddles of the Sphinx* and *The Bad Sister* and she recently directed a Channel 4 documentary, *Disgraced Monuments*.

Marc O'Day is a freelance lecturer, writer and educational organiser based in Norwich. He teaches and organises adult education courses for two of East Anglia's regional film theatres, and is currently gathering bits and pieces for a study on bricolage in consumer culture.

Sue Roe is a novelist, poet and critic, and a Lecturer in Literature and Creative Writing at the University of East Anglia. Her publications include *Estella, her Expectations* (a novel) and *Writing and Gender: Virginia Woolf's Writing Practice*. Her latest book (with Susan Sellers and Nicole Ward Jouve), about the creative process, is *The Semi-Transparent Envelope* (Marion Boyars, 1994).

Susan Rubin Suleiman is Professor of Romance and Comparative Literatures at Harvard University, and is currently Chair of the Committee on Degrees in Women's Studies. Her books include *Authoritarian Fictions: The Ideological Novel as a Literary Genre, Subversive Intent: Gender, Politics, and the Avant-Garde*; and most recently, *Risking Who One Is: Encounters with Contemporary Art and Literature* (Harvard, 1994).

Marina Warner is a novelist and critic. Her most recent study, *From the Beast to the Blonde: On Fairy Tales and their Tellers* was inspired by the writing of Angela Carter.

Kate Webb is a graduate student at the University of East Anglia. She has worked for Rock Against Racism, Brixton's Ritzy Cinema, the London Film Co-Op, the Bandung File, and Faber & Faber. Angela Carter was a family friend for whom she occasionally babysat.

A Basic Bibliography

Novels

Shadow Dance, London: Heinemann, 1966; reprinted as
    Honeybuzzard; New York: Simon & Schuster, 1966; London:
    Pan, 1968.

The Magic Toyshop, London: Heinemann, 1967; New York: Simon
    & Schuster, 1968; London: Virago, 1981.

Several Perceptions, London: Heinemann, 1968; New York: Simon
    & Schuster, 1969; London: Pan, 1970.

Heroes and Villains, London: Heinemann, 1969; New York: Simon
    & Schuster, 1969; Harmondsworth: Penguin, 1981.

Love, London: Hart-Davis, 1971; revised edition London: Chatto &
    Windus, 1987; New York: Viking Penguin, 1988; London:
    Picador, 1988.

The Infernal Desire Machines of Doctor Hoffman, London: Hart-Davis,
    1972; reprinted as *The War of Dreams*, New York: Bard/Avon
    Books, 1977; Harmondsworth: Penguin, 1982.

The Passion of New Eve, London: Gollancz, 1977; New York:
    Harcourt Brace Jovanovich, 1977; London: Virago, 1982.

Nights at the Circus, London: Chatto & Windus, 1984; New York:
    Viking, 1984; London: Pan, 1985.

Wise Children, London: Chatto & Windus, 1991; New York: Viking
    Penguin, 1993; London: Vintage, 1992.

Short Stories

Fireworks: Nine Profane Pieces, London: Quartet Books, 1974; New
    York: Harper & Row, 1981; revised edition London: Chatto
    & Windus, 1987; London: Virago, 1988.

The Bloody Chamber and Other Stories, London: Gollancz, 1979; New
    York: Harper & Row, 1980; Harmondsworth: Penguin, 1981.

Black Venus, London: Chatto & Windus, 1985; reprinted as *Saints
    and Strangers*, New York: Viking Penguin, 1987; London:
    Pan, 1986.

American Ghosts & Old World Wonders, London: Chatto & Windus,
    1993; London: Vintage, 1994.

Children's Stories

Miss Z. The Dark Young Lady, London: Heinemann, 1970; New
    York: Simon & Schuster, 1970.
The Donkey Prince, New York: Simon and Schuster, 1970.
Martin Leman's Comic and Curious Cats (Text by Angela Carter,
    illustrations by Martin Leman) London: Gollancz, 1979;
    London: Gollancz paperback, 1988.
Moonshadow (Text by Angela Carter, idea and paintings by Justin
    Todd) London: Gollancz, 1982.

Verse

Unicorn, Leeds: Location Press, 1966.

Radio Plays

Come Unto These Yellow Sands: Four Radio Plays, Newcastle on
    Tyne: Bloodaxe, 1985; Dufour Editions, 1985; Newcastle on
    Tyne: Bloodaxe paperback, 1985.

Non-Fiction

The Sadeian Woman: An Exercise in Cultural History, London: Virago
    1979; reprinted as *The Sadeian Woman and the Ideology of
    Pornography*, New York: Pantheon, 1979.
Translator and Foreword, *The Fairy Tales of Charles Perrault*,
    London: Gollancz, 1977; New York: Bard Books, 1979.
Nothing Sacred, London: Virago 1982; revised edition London:
    Virago, 1992.
Editor and Translator, *Sleeping Beauty and Other Favourite Fairy
    Tales*, London: Gollancz, 1982; New York: Schoken, 1989;
    London: Gollancz paperback, 1991.
Introduction to Walter de la Mare, *Memoirs of a Midget*, Oxford
    University Press, 1982.
Introduction to Christina Stead, *The Puzzleheaded Girl*, London:
    Virago, 1984.
Editor, *Wayward Girls and Wicked Women*, London: Virago, 1986.
Introduction to Gilbert Hernandez, *Duck Feet*, London: Titan
    Books, 1988.
Images of Frida Kahlo, London: Redstone Press, 1989.
Editor, *The Virago Book of Fairy Tales*, London: Virago, 1990;
    reprinted as *Old Wives' Fairy Tale Book*, New York: David
    McKay, 1987; London: Virago, 1991.

Introduction to Charlotte Brontë, *Jane Eyre*, London: Virago, 1990.
Expletives Deleted: Selected Writings, London: Chatto & Windus,
    1992; London. Vintage, 1993.
Editor, *The Second Virago Book of Fairy Tales*, London: Virago, 1992;
    London: Virago, 1993.

Index

Works by Angela Carter are individually alphabetised and indicated in **bold** type